Education

AND THE

Future OF
Latin America

Education

AND THE

Future OF Latin America

Alejandro Toledo Manrique

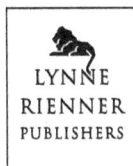

LYNNE
RIENNER
PUBLISHERS

BOULDER
LONDON

Published in the United States of America in 2021 by
Lynne Rienner Publishers, Inc.
1800 30th Street, Suite 314, Boulder, Colorado 80301
www.rienner.com

and in the United Kingdom by
Lynne Rienner Publishers, Inc.
Gray's Inn House, 127 Clerkenwell Road, London EC1 5DB
www.eurospanbookstore.com/rienner

Library of Congress Cataloging-in-Publication Data
Names: Toledo Manrique, Alejandro, author.
Title: Education and the future of Latin America / Alejandro Toledo
    Manrique.
Description: Boulder, Colorado : Lynne Rienner Publishers, Inc, [2021] |
    Includes bibliographical references and index. | Summary: "Addresses the
    question: What will it take to overcome the many challenges that Latin
    America faces in developing quality, inclusive education for its diverse
    population?"— Provided by publisher.
Identifiers: LCCN 2021015773 (print) | LCCN 2021015774 (ebook) | ISBN
    9781626379572 (Hardcover : alk. paper) | ISBN 9781626379725 (eBook)
Subjects: LCSH: Education—Latin America. | Education and state—Latin
    America. | Educational equalization—Latin America. | Social justice and
    education.
Classification: LCC LA541 .T65 2021 (print) | LCC LA541 (ebook) | DDC
    370.98--dc23
LC record available at https://lccn.loc.gov/2021015773
LC ebook record available at https://lccn.loc.gov/2021015774

British Cataloguing in Publication Data
A Cataloguing in Publication record for this book
is available from the British Library.

Printed and bound in the United States of America

The paper used in this publication meets the requirements
of the American National Standard for Permanence of
Paper for Printed Library Materials Z39.48-1992.

5 4 3 2 1

This book was written during very difficult times for my family and me. It would not have been possible without the ongoing support of many individuals. I want to specifically thank a few of them from the bottom of my heart.

It is to them that I dedicate this book.

First, I thank Martin Carnoy, who was my professor and is now my close friend. He is forever connected to the Graduate School of Education at Stanford University, and so am I. I have had the privilege of working in many renowned academic institutions and international organizations during my life, but Stanford has played such an important role in my education and in helping me chart my path that I am forever indebted to it and particularly to the Graduate School of Education.

Second, after concluding my term as presidenct of Peru in 2006, I had the honor of being a visiting scholar at Stanford's Center for Advanced Study in the Behavioral Sciences and also at Stanford's Center on Democracy, Development, and the Rule of Law (CDDRL) at the Freeman Spogli Institute. I am deeply grateful to both centers and especially to Larry Diamond, head of CDDRL at the time, who has been a friend and a source of intellectual inspiration with his insightful work on democracy, for making it possible for me to write two earlier books, *The Shared Society* and *Growing for Inclusion*.

Third, and with a profound depth of feeling, I dedicate this book to the vision of President John F. Kennedy as symbolized by my dearest friends, Joel and Nancy Meister, as well as Marjorie Lamb and all the former and current Peace Corps volunteers. Their philosophy of respect for cultural differences in the world and their dedication to better human understanding has always been an inspiration to me.

Fourth, I dedicate this book to the woman of my life, Eliane, who has supported me through thick and thin and with whom I share an immense love and so many dreams.

Fifth, I dedicate this book to the poor children in the world, who deserve access to the same quality of educational opportunities that I had, not as an anomaly, but as a human right.

Sixth, I dedicate this book to the teachers and professors of the world, especially those in Latin America and in my beloved country, Peru. They are the key to a better future.

Contents

Tables and Figures

Tables

Figures

Preface

I was born in a small village, 11,000 feet above sea level, in the High Andes, one of sixteen children. Seven of my siblings died in childhood. But I was extraordinarily lucky. My father decided that he could no longer tolerate the precarious life of extreme poverty in our village. There was no potable water or proper sanitation, and, along with the other villagers, our family faced malnutrition and high child mortality. The village had no schools at that time; we had to walk hours each day to a larger town to attend a primary school. My father and mother decided to migrate to the seaport of Chimbote. I was four years old.

That move was the first in a series of events that allowed me to become a statistical anomaly. In Chimbote, we lived in the poverty of an urban shantytown, but we had the sea, and the sea was a source of healthy food. I also could help my family by earning money. When I was six years old, I joined my brothers in shining shoes and selling newspapers and lottery tickets in the streets of the port at night. During the day, we attended schools that had no potable water, but did have schoolteachers who cared about us and pushed me forward.

When I was fourteen, in 1964, by sheer chance I met two Peace Corps volunteers—Joel Meister and Nancy Deeds—who were working in our shantytown. Nancy needed a place to live, and I convinced my mother to rent her a small area in our overcrowded house. Perhaps as a consequence of my persistent and at times impertinent questions about the philosophy of the Peace Corps and about life in

general, Joel and Nancy and the rest of the Peace Corps group in
Chimbote took me under their collective wing and helped me eventually to attend university in the United States. That allowed me to
work for the United Nations Development Programme and the World
Bank; to become a university professor in Peru at an internationally
renowned graduate business school, ESAN; and to be a visiting scholar
at such universities as Harvard, Waseda in Tokyo, and Tsinghua in Bei-
jing. Ultimately, with almost no previous political experience, I was
elected to the presidency of my country—making me the first South
American president of Indigenous descent ever to be democratically
elected.

As president, I was able to restore democracy and reconstruct civil
society in Peru after the tumultuous period in which my predecessor
had tried to overturn the national constitution. Yet, I was not able to
accomplish many things that I wanted to during those five years.
Although I helped lift the incomes of the poorest groups in my country, I had only limited impact on what I consider one of the most
important factors in social mobility and human progress, especially for
Latin America's marginalized groups: improving their quality of education. I was able to double teachers' salaries, and that was important,
because teacher salaries were abysmally low at the end of the previous
regime. Those abysmal salaries had left teachers' morale so low that
the educational system was barely functioning. Raising teacher earnings helped, but there were many other steps that I would have liked
to take. Teachers are key to enacting any educational-improvement
policies, and a crucial lesson I learned is that building confidence in
teachers and making them part of the reform process must precede
any meaningful strategy to improve educational quality.

Now, an important note: My popularity in Peru today is at a low
point. I have been accused of taking a large bribe from Odebrecht, a
Brazilian construction company, which received a contract near the
end of my presidency for building a part of the Trans-Oceanic High-
way between Peru and Brazil. This was an important project that
Brazil's president Lula and I helped realize to bring the east and west
of Latin America together. Thus, I am writing the preface to this book
from lockdown in a small apartment in the United States. At the
request of the Peruvian government, I have been arrested and face
extradition to Peru. I have not been charged with a crime in Peru (just
accused and under investigation), and all the money from the alleged
bribe has been found, not in my bank accounts, but in the Swiss
accounts of the person who claims that he acted as my intermediary in

asking for the bribe more than fifteen years ago. He conveniently turned state's evidence to avoid going to prison himself. To be clear: I never asked for or took any money from Odebrecht or any other company or individual. The accusations against me are false and, indeed, have been shown to be full of obvious contradictions. Unfortunately, in today's Peru, these facts don't matter. I have been tried and found guilty in the Peruvian media many times over, and, of course, my reputation is in ruins. Ironically, however, Peruvians still rate me as being the best president the country has had in the past generation.

Now that I have put that disclaimer on the table, I want to make something else perfectly clear. None of this has dampened my passion to ensure that Latin America's poor and Indigenous peoples gain the opportunities that I had and many more. I do not want my case to serve as a model for the marginalized and have nots—the current system, which allows only a few to somehow overcome so many barriers, should not be held up to be admired. That extremely unequal and unfair system relies too much on luck. It must be drastically transformed. I want to see this transformation take place through visionary leadership and social and political movements across society.

This visionary leadership demands that world leaders—in this case, especially in Latin America—make decisions that are not based on quick, short-run returns or what may influence the next election, but rather that take on the challenges of human development of the next generations. Such leadership is what is needed for the poor and the Indigenous to gain their freedom—the freedom afforded by adequate nutrition, proper health care, an end to ethnic and racial discrimination, and not least, a quality education. Democracy is an empty word if democratic governments do not have the capacity to deliver concrete and measurable long-term results, beginning with significant investments in the minds and lives of our region's poor and marginalized.

This great challenge will not be cheap, and it requires enormous commitment over a long period of time. The challenge has been made even greater by the huge impact of the global Covid-19 pandemic on education in Latin America—especially the education of the marginalized and the poor, who do not have the digital or other resources needed to confront school closings. The adverse effect of the pandemic on Latin America's economies will, in turn, make it more difficult to mobilize resources for the investments we need in order to meet the challenge. Yet, difficult as it will be, we must find a way to do it—and it is possible to do it, as evidenced by the decision of my own country's Congress to dedicate 6 percent of GDP to the education sector.

In addition to our health and education institutions just catching up, the life profile of our children thirty years from now will be different, and to be successful, this generation will need even more complex skills than today, including being much better prepared in using digital technology, being more flexible in the kinds of work they can do, and perhaps confronting social and economic problems far greater than today's. Furthermore, on the input side, the costs of providing clean drinking water and decent housing are likely to go up, and the degradation of our environment will be greater, making it more difficult to mobilize the resources necessary to effect the transformations I am proposing. On the positive side, hopefully the provision of health care will be more efficient, and we should be able to solve the most common medical problems of the poor more economically than we can today.

Another major transformation we have to achieve in Latin America is to learn to view ourselves differently, namely as multicultural, diverse societies that can be more productive, safer, more sustainable, and more deeply democratic when we are inclusive, tolerant, and recognize cultural differences as an important part of who we are. I believe that a great educational system can contribute a lot to promoting this new view of ourselves, and that the secret to achieving future greatness in education is to ensure that everyone—from those living in our poorest rural areas to those living in urban middle-class neighborhoods—gets the best schooling that money can buy. I also believe that a great educational system with great teachers well trained in great universities is important, but it is not enough to create the kind of Latin America I am talking about.

To complete the picture, we as societies have to ensure that our children, from the time they are forming in their mothers' wombs to their crucial early childhood development to their years in school, must have good nutrition and access to clean water, live in healthy violence-free environments, and receive excellent preventive health care so that they can flourish in much improved schools. We also have to foster and train teachers to deliver a curriculum that inculcates our children with basic human values of mutual respect for our differences in social background and culture. And that curriculum needs to teach students at all levels how to learn in a global environment, for we are all becoming global citizens. For better or worse, the nature of jobs is dramatically changing—increasingly they require people to learn new skills at several different times in their lives and to be intimately familiar with information technology. Our schools need to greatly strengthen their capacity to provide high levels of academic and socio-emotional skills so that even the graduates of schools in our small towns and villages are ready to effectively confront these new realities and to do so without losing the power of their cultural identities.

As I mentioned earlier, making this happen is going to take a new mindset in our leadership. The world is desperately hungry for such a new visionary mindset, which has to move beyond solving the many short-term problems facing all politicians during their terms in office. The payoffs to the kinds of changes I am talking about take a generation to produce big results and require envisioning how the world may look a generation from now in order to shape our institutions to meet those challenges. Thirty years is a split second in human history. Today's leaders have to see themselves as preparing today's children and societies for this next split second.

—Alejandro Toledo Manrique

1

A Vision for Quality Education in Latin America

This book is about a vision for quality education in Latin America. Why devote a whole book to education, when there are so many other problems in the region? For me, the answer to this question is very personal. I was born in a small village in the Peruvian Andes mountains. My parents were poor, and I was among the youngest of sixteen children. Only nine of my siblings survived to adulthood. In the parlance of Latin America, I am *Indigena*—of indigenous origin—and because of that, I was almost certain to remain poor and socially marginalized as an adult. My children would also be likely to be poor and marginalized.

When I was four years old, my family moved to Chimbote, a port town on the Peruvian coast north of Lima. In Chimbote, I shined shoes to earn money for my family, and we lived in a *población marginal*, a sprawling shantytown at the edge of the city. But in Chimbote I got to go to school, and I was fortunate enough to have some teachers who encouraged me to continue into secondary education. I also—purely by chance—got to know two Peace Corps volunteers living in our barrio. They performed a miracle for me—they helped me get into a US university, the University of San Francisco, and after graduation from USF, I was accepted to Stanford, first into the master's program in international education, then to do a PhD.

Thus, access to education changed my life. It's a great story of a poor kid making good. Without education, I would have ended up never fully using my God-given intellectual capacity. I could have

1

never been a university professor, worked for the United Nations, or helped my country change course at a very difficult time. My contribution to my country's economic growth and political development would have been far less. That is why I am such a strong believer in the enabling and transformative power of schooling.

Yet, for all its uplifting qualities, my story is also one set in a harsh overriding reality. In the 1960s and 1970s, when all this happened for me, my case was dishearteningly unique. Few of my friends in that Chimbote barrio made it to secondary school, and not one to university. True, many changes have occurred since then. Education in Latin America has greatly expanded access to secondary school and university. In the past two decades, many countries in Latin America, including Peru, also had a long period of economic growth, and that has helped us pay teachers more reasonably and to improve somewhat the quality of schooling than what was available to me and my friends. But even today, Indigenous children in my country and in other parts of Latin America are far behind European-origin children in access to educational and economic opportunities. Rural children—and there are many of them in Latin America—are typically denied the same quantity and quality of schooling as children in urban areas. And low-income urban children, no matter their race or ethnicity, attain much lower levels of schooling than children from middle- and upper-class families.

Every year that this unequal access to educational opportunity continues in Latin America is another year that we lose in harnessing the massive intellectual potential of children effectively excluded from the education they deserve. I am fully aware that educational access alone is not nearly enough to develop this intellectual capacity or to transform it into productive, satisfying lives. We need to continue to grow our economies and to do so more equitably and in a more environmentally sound way. We also need to commit ourselves to ensuring that all families get adequate nutrition, clean water, and decent housing, and that we both build the underlying infrastructure to promote investment in good jobs and empower our most vulnerable populations to resist the environmental degradation of their communities. That said, I am a firm believer that, done correctly, schooling and other forms of education can play a key role in making life much better for children like those I grew up with but who did not have my opportunities.

In the pages that follow, I will present my ideas for how we can achieve this lofty goal over the next generation. Before I do that, I briefly assess where Latin American education stands now, including its accomplishments over the past generation, and I will lay out the most important obstacles I see impeding serious educational change. Many of these obstacles are outside the public schooling systems that form the backbone of Latin American education. But we also need our public and private schools and universities to change if we are to move forward.

Probably the greatest impediment to improving the health of poor children and raising the quality of education they receive is political. As a former head of state, I am well aware of the pressure to produce results in the short term. Most elected leaders have only four years, some five, and a few, eight, to realize politically visible gains that they can point to as their accomplishments. However, most investments in the young and the poor—so important for society's progress—take a long time to pay off. The economic and social gains will come fifteen, twenty, even thirty years down the road. Politicians know that if they make these investments for the long term they probably will not get credit for them. Unfortunately, this means that it will take exceptional leaders with vision and dedication to the public good to mobilize the resources needed for the policies I propose.

Others have noted that to get politicians to change their political horizon and to reduce inequality in Latin America would require a significant change in the political consciousness of Latin America's elites (Tedesco, 2014). There is a lot of truth in that argument, but it does not explain the dynamic through which elite consciousness would change. I think that the one source of change will be social movements working within democratic institutions, such as occurred in Peru in the late 1990s, in Brazil in the early 2000s, and in the past decade or even two decades in Chile. These pushed the political systems to implement policies favoring lower income groups within the confines of ongoing democracy. The second source will be exceptional leaders that lead broad coalitions, including more socially conscious factions of elite groups, to reconstruct the long-run development process in the region. I will discuss examples of such leadership in the course of this book.

In my assessment of the current situation and suggestions for reform, I try to keep in mind that Latin America is a very large and diverse region. Countries' population sizes vary greatly, as well as the race/ethnic compositions of their populations. The income and wealth of countries in the region also vary greatly, and so does the quality of their national education systems, at least as measured by student performance on international tests. I realize that many of the policies I recommend do not apply equally to large, federal Brazil and to compact Costa Rica, or to mainly European-origin Chile and to Bolivia or Peru, with their important Indigenous populations. That said, there is enough commonality among nations in the region that I intend to use the diversity in educational and social improvement to spread those policies that seem to have worked in the countries and subregions making the most progress. I also devote a chapter to the politics of Indigenous education and how it relates to the definition of the nation-state in my own society, Peru, and in Bolivia, Guatemala, Mexico, Ecuador, and other countries with smaller proportions of Indigenous peoples.

The Great Expansion of Latin American Education

As in much of the rest of the world, the expansion of secondary and tertiary education in Latin America since 1980 has been remarkable. The average teenager in most of Latin America today completes lower secondary school, and in some countries, such as Argentina, Chile, Colombia, Cuba, Dominican Republic, and Jamaica, more than half complete upper secondary schooling.

The region as a whole has increased access to schooling and so has every country in the region. Access to primary schooling is essentially universal, even in poor rural areas, although in Guatemala, Honduras, and Nicaragua, about 15 to 20 percent of students still do not complete primary school. Access to secondary and tertiary education among countries has been generally transformed as well, but this varies greatly across the region.

Figures 1.1 and 1.2 show how enrollment growth in Latin America compared to North America (excluding Mexico) plus Western Europe in 1980 to 2017. The two populations are of different size, obviously, but the notable feature here is that secondary enrollment exploded in Latin American during this period, and tertiary-level enrollment in Latin America began to catch up with the United States and Europe. In the UNESCO definition we use, tertiary education includes some non-university higher education in Latin America and a lot in the United States (community colleges), so it is not exactly a measure of university enrollment. Yet, it does indicate that enrollment in institutions beyond high school in Latin America jumped from less than 5 million in 1980 to over 25 million in 2017.

Figure 1.1   Secondary School Enrollment, by Region, 1980–2017 (millions)

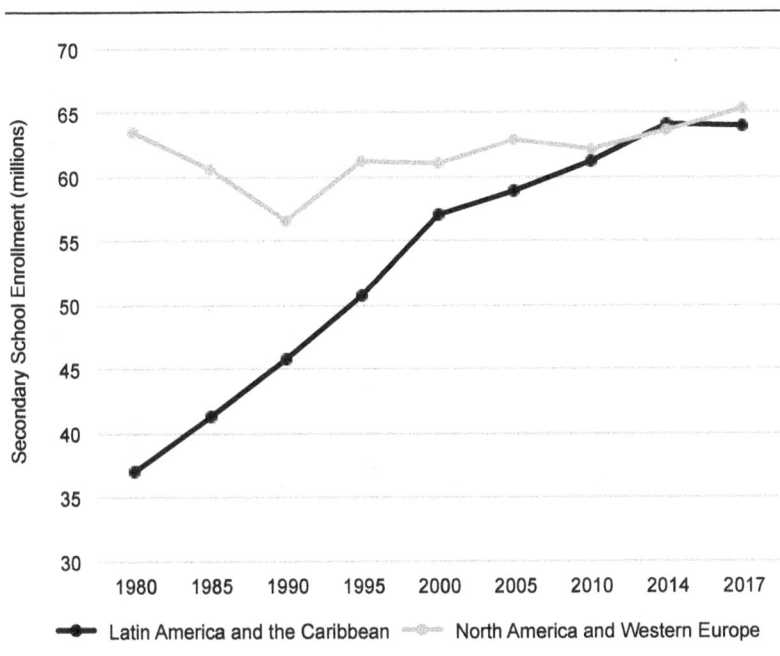

Source: UNESCO Statistical Institute, 2021.

I already mentioned that the enrollment rate in both upper secondary and tertiary education varies greatly among countries in the region. Figures 1.3 and 1.4 show how big this variation is. The bars in Figure 1.3 represent *net* enrollment rates in upper secondary school. Net rates adjust the number of students in school for student repetition (hence age) and divide that adjusted enrollment by the total number of young people of upper secondary school age. These figures are therefore a good estimate of the percentage of the age group in school in 2014. Chile and Cuba had more than 80 percent of the age group in upper secondary school, and a number of countries have over 50 percent in school, but there are three Central American countries with barely more than one in five young people in school after the eighth or ninth grade.

In Figure 1.4, I show gross enrollment rates (GER) for tertiary education (net rates are not available), which is the percentage of all the students enrolled in tertiary education institutions divided by the number of young people eighteen to twenty-four years old. Thus,

Figure 1.2 Tertiary Education Enrollment, by Region, 1980–2017 (millions)

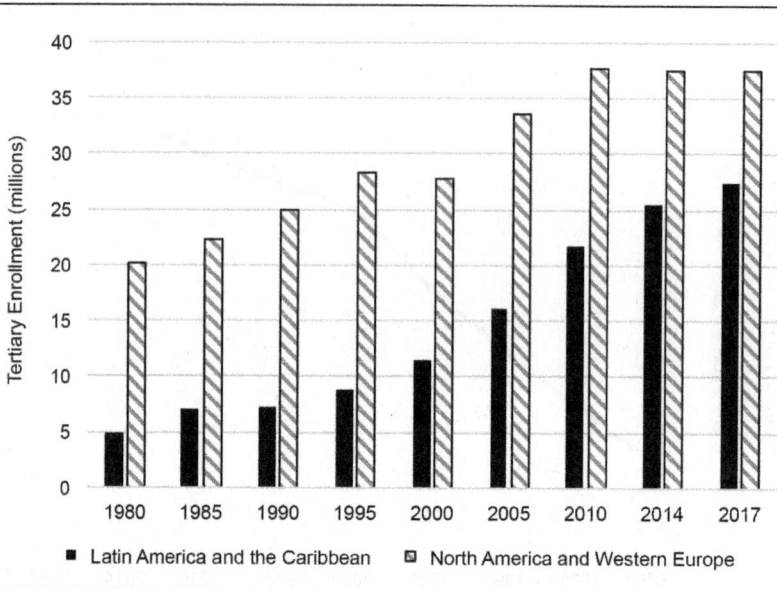

Source: UNESCO Statistical Institute, 2021.

Figure 1.3 Net Upper-Secondary Enrollment Rate, by Country, 2014 (percent)

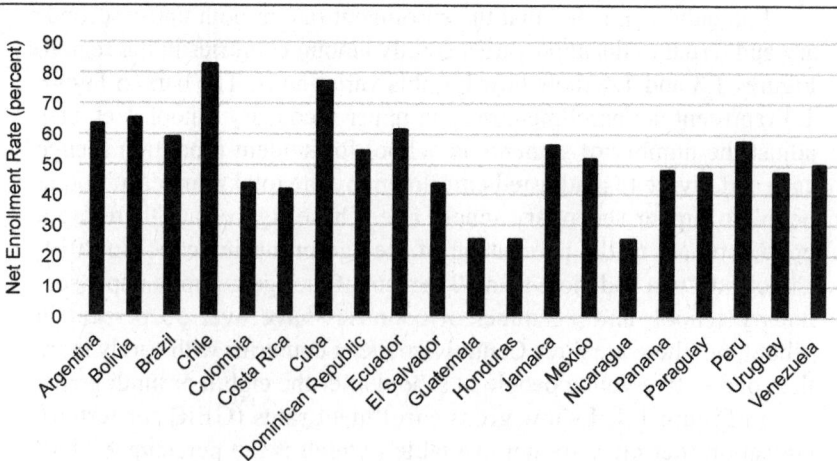

Source: UNESCO Statistical Institute, 2021.

Figure 1.4 Tertiary Gross Enrollment Rate, by Country and Region, 2017 (percent)

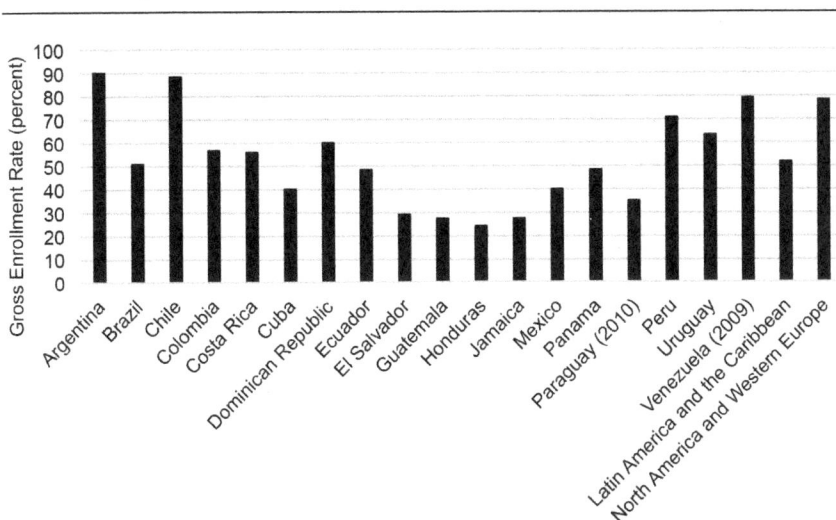

Source: World Bank, 2021.

these are overestimates of the "true" percentage of young people in higher education, mainly because there are significant numbers of students in tertiary education who are outside the six years covered in the eighteen-to-twenty-four-years age group. The more students who work while studying and take more than six years to finish their course work, the greater the overestimate. Keeping this in mind, the GER for tertiary education for Latin America as a whole is quite high, at 50 percent. Even if the "true" rate was as low as 35 percent, that is about half the GER for the United States and Western Europe. And unless the GERs are highly overestimated in Argentina, Chile, and Uruguay, those countries incorporate a high percentage of their age group in some form of education after they leave secondary school. At the other extreme, the poor Central American countries had rates of tertiary attendance well below 30 percent even in 2017.

The story of the past thirty plus years is therefore one of a rapidly changing educational landscape, where today in most Latin American countries a typical young person reaches upper secondary education (tenth to twelfth grade) but probably does not complete it. For those students who do complete upper secondary, going to some form of tertiary education is also very likely. This means that probably 35 percent of Latin American young people take education beyond high school. This is not European levels, but it is still a major accomplishment for a "developing" region of the world. It also means that from here on out, the labor force in Latin America is going to become secondary school educated, probably easier to train than in the past, and more able to take on complex tasks.

Educational Quality

Latin American students score lower (and in some countries, *much* lower) on international tests than students in highly developed countries, even when the scores are adjusted for the fewer academic resources that Latin American students' have in their families (books in the home and parents' education) compared to students in highly developed countries. For example, on the Organization for Economic Cooperation and Development (OECD) 2018 PISA test (Programme for International Student Assessment), if we assume that fifteen-year-olds in Spain and Portugal and in the highest scoring Latin American countries (Chile, Mexico, and Uruguay) all had similar family academic resources, students in Spain still score 40–50 points higher in mathematics than students in these top scoring Latin American countries, and students in Portugal, another 20 points higher than in Spain. The differences are smaller in reading (20–40 points), but even students in Chile, with the highest PISA reading score in Latin America, score significantly lower in reading than students in Spain and much lower than students in Portugal.

As far as Peru is concerned, fifteen-year-old students' performance, adjusted for family resources, on both the PISA reading and math is significantly lower than in either Chile or Mexico, even in the PISA 2018, when Peruvian students' scores increased compared to student achievement in both those countries. International tests are only one measure of student learning, and there are factors other than schooling that impact student learning, even when we adjust for home academic resource differences. Peru has made a lot of progress in raising the quality of its primary and secondary schooling, but I have visited many classrooms in Peru, and I have witnessed the lack of resources in most of them. Teachers are still poorly trained to work with the many low-income children who attend Peruvian schools, and the teachers are also still greatly underpaid. The curriculum is not up to international standards, and many teachers, especially those working in low-socioeconomic schools, do not complete the required curriculum during the academic year. My personal experience, although many years ago, was that I had some very caring teachers, but I was rarely challenged by what they were teaching—I could have done a lot more, and so could many other students in the class. The main point I want to make is that what I have seen in Peruvian schools and my own experience suggest that the results of the PISA tests and other international tests in Peru are not distorting the reality of how much Peruvian students are learning in Peruvian classrooms.

It is fair to ask what I did about this as president of Peru. To start, I did two very important things that had short- and long-term effects on Peruvian education. The first is that I doubled teachers' salaries over a three-year period during my presidency. This may seem far removed from the issue of educational quality, but teacher salaries were so low when I assumed the presidency in 2001 that teachers were completely demoralized and their work (hence student learning) suffered greatly. I also initiated a major program of conditional cash transfers (CCTs) for Peru's very poor. Again, this does not seem to have much to do directly with the quality of schooling. Yet, by requiring families receiving the transfer to keep their children in school, and conditioning the money on families' taking children in for regular checkups at clinics that we built around the country, I believe that CCTs did have an important effect on children's capacity to learn.

It is also fair to ask why I did not do more for education during my five years. I provide some answers to that question throughout this book. They focus mainly on the lessons I learned about how difficult it is to improve the process of schooling, despite my training at Stanford in the economics of education and educational policy. I also discuss how we might change the disincentives to politicians to invest in educational improvement when the fruits of that improvement take so much longer to realize than the single term of an administration (in Peru, five years).

Is the Quality of Schooling the Problem or Is It Poverty?

The low level of student learning in Latin America is the main issue I focus on in this book. Schooling quality is an important reason that students in some countries learn more than others and that students in some school districts and schools learn more than others. But there are other aspects of student learning that we should keep in mind as we address the issue. First, schooling quality is only part of the learning problem. Many analysts, including economics Nobel Prize–winner James Heckman (Heckman, 2011) have identified the conditions in which children develop in their early years are crucial to their development, and hence their later learning. Even once children enter primary school, the conditions they face outside school greatly affect their learning. The bottom line is that a child that has been malnourished or suffered poor health in his or her early years is not going to be able to learn as much in school as a well-nourished healthy child. Outside of school opportunities to learn during the school years are also an important component of student learning. School meets about thirty-six to forty weeks per year in almost every country. The activities that students engage in during the other twelve to sixteen weeks per year and in the hours after school on the days that school meets are key to the gains that students make over the course of each year (Alexander, 2007). Families in many countries of Asia, for example, enroll their children in after-school and vacation tutoring and cram courses beginning in primary school (Bray and Lykins, 2012).

Outside of school opportunities to engage in enriched learning stimuli is the positive end of a spectrum of "educational context" that I believe has an enormous impact on how much young people learn overall as they are growing up, and these opportunities may even affect how much they learn in school. For children growing up in poor families, and that is still 40 percent of Latin American families, the spectrum of educational context not only lacks positive opportunities for academic learning, it largely consists of *negative* experiences around violence, hunger, poor health, and the necessity to work many difficult hours weekly to help their families to survive. Rather than focusing on how to give their children opportunities for learning in their early childhood before they enter school and opportunities for learning in activities outside of school once enrolled in school, a typical poor family, for all its desires to do these things for their children, is forced to focus all its energy on physically surviving. I have asserted elsewhere (Toledo, 2015) that child poverty is the greatest barrier to making education work for social mobility in our Latin American societies. No education policy can be successful for the mass of Latin American children without simultaneously changing the conditions they face in their daily lives outside of school.

Student Performance in Latin America

Keeping these caveats in mind, the evidence also suggests that schooling does vary in quality, meaning that students in some countries and localities do learn more mathematics and reading in their schools because of better-skilled teachers; better curriculum and teaching methods; and better organized schools, school districts, and state and national educational administrations. We can show two simple examples of this at the national level. The first shows the relationship between UNESCO's Third Regional Comparative and Explanatory Study (TERCE) sixth grade mathematics test score averages by country relative to their gross domestic product (GDP) per capita in the same year the test was given, 2013, with the GDP per capita expressed in 2011 PPP dollars—this means that the GDP per capita is adjusted for cost of living differences among countries. Figures 1.5 and 1.6 show this relationship, and they suggest that sixth grade students in some countries are performing better than predicted in mathematics and reading given the gross product per person in that country, and sixth grade students in some countries are performing much worse than predicted. Chilean, Uruguayan, Mexican, Costa Rican, and Peruvian students are performing considerably above the prediction line in mathematics, and students in Paraguay, Dominican Republic, and Panama are performing far below the prediction line.

In reading, Chilean, Colombian, Costa Rican, and Mexican students do better than predicted, and Argentina joins the other three poorer than predicted performers. GDP per capita is only one measure of a country's capacity to produce good education, but other measures, such as the social class of the sixth grade students who took the TERCE test in each country put the same countries above and below the trend line. Thus, there are education systems in Latin America that seem to be producing relatively better student performance on this test and some countries whose educational systems are doing much worse than they should be. If we had shown the scores from UNESCO's Second Regional Comparative and Explanatory Study (SERCE) test, taken seven years earlier in 2007, we would see that sixth graders in Cuba scored much higher than students in any other Latin American country, especially in mathematics. Cuba did not participate in the 2013 TERCE test, but there is no reason to believe that scores would have been any lower. I will talk about the lessons that we can learn from Cuban education in a later chapter on teacher education and curriculum.

Figure 1.5   UNESCO TERCE Sixth Grade Math Score vs. GDP per Capita, by Country, 2013

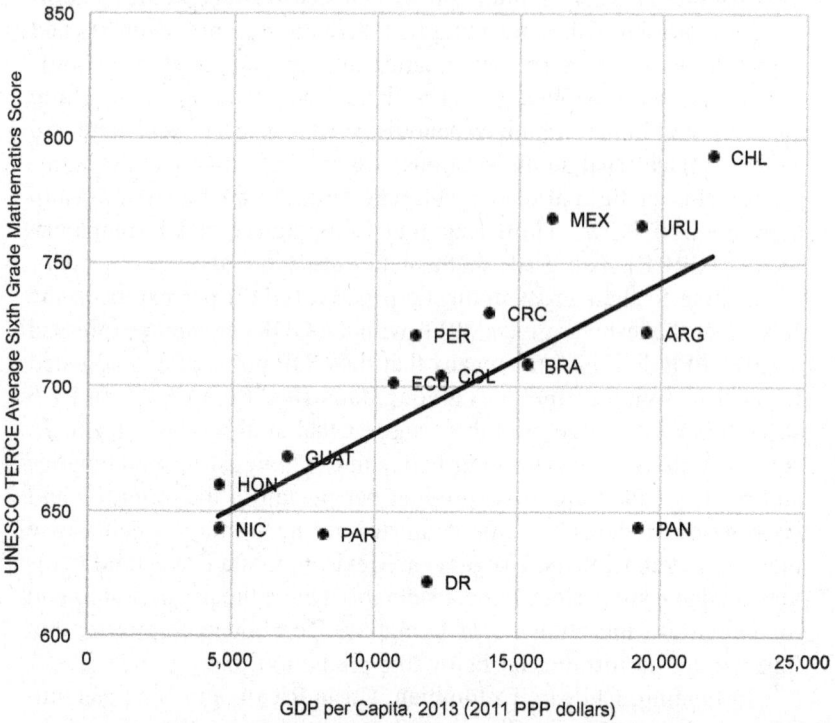

Sources: Average test scores: TERCE, 2015. *Logros de Aprendizaje.* Santiago de Chile: UNESCO, OREALC; GDP per capita: World Bank, *World Development Indicators.*
Notes: ARG = Argentina, BRA = Brazil, CHL = Chile, COL = Colombia, CRC = Costa Rica, DR = Dominican Republic, ECU = Ecuador, GUAT = Guatemala, HON = Honduras, MEX = Mexico, NIC = Nicaragua, PAN = Panama, PAR = Paraguay, PER = Peru, URU = Uruguay.

Again, we need to be careful in attributing these high and low performances strictly to schooling, but they do suggest something about the quality of the educational systems.

Another example shows how students in those Latin American countries who took the PISA math test in the years 2003 to 2018 compared to each other, both in their level of performance and the change in student performance over time. To control for social class differences among students taking the test—over time in the same country and across countries—we estimate the average scores in each country as if the sample of students who took the test in each country and in each year had the same family academic resources as students

Figure 1.6   UNESCO TERCE Sixth Grade Reading Score vs. GDP per Capita, by Country, 2013

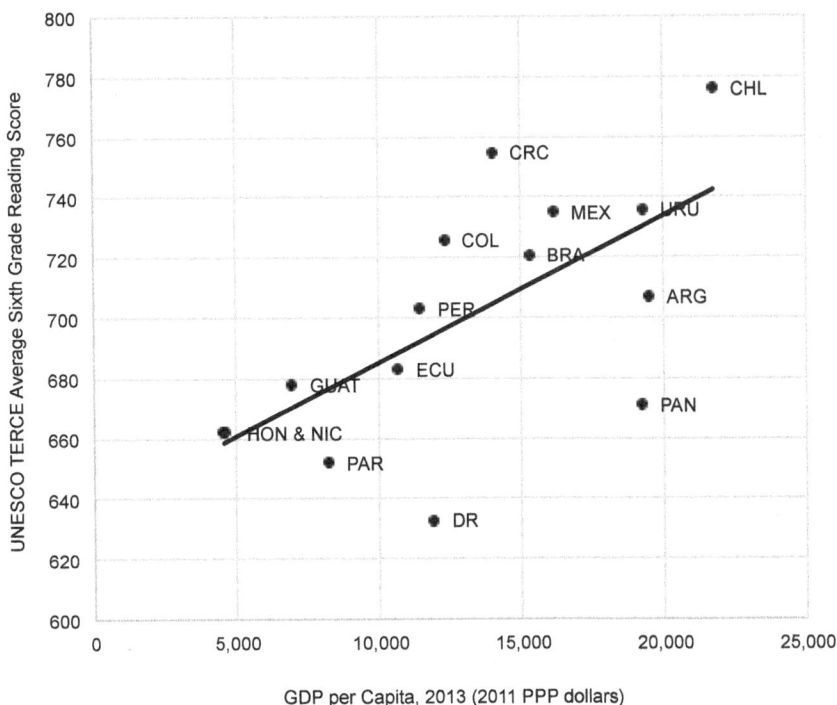

GDP per Capita, 2013 (2011 PPP dollars)

Sources: Average test scores: TERCE, 2015. *Logros de Aprendizaje.* Santiago de Chile: UNESCO, OREALC; GDP per capita: World Bank, 2021.

Notes: ARG = Argentina, BRA = Brazil, CHL = Chile, COL = Colombia, CRC = Costa Rica, DR = Dominican Republic, ECU = Ecuador, GUAT = Guatemala, HON = Honduras, MEX = Mexico, NIC = Nicaragua, PAN = Panama, PAR = Paraguay, PER = Peru, URU = Uruguay.

in a developed country such as Spain in a constant year, 2012. Table 1.1 shows these levels and trends for seven Latin American countries, two of which were below the GDP per capita trend line in Figure 1.5 (Argentina and Brazil) and the rest on or above the trend line. The average scores in the two graphs are all estimated on the assumption that the average family resources (books in the home) of students in each country and in each PISA test year were distributed as they were among the PISA sample of Spanish students in 2012.

Table 1.1 shows us that, as in the TERCE test, there are some countries in Latin America where schools might be better than in other countries. In reading, for example, students in Chile (adjusted

Table 1.1   PISA Average Mathematics and Reading Scale Scores Adjusted for Family Academic Resources (equal to the Spanish 2012 PISA sample distribution), by Country, 2003–2018

Country	2003	2006	2009	2012	2015	2018
PISA Adjusted Mathematics Score by Year						
Argentina		415	417	412		407
Brazil	396	399	409	412	402	414
Chile		438	440	447	445	441
Colombia		398	406	404	413	417
Mexico	414	433	443	433	425	425
Peru			398	398	412	426
Uruguay	441	450	452	442	449	446
Spain	479	478	482	485	487	485
PISA Adjusted Reading Score by Year						
Argentina		410	430	423		432
Brazil	432	422	436	430	432	447
Chile		467	468	463	480	475
Colombia		418	440	431	452	440
Mexico	430	437	451	444	440	440
Peru			405	414	426	430
Uruguay	454	439	453	444	471	461
Spain	475	459	480	490	496	NA[a]

Source: OECD PISA microdata, https://www.oecd.org/pisa/data/. Accessed April 12, 2021.
Note: a. Reading scores for Spain in 2018 have been withheld by PISA for further verification.

for family resources) are doing almost as well as in a lower scoring European country, such as Spain. In mathematics, when we adjust for family resource differences, students in Chile, Mexico, and Uruguay are still far behind Spain on the PISA test, but they do much better than the other four Latin American countries where students took this test. Especially interesting is why Argentinian fifteen-year-olds seem to perform lower in math than fifteen-year-olds do in Argentina's neighbors, Chile and Uruguay. In reading, Latin American students' performance adjusted for family academic resources is better compared to Spanish students than in math. As mentioned, Chilean students do particularly well in reading, but again, the highest scoring students are in Chile, Uruguay, and Mexico.

Table 1.1 also gives us some information about whether test scores are rising in Latin American countries. On the PISA mathematics test, students in Brazil, Colombia, Peru, and Mexico (in 2003–2009) have made gains, but Chile and Uruguay's gains have been modest, and Argentine students have lost ground. In reading, almost all countries have made some gains, but they are generally modest in recent years except for Peru, which started at a low level, made gains, but remains at the lower end of the Latin American PISA spectrum. One important factor to keep in mind: when we look at gains in scores in this period for fifteen-year-olds, we need to take account of the fact that access to secondary education has been expanding rapidly in many of these countries, so that even if we are adjusting for the family academic resource composition of the student sample across countries and years of the test, the average grade the fifteen-year-olds are attending is rising over time (Klein, 2011), and that has a positive effect on test scores.

Is the level of Latin American students' learning in school increasing? There is some indication from PISA and the UNESCO SERCE (2007) and TERCE (2014) tests that learning is increasing, but not universally and not greatly, even though the OECD has featured Brazilian gains in mathematics as one of its "examples" of great improvement in the quality of education (OECD, 2012). Students in Peru have also shown large gains, even more so were we to reference the PISA 2000 mathematics and reading test results, in which Peruvian students did quite poorly. There are also indications from national tests, such as the Prova Brasil and Chile's Sistema de Medición de la Calidad de la Educación (SIMCE) test, that students made progress in how much they learn by the end of fourth and eighth grades (Carnoy, Khavenson, Fonseca, Costa, and Marotta, 2015, for Brazil; Bellei and Vanni, 2015, for Chile).

These are hopeful signs, but it is clear that when it comes to the quality of education—if these test scores provide a valid indicator of educational quality—Latin American education has to make much greater improvements in its classrooms in the next generation than it has in the past generation if it hopes to have students learning at the level of lower scoring European countries such as Spain. And we will show that this is only part of the story, since one of the reasons that students learn less in a typical Latin American school than they would in a Southern European or US school is that the training of a typical teacher in Latin America and the curriculum the teacher is teaching are even more inadequate to the task than in schools of developed nations. That goes not only for schools attended by low-income students, but also for high-income students. Maybe the biggest surprise is how poorly high-income students in Latin America attending private schools perform on international tests, especially in mathematics.

The Major Challenges

Latin American education will continue to expand access. I believe that the process is unstoppable, and it is to the credit of Latin American governments that they have managed to increase the average level of schooling for young people so much in the past generation. Generally, educational expansion is beneficial for all children, and especially for disadvantaged children. There are many problems with the way educational expansion is taking place, especially at the university level, and I will talk about those in dealing with private versus public postsecondary education. However, the truly difficult problems in Latin American education we need to address in the next generation are three: (1) How do we change the conditions in which the mass of Latin America's low-income children—children living in poor rural areas and the sprawling *poblaciones* and *favelas* of urban areas, many of them Indigenous people and Blacks—grow up and learn the ways of the world? (2) How do we make the quality of schooling in Latin America—including the education of Latin America's upper-middle class but especially for low-income students—substantially better? And (3) how do we do this in a world confronting the negative impact of climate change, possibly future pandemics, and changing labor markets due to rapid technological changes requiring workers who need to readapt and learn how to learn?

I cannot claim that I have the solutions to these three fundamental issues. Yet, in what I have been able to learn in my many discussions with political and educational leaders in the region and in what I have been able to read about education in the years since my presidency, we know a lot more today about what works and does not work to reduce poverty effectively and to improve the schooling that Latin American children take for more and more years. In this book, you will find empirical evidence for the interrelationship in Latin America between investments in poverty reduction, in better education for teachers, in health care, in nutrition, in the reduction of violence, in access to digital technology, and in human dignity and democratic participation—these are all required to increase learning to high levels for every child in our societies.

I will focus on nine major challenges facing us as we try to move beyond increasing classroom seats and university places, take on improving what happens inside the classroom for all students, and drastically change the experience of low-income students both inside and outside the classroom.

1. Access to the new norm of secondary education is still very unequally distributed, and access to tertiary education, particularly university education, is even more unequally distributed.
2. Reasonable quality early childhood education and out of school enrichment experiences, which can have an important positive effect on student learning in early childhood and in primary school and beyond, is very unequally distributed in Latin America. The children who could probably benefit most from these opportunities are least likely to have access to them.
3. To the contrary, outside of school experiences for low-income children tend to be significantly *detrimental* to school learning and social mobility in the larger Latin American society. The level of violence in low-income schools in most Latin American countries is also a major detriment to student learning. These educational contexts contribute to student anxiety and detract from low-income students' ability to focus on their education.
4. The average quality of primary and secondary education in Latin America, although perhaps gradually improving, is still low, and the average quality even of elite private schools is no better than the schooling available to students from families with average income in most developed countries.
5. The quality of schooling resources available is unequally distributed among higher and lower social class students. One example of this is that teachers teaching in lower-income schools tend to be less well trained and more likely to be on temporary contracts than in higher income schools. In addition, schools in Latin America are highly social class segregated— this problem is exacerbated by the relatively high percentage of middle and higher class students attending private schools.
6. The quality of rural education is especially low in most of Latin America, and access to secondary education for rural students remains a major challenge in much of the region, in large part because of the much higher cost of quality education in rural areas.

7. In those countries with Indigenous populations, the question of improving the quality of education is made even more complex. In defining education for both Indigenous and non-Indigenous populations, nation-states need to recognize the importance of Indigenous knowledge and the meaning of the nation-state itself.
8. In a world increasingly dominated by information technology (IT), the digital divide between urban and rural students and between lower social class and higher social class students in urban areas can have serious negative implications for these students in their job market success, and it may influence who and how many go into science, technology, engineering, and math (STEM) careers.
9. University education has a high economic payoff to graduates and has been expanding rapidly in Latin America. But the expansion has taken place very unequally, both in access by different groups in society and in the distribution of quality. Good university education is expensive, and a major question is who should pay for it, students and their families or the government through general taxation. Many countries in the region have turned to private institutions to expand access—is this the right solution?

In the chapters that follow, I want to deal with each of these topics. It is important to be realistic in trying to overcome these problems. My way of doing that is to draw on carefully researched studies that analyze the nature of the challenges and how to overcome them. It is also important to be realistic about the overall impact that better education in the region can have in solving broader Latin American social and economic issues such as economic growth, environmental degradation, or unequal income distribution.

Improving the education that young people get is a useful end in itself. Yet, arguing for a better-educated population for the sake of education is probably not going to convince the minister of economics that we should invest heavily in better and more equal education just because it will produce many more bright people. The minister wants to know how that investment will increase worker productivity, produce better citizens, and reduce the unemployment rate, among other good outcomes. I am going to argue that we need to make sure that we do not overstate the "savior" aspects of education, but rather insist on the potential beneficial effects that a better educated labor force and citizenry might contribute to making life better for everyone.

2

The Inequality of Educational Outcomes

A key feature of the world's national educational systems is that they do not provide the same quantity or quality of schooling to all children. I have always considered, given my own history, that high levels of schooling are desirable for all. But probably not everyone wants to attend university or take postgraduate courses and not everyone does. If these different levels of attainment or access to educational quality were just due to such individual differences in taste for education or of randomized differences in student academic ability, it would not be much of a problem.

However, the differences in attainment and quality are not mainly due to taste and innate differences in abilities. Family social class and race/ethnicity are consistently shown to be important determinants of how far young people go in school—as or even more important than academic ability, and, it turns out, academic ability is also affected by social class because higher social class children have better opportunities to learn than lower social class children. When inequities of access to schooling and quality schooling are based on social class and race/ethnicity, this threatens the meritocratic ideals of democracy. It is also socially inefficient, since it allocates too few educational resources to more qualified, yet overlooked, young people in disadvantaged groups and too many resources to less qualified, but socially favored young people in advantaged groups.

Latin American countries are no exception to this pattern of educational access and quality. In this chapter, I show that educational systems in Latin America have greatly expanded since the 1980s, incorporating a much higher fraction of school age children into secondary school and, after the 1990s, into higher education. I also try to show that rural and lower social class Latin Americans attain systematically fewer years of schooling and score significantly lower on achievement tests than their urban and higher social class counterparts in every country in the region. The good news is that these differences are declining in many Latin American countries and that they are much smaller in some Latin American countries than in others. This means that it is possible to realize smaller differences between regions, rural and urban, and the socially advantaged and disadvantaged.

I try to make a strong case through the book that educational attainment and achievement levels and differences among groups and the way they are changing in each society are at least partly due to government policies. These policies, by omission or commission, fail to allocate sufficient resources that would help improve educational outcomes and to make them more equal. Because they are partly to blame, Latin American governments can and need to take specific actions to remedy the unnecessarily low and unnecessarily unequal outcomes. I make some suggestions at the end of the chapter and develop them in greater detail throughout the book. Without such actions in education and broader actions to remedy the immense social class and ethnicity/racial differences in the region, democracy and economic development will never come near to reaching their full potential.

The Expansion of Education Enrollment in Latin America

Unequal Educational Attainment

Urban-rural differences. It is difficult to estimate educational attainment by social class groups in Latin America, but one indicator of these differences is the unequal attainment of adults twenty-five to fifty-nine years old living in urban and rural areas. For our purposes, it is also important to understand how urban-rural educational attainment has changed in recent years. Rural populations have declined substantially in every Latin American country in the past twenty-five years, but many countries in 2015 still had more than 20 percent of their populations living in rural areas, and, not surprisingly, the less developed countries of Central America still had 40 percent in rural areas. Those living in rural areas tend to be poorer and have far less access to services such as education and health care.

We need to understand as well that in Central America, Mexico, and Peru, the populations of rural areas are primarily Indigenous peoples. Indigenous peoples are—plain and simple—marginalized from the European-origin mainstream of Latin American society. In those countries with large Indigenous populations, many of them now living in urban areas, coming up with ways to value their potential contribution to the broader society and to provide them with dignity and instill pride in their culture are essential to the future of these nations.

Table 2.1 shows the percentage of the population in rural areas in 1990, 2015, and 2019 for twelve countries in the region. This percentage varies considerably between countries such as Uruguay, with a very low fraction in rural areas, and Bolivia and Guatemala, with high fractions in rural areas, still in 2019. My country, Peru, had more than 20 percent of the population living in rural areas in the second decade of the twenty-first century. Since *rural* is defined as very small communities (less than 5,000 population), these figures may underestimate the population of what we might think of rural areas, which would include some slightly larger towns but far from any urban-type services.

Table 2.1 Population in Rural Areas, by Country, 1990, 2015, and 2019 (in percent)

Country	1990	2015	2019
Bolivia	44.5	30.9	30.2
Brazil	25.3	14.3	13.2
Chile	16.8	11.1	12.4
Colombia	30.5	20.6	18.9
Costa Rica	50.0	23.4	19.9
Cuba	28.1	23.0	22.9
Dominican Republic	44.9	21.2	18.2
Guatemala	65.6	44.0	48.6
Mexico	29.1	22.7	19.6
Panama	46.1	33.4	31.9
Peru	31.1	21.3	21.9
Uruguay	11.1	4.7	4.6

Sources: Economic Commission for Latin America. (2021). CEPAL STAT. https://estadisticas.cepal.org/cepalstat/portada.html?idioma=english. Accessed April 12, 2021; World Bank. (2021). *World Development Indicators.* https://databank.worldbank.org/reports.aspx?source=World-Development-Indicators. Accessed April 12, 2021.

Table 2.2 shows the average years of schooling in the population twenty-five to fifty-nine years old for eleven countries and Latin America as a whole over the period 1990–2018. I see the good news in Table 2.2 as the steady rise in educational attainment in both urban and rural areas in the past generation. If the data are accurate, Bolivia's urban adult population has increased its average education from nine years in 1990 to more than eleven years in 2018, followed by Chile's urban population, which has twelve years of schooling, on average, up from less than ten years in 1990. The education level of the rural population has also increased steadily in this period—up three years in Bolivia since 1999, more than three years in Bolivia and Chile, and somewhat less in other countries. The bad news is that the difference in educational attainment between urban and rural populations—between the richer part of the population and the poorest part of the population—has barely decreased in the past fifteen to twenty-five years. The smallest gaps are in countries such as Costa Rica and Uruguay, and the largest in Brazil and my own country, Peru, where urban Peruvians have a relatively high level of educational attainment, but rural Peruvians on average only completed six years of primary schooling in 2018.

The gap between rural and urban Latin Americans has serious implications for the structure of economic and social development. The worst situation is in countries such as Guatemala, where both urban and rural populations have low levels of education, and the rural population attains, on average, only a few years of primary school, probably not enough to know how to read or do simple arithmetic. Furthermore, almost half the population lives in rural areas, and this population faces additional social barriers because it is Indigenous. In Peru and Bolivia, where the gap is large in part because of the relatively high levels of educational attainment in the urban population, the nature of the gap suggests that rural primary education is widely accessible, but that secondary education is still largely an urban phenomenon. In these two countries, we also have large fractions of the population in underserved rural areas, and, as in Guatemala, most of them are Indigenous peoples.

Costa Rica is also an interesting case, since its rural population, after Chile and Uruguay, has one of the highest levels of education in the region and is relatively high compared to the education of the urban population. If we compare Costa Rica with its neighbor, Panama, its urban population has higher levels of schooling than urban Costa Ricans, but its rural population, relatively much larger

Table 2.2   Years of Schooling in the Population Twenty-Five to Fifty-Nine Years Old, by Country and Urban/Rural, 1990–2018

Country/Area	1990	1994	1999	2004	2009	2014	2018
Bolivia urban	*8.8*	9.3	9.4	8.9	10.5	*10.9*	11.2
Bolivia rural			3.5	4.9	5.4	*6.2*	6.7
Brazil urban	6.2	*6.4*	7	7.7	8.8	9.2	10.8
Brazil rural	2.6	*2.8*	3.3	3.7	5.2	5.5	6.9
Chile urban	9.7	10.2	*10.8*	*11.1*	11.4	*12.0*	12.4
Chile rural	6.2	6.6	*6.7*	*7.4*	8.4	*9.2*	9.7
Colombia urban	*8.1*	8.3	8.6	9	9.3	10	10.4
Colombia rural	*4.1*	4.4	4.8	4.7	4.7	5.5	6.1
Costa Rica urban	8.8	9.1	9.3	9.5	9.9	9.8	9.8
Costa Rica rural	5.6	6	6.5	6.6	7.2	7.4	7.5
Dom. Republic urban			*8.9*	9.2	9.6	10	10.3
Dom. Republic rural			*5.2*	6.4	6.4	7	7.5
Guatemala urban			*6.7*	7.2	*7*	6.3	NA
Guatemala rural			*2.1*	*2.5*	*2.6*	3.1	NA
Mexico urban		8	*8.6*	*9.4*	*10*	10.6	10.6
Mexico rural		4	*5.6*	6.2	*6.5*	7.2	7.4
Panama urban	10.4	10.6	11	11.1	*11.4*	12	12.1
Panama rural			*6*	6.8	7.3	7.5	· 8.0
Peru urban			10.1	*10.8*	11.2	11.2	11.4
Peru rural			4.6	*5.4*	5.8	6	6.4
Uruguay urban	8.3	8.6	9.2	9.9	9.9	10.4	10.4
Uruguay rural					7.2	8	8.0
Latin America urban	8	8.2	8.8	9.2	*9.7*	10.1	10.4
Latin America rural			4.3	5	*5.6*	6.2	6.7

Source: CEPAL STAT. https://estadisticas.cepal.org/cepalstat/portada.html?idioma=english. Accessed April 12, 2021.

Note: Numbers in italics and lighter type are interpolated.

than Costa Rica's, has about the same level of education. As I will show later in the chapter, a key difference between the two countries' education systems is that Costa Rican students score near the top of Latin American countries, and Panama, near the bottom. The reasons for this and the impact that it might have on development patterns and the distribution of the fruits of growth in the two countries can help us understand a lot about education and the future of social development in the region.

The data in Tables 2.1 and 2.2 provide one view of educational inequalities in the region, but it is an important one because living in a rural area in Latin America is associated with poverty and a lack of services, such as quality education and health care, potable water, waste systems, and good transportation, all of which are crucial to reducing inequality and laying the groundwork for more rapid economic development in these areas. The gap in levels of educational attainment is one indicator of how great is the inequality in the provision of such services to lower and higher income groups in various countries. There are other indicators of this inequality, and I want to turn to some of these now.

Social class differences in attainment. As I noted earlier, it is difficult to find studies in Latin America of educational attainment differences by social class. But it is not impossible to find evidence that such attainment differences exist. One source is the information from the OECD's Programme for International Student Assessment (PISA). Because PISA tests and surveys fifteen-year-olds in school in each participant country, no matter their grade, we can estimate for the seven Latin American countries participating in the PISA, the grade of students by their social class background (socioeconomic status, SES), with SES measured by books in the home and mother's education. The results show that those lower SES students still in school when they are fifteen years old are significantly behind in grade attainment compared to higher SES students—and we have to remember that many lower SES students in Latin America are not in school at fifteen years old. This means that by just observing those lower social class students who are still in school at fifteen years old we are greatly underestimating the true gap in attainment of lower social class students at that age. Our estimates do not include all the unobserved lower social class students who already dropped out.

Table 2.3 shows the attainment gap between students in a low family academic resource (FAR) group—those who reported zero to ten books in the home—and those in a high family academic resource group—those who reported more than 100 books in the home. We can disagree whether books in the home is a good measure of social class, but it is highly correlated with other measures, such as mother's education, and these two categories describe students with very different academic home environments. The average number of years of schooling attained by fifteen-year-old students sampled by PISA and in the advantaged FAR category was around ten years of schooling in all the Latin American countries participating in PISA except Brazil, in part because Brazilian students began primary schooling at seven years old until 2007, when the law was changed to admit first graders at six years old. Students from low FAR families, on the other hand,

Table 2.3   Average Years of Schooling of Students Taking the PISA Test, Gap Between Very Disadvantaged and Advantaged Students, 2000–2015 (gap measured in years of schooling)

Country/SES of Students' Group	Year of PISA Test						
	2000 Math	2000 Reading	2003	2006	2009	2012	2015
Argentina very disadvantaged	9.33	9.32		9.31	9.20	9.33	
Argentina advantaged	9.86	9.86		9.87	9.64	9.78	
Gap Argentina	0.53	0.55		0.56	0.44	0.46	
Brazil very disadvantaged	8.38	8.39	8.57	8.63	8.93	9.04[a]	8.93[a]
Brazil advantaged	8.66	8.75	8.87	8.99	9.28	9.40[a]	9.24[a]
Gap Brazil	0.28	0.36	0.30	0.36	0.35	0.36	0.31
Chile very disadvantaged	9.23	9.21		9.63	9.58	9.54	9.46
Chile advantaged	9.71	9.67		9.90	9.85	9.79	9.76
Gap Chile	0.49	0.45		0.27	0.27	0.24	0.30
Colombia very disadvantaged				9.20	9.39	9.36	9.36
Colombia advantaged				9.93	9.89	9.87	9.73
Gap Colombia				0.73	0.51	0.51	0.37
Mexico very disadvantaged	9.17	9.13	9.18	9.39	9.35	9.53	9.47
Mexico advantaged	9.58	9.60	9.45	9.74	9.65	9.66	9.59
Gap Mexico	0.42	0.47	0.27	0.35	0.30	0.14	0.13
Peru very disadvantaged	9.02	9.02			9.45	9.59	9.70
Peru advantaged	9.75	9.74			10.13	10.07	10.10
Gap Peru	0.73	0.72			0.68	0.47	0.39
Uruguay very disadvantaged			9.20	9.12	9.05	9.16	9.15
Uruguay advantaged			9.79	9.82	9.78	9.68	9.72
Gap Uruguay			0.59	0.70	0.72	0.52	0.58

Source: OECD PISA microdata, 2000–2015, https://www.oecd.org/pisa/data/. *Note:* a. Brazil's estimated years of schooling reduced by one year in 2012 and 2015 to make comparable with previous years, since educational system reform added a year of schooling as students entering first grade entered at six years old rather than seven years old.

averaged anywhere from about one-third to almost three-quarters of a year less. This could have been true for many reasons, including starting school later and a greater likelihood of repeating grades.

The good news is that in these seven countries, the gap has generally declined, mainly because students in the lower FAR group are increasing their grade level more than the higher FAR group of students. One exception is Brazil, where the gap has been constant since PISA 2000. At the other extreme, in Mexico, the gap has declined to only 0.13 years.

We know, of course, that lower social class students take fewer years of schooling than higher social class students. A smaller proportion of lower SES students completes high school and goes on to college, for example. A much higher percentage of lower SES students also drops out in middle school. What I am trying to show here is even for those students who make it to the last years of middle school and to high school, at a given age, even though they are still in school, lower SES students are likely to be in a lower grade than their higher SES counterparts. This is one reason contributing to the higher level of dropout for lower SES students in high school, and is a possible indicator of unequal access to high-quality resources in primary and middle school.

Unequal Academic Achievement

Fewer years of schooling. Why is it important to adjust test scores for differences in students' family resources when analyzing student academic achievement? Students from low-income families not only get fewer years of education than their better off counterparts, they perform at a lower level on national and international tests. This indicates that they have learned less of what they were supposed to be taught in school by the time they reach a certain age or complete a certain number of years of schooling. However, much of their so-called learning less is due to the fact that they start school already behind higher social class children entering kindergarten or first grade, and in Latin America, they are also likely to start school later and repeat grades. Yet, part is the result of attending schools that are not as good at teaching students academic skills, and another part is due to the kinds of activities that students engage in during their vacations and after school.

When I was going to school, I had to work shining shoes to help out my family financially. I was no different than many low-income children in Latin America even today. They work after school at informal jobs, badly paid but maybe enough to help buy food and clothing for themselves and younger siblings. This affects their time to do schoolwork at home, and it precludes participating in enriching activities when not attending school.

Low-income children are also more likely to live in neighborhoods marked by violence during the school year. The violence is often associated with gang, or turf, wars that erupt in neighborhoods. Stanford student Sophia MacGregor showed, using Mexican data, that if a turf war erupted in a neighborhood in the month before students in schools there took the national mathematics evaluation test (ENLACES), their scores were significantly lower than for students in neighborhoods where turf wars erupted after the ENLACES test. Not surprisingly, boys' performance on the test was more affected by the violence than were girls' scores (MacGregor, 2017).

As important, schools in neighborhoods marked by violence are more likely to have more violence among students and between students and teachers. And this violence has a significant effect on students' average achievement levels in these schools, even when controlling for the lower social class of students attending them. It is difficult to unravel the effect on individual achievement of being in a low-income school from the effect of higher levels of violence associated with low-income schools, but MacGregor's (2017) and others' studies show that violence itself has a negative influence on student achievement over and above being in a school with mostly low-income students. This is important to know because it means that if we can make low-income neighborhoods more secure, students will achieve at higher levels even if they remain low-income and continue to attend a low-income school. Of course, we also know that much of the violence associated with drugs and other criminal behavior is the direct result of long-term poverty and income inequality, so reducing poverty is an important factor in reducing violence.

Thus, when I analyze student achievement on tests, I "adjust" the reported scores for socioeconomic background differences between countries. In the PISA test, we assume that each Latin American country's fifteen-year-olds have the same distribution of family academic resources as fifteen-year-olds in Spain in a given test year, 2012. For the United Nations Educational, Scientific and Cultural Organization (UNESCO) Latin American tests, I assume that in every country, third and sixth graders had the same distribution of students by socioeconomic background as in the distribution for the entire Latin American sample taken together in each grade. In order to compare the SERCE test, given in 2007 with the TERCE test given in 2014, I assume that the TERCE sample had the same distribution of students by SES as the entire Latin American sample in the SERCE test.

Why adjust the scores? I think that the adjusted scores give a better picture of how well the educational system is doing with the children it receives into the educational system in first grade. I don't think it is fair to say, for example, simply based on average unadjusted test scores, that Peru's educational system is "much worse" than the Chilean education system. An average Peruvian student comes to first grade with many fewer academic resources invested in him or her and has many fewer resources invested in them outside school while they proceed through primary and into secondary education.

International data on student achievement in Latin America. In recent years, students in Latin American countries have regularly participated in international tests such as the OECD's Programme for International Student Assessment and UNESCO's Latin American Laboratory for Assessment of the Quality of Education (LLECE) test (1997), the SERCE (2007), and TERCE (2014). The PISA tested fifteen-year-olds every three years in randomly selected schools in each of seven Latin American countries in the years 2000 to 2018. Not every country participated in the PISA every test year, but students in two countries, Brazil and Mexico, took the test in all six years it was given. Brazil and Mexico applied much larger samples than other countries because they were interested in state differences. The PISA sampling is complicated because fifteen-year-olds in Latin America are found in the eighth to eleventh grades, and in most countries the eighth and ninth grades are part of basic education schools and the tenth and eleventh grades in upper secondary schools.

LLECE (now called PERCE) sampled and tested students in third and fourth grades in 1997, and SERCE and TERCE, in third and sixth grades in 2007 and 2014. Almost every Latin American country took the SERCE and TERCE. There is a good analysis of the LLECE test results in Carnoy, Gove, and Marshall (2007), which shows Cuban third and fourth grade students performing much better in both math and reading than students coming from families with similar levels of mother's education in Argentina, Bolivia, Brazil, Chile, Colombia, and Mexico. However, I will focus on the third and sixth grade performance of students in the more recent SERCE and TERCE surveys because they cover the same seven countries that took PISA.

The main results I want to show are the differences between "very disadvantaged," "disadvantaged," and "advantaged" students taking these tests and how they have changed over the past two decades. I use the PISA test for one of my comparisons and the

SERCE and TERCE tests for my other comparison. The students who took the PISA test were fifteen years old when they sat the test. As I discussed earlier, lower social class fifteen-year-olds taking the PISA have attained somewhat fewer years of schooling when they took the test, so we would expect them to score lower. But the differences in test score on the PISA is much larger between advantaged students coming from families with high levels of family academic resources (more than 100 books in the home or mother with college education) and students coming from families with very low levels of family resources (ten or fewer books in the home or mother with less than complete high school education) than could be explained by the one-third to one-half grade difference in attainment we showed in Table 2.3 between very disadvantaged and advantaged students.

PISA scores for advantaged and disadvantaged students. Figures 2.1a, 2.1b, 2.1c, and 2.1d show the achievement differences among students in seven countries by family academic resource levels, when we define the students' family academic resources by books in the home. The results when we use mother's education to define advantage and disadvantage are very similar. In each graph, I compare the PISA scores in mathematics by year of the test by level of family academic resources (in this case, books in the home) for two countries at a time. I included a comparison with Colombia, even though students there only started taking the test in 2006. Peru did not participate in the PISA in 2003 and 2006, so the scores for Peru in 2003 and 2006 shown in the Peru-Colombia comparison (Figure 2.1c) are interpolations. The same is true for Chile in 2003 and Argentina in 2003 and 2015.

These graphs prove to be very interesting, especially in what they suggest about how Latin American schooling may or may not be improving and becoming more or less equitable. One very important result, which should be no surprise, is that students with lower family resources do not do as well on the mathematics test as students with higher family resources. Not all very disadvantaged fifteen-year-old students, representing about 25–40 percent of the PISA sample, are still in school at fifteen years old in some of these countries. If all were in school, their scores might be lower. But taking the scores as they are, the differences in recent years (2012 and 2018) between the scores of advantaged students—the students from the top 15–20 percent of family academic resource families—and the very disadvantaged—the bottom 30–40 percent of FAR families, were anywhere from about 40 points (Mexico) to 80–90 points (Chile, Peru, and Uruguay). This

Figure 2.1a   Brazil and Mexico: Average PISA Mathematics Scale Score, by Students' Family Academic Resource Group, 2000–2018

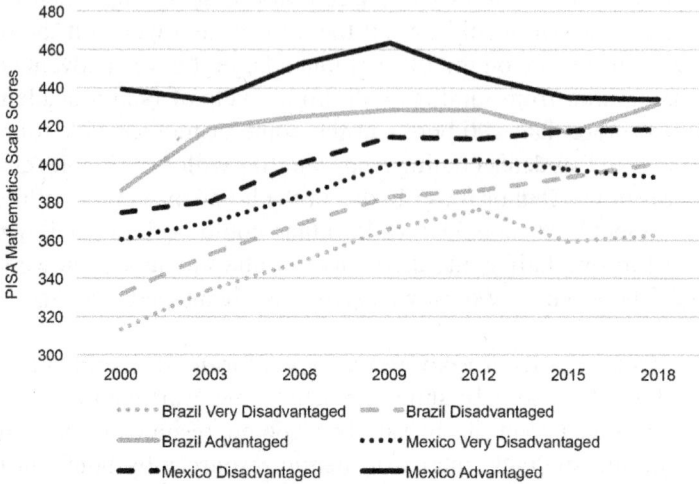

Source: OECD PISA microdata, 2000–2018.

Figure 2.1b   Argentina and Chile: Average PISA Mathematics Scale Score, by Students' Family Academic Resource Group, 2000–2018

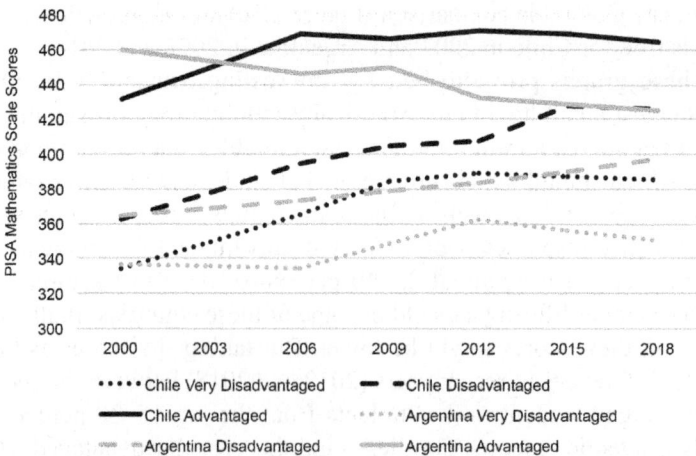

Source: OECD PISA microdata, 2000–2018.
Note: Chilean and Argentine scores are interpolated in 2003 and Argentine scores are interpolated in 2015, since Chile and Argentina did not participate in the PISA in those years.

Figure 2.1c   Peru and Colombia: Average PISA Mathematics Scale Score, by Students' Family Academic Resource Group, 2000–2018

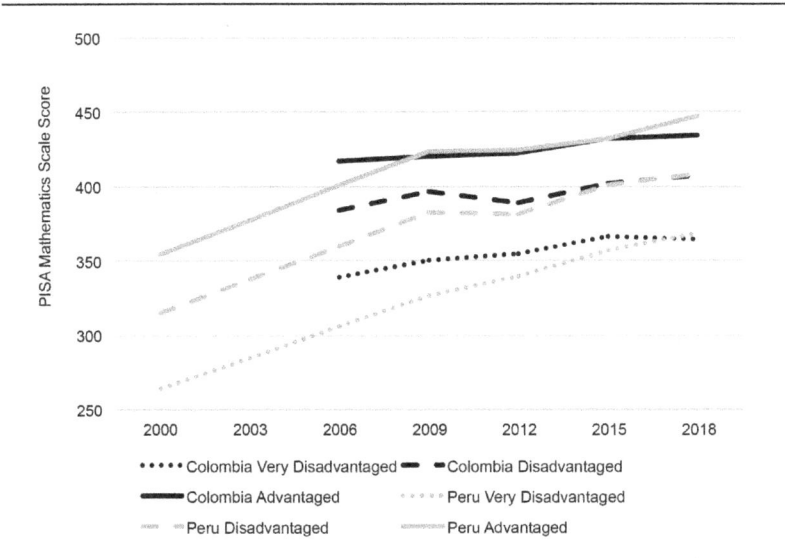

Source: OECD PISA microdata, 2000–2018.
Note: Peruvian scores in 2003 and 2006 are interpolated linearly between 2000 and 2009 scores, since Peru did not participate in the PISA test in those years.

represents 0.4 to 0.9 standard deviations (SDs). The differences in Chile, Peru, and Uruguay are very large by international standards, and the difference in Mexico is small by international standards. The difference is so much larger in Chile and Uruguay not because very disadvantaged students are scoring so much lower than students in other countries—in fact, they do better than in Brazil, Colombia, and Peru—but that the advantaged students are doing so much better on the PISA math test in Chile than in the rest of the region. In Peru, the opposite is true: Peruvian advantaged students do not do particularly well, but very disadvantaged students score very low.

We also have to take into consideration the fact that lower social class students in these PISA samples of fifteen-year-olds are much more likely to be in a lower grade than their higher social class counterparts. If we go back to Table 2.3, we can see that the grade gap in Mexico between advantaged and very disadvantaged students has declined substantially and is now very small. Similarly, PISA scores in Mexico for very disadvantaged and advantaged in Mexico have

Figure 2.1d   Argentina and Uruguay: Average PISA Mathematics Scale Score, by Students' Family Academic Resource Group, 2000–2018

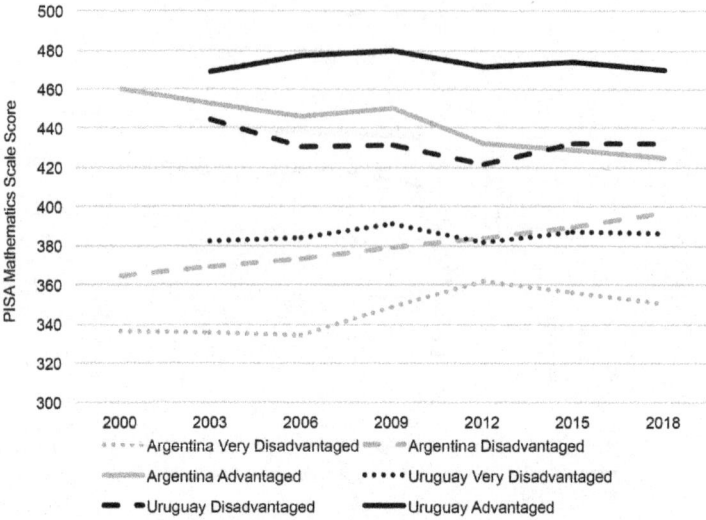

Source: OECD PISA microdata, 2000–2018.
    Note: Argentine scores are interpolated in 2003 and 2015, since Argentina did not participate in the PISA in those years.

become more equal. Peru is another example of a declining gap in grade attained and math test scores for the very disadvantaged and advantaged. On the other hand, both the grade gap and test score gap has changed little in Brazil. Thus, decreasing the grade gap between lower and higher family resourced students, as in Mexico or Peru, is likely to decrease the gap in their PISA achievement.

SERCE and TERCE scores for third and sixth graders. PISA is not the only test used to measure how well students are doing in the region's schools. UNESCO surveyed and tested third and fourth graders with the LLECE test in 1997, and since then has followed up with two more tests, the SERCE in 2007 and the TERCE in 2014, applied to third graders and sixth graders. Fortunately, with these last two tests their scores are comparable and, unlike the LLECE survey, almost all countries in Latin America participated. I am going to compare mathematics scores for sixth graders who have less and more educated mothers on the SERCE and the TERCE. This will help us see whether the socioeconomic difference in test scores looks similar in elementary school and high school (PISA). These two Latin American tests also allow us to look at some countries that did not participate in the PISA.

The results in Figure 2.2 show that as in the PISA, the difference in the math test score between disadvantaged sixth grade students—in this case, students with mothers that had not completed high school—and advantaged sixth grade students—in this case, students whose mothers had completed high school or attended university—varies a lot among countries. At least in two countries, Peru and Uruguay, large differences between the two groups are consistent with the large test score differences between advantaged and disadvantaged students on the PISA. I did not include Cuba because Cuba participated in the SERCE but not the TERCE. I could not include Mexico in the comparisons because Mexico did not apply a parent questionnaire in the SERCE so I could not estimate the average scores for disadvantaged and advantaged students. On the sixth grade TERCE math and reading tests, Mexican advantaged students were right up there among the highest scoring countries. Mexico's disadvantaged students were also among the highest scoring in math, but were significantly behind Costa Rica and Chile in sixth grade reading. The third grade mathematics scores in the various countries behave about the same as sixth grade scores and so do the third and sixth grade reading scores.

I find that the most interesting feature of the SERCE and TERCE scores in both math and reading when comparing disadvantaged and advantaged students is that several of the countries where both groups of students perform quite poorly, such as Guatemala, Nicaragua, Panama, Paraguay, and the Dominican Republic, not shown here, the test score differences between the groups are quite small, and countries that perform on average very well, such as Chile and Uruguay, are marked by very large differences between performance of advantaged and disadvantaged students. One interesting case is Costa Rica, where disadvantaged students do very well compared to sixth graders in other Latin American countries but advantaged students do not do that well, especially compared to Uruguay and Chile.

We can also adjust SERCE and TERCE scores for students' family academic resource differences among countries as I discussed earlier. I recalculate the average test score for each country assuming that students in every country have the same average FAR plus the same urban/rural and Indigenous/non-Indigenous composition as in the overall Latin American sample in the SERCE test in 2007. How do test scores differ among countries when the results are adjusted

34

Figure 2.2 Average SERCE and TERCE Mathematics Score, by Family Academic Resource Group and Country, 2007 and 2014

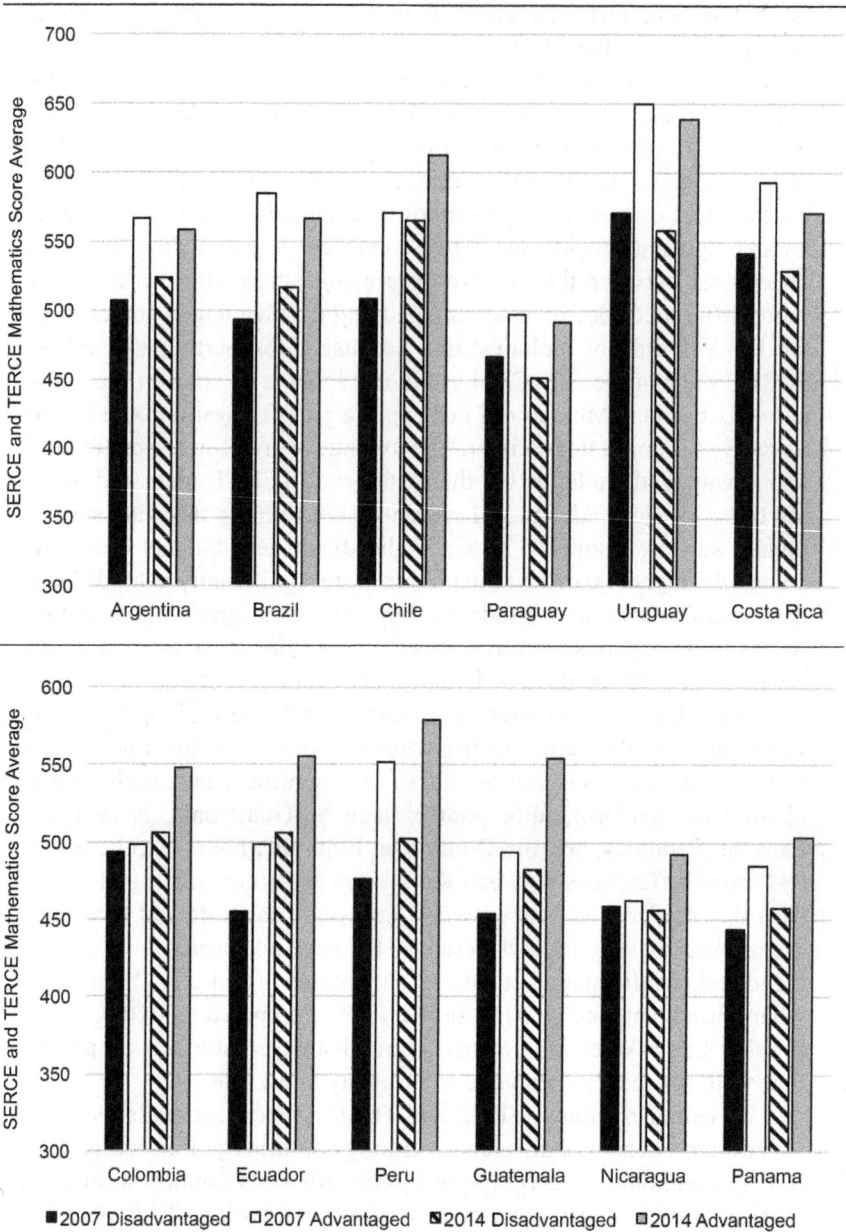

Source: UNESCO, SERCE and TERCE microdata.

for such sample composition differences across countries and across time (2014 versus 2007)?

Tables 2.4 and 2.5 show the scores as they were reported in SERCE and TERCE and the scores estimated by adjusting for FAR, race, and locality differences. Students in the richer countries don't do as well as reported in the raw scores, and students in the poorer countries do better than reported. The changes are not big, but some countries move up and down in the rankings, and the variation in scores among the countries is much smaller, as we would expect. In Peru, for example, once we adjust students' scores in TERCE sixth grade math, the gap between their average math achievement and students' achievement in the high scoring countries, Chile and Uruguay, was reduced to 34 points from 54 in Chile, stayed at 40 points compared to Uruguay, but increased compared to Mexico's students from 39 to 48 points. This is still a big average gap, true, but Peru has made large gains in student achievement in the years between SERCE and TERCE (along with a number of other countries—for example, Argentina, Brazil, Colombia, and Ecuador in math; and Ecuador in reading).

Table 2.4   Reported and Adjusted SERCE Sixth Grade Mathematics and Reading Scores, Ranking by Country, 2007

Ranking SERCE Sixth Grade Mathematics				Ranking SERCE Sixth Grade Reading			
Reported Scores		Adjusted Scores		Reported Scores		Adjusted Scores	
Uruguay	578	Uruguay	571	Costa Rica	563	Costa Rica	574
Costa Rica	549	Costa Rica	559	Chile	546	Brazil	532
Chile	517	Brazil	512	Uruguay	542	Uruguay	532
Argentina	513	Argentina	503	Brazil	520	Colombia	520
Brazil	499	Colombia	498	Colombia	515	Chile	520
Colombia	493	Paraguay	493	Argentina	506	Argentina	494
Peru	490	Guatemala	492	Peru	476	Guatemala	492
Paraguay	468	Chile	491	Nicaragua	473	Nicaragua	491
Ecuador	460	Peru	488	Panama	472	Paraguay	485
Nicaragua	458	Nicaragua	473	Paraguay	455	Peru	474
Guatemala	456	Ecuador	455	Guatemala	451	Panama	472
Panama	452	Panama	451	Ecuador	447	Ecuador	445
Dominican Republic	416	Dominican Republic	428	Dominican Republic	421	Dominican Republic	435

Source: UNESCO SERCE microdata, 2007. These data were made available to the author by request from UNESCO LLECE. Also available from http://gaml.uis.unesco.org/learning-data/. Accessed April 12, 2021.

Note: Adjusted scores are adjusted to Latin American SERCE sample means of mother's education, books in home, age in grade, Indigenous, urban/rural, and private/public school.

Table 2.5   Reported and Adjusted TERCE Sixth Grade Mathematics and Reading Scores, Ranking by Country, 2014

Ranking TERCE Sixth Grade Mathematics				Ranking TERCE Sixth Grade Reading			
Reported Scores		Adjusted Scores		Reported Scores		Adjusted Scores	
Chile	581	Mexico	564	Chile	557	Costa Rica	534
Uruguay	567	Uruguay	556	Costa Rica	546	Brazil	519
Mexico	566	Chile	550	Uruguay	532	Mexico	516
Costa Rica	535	Costa Rica	536	Mexico	529	Chile	514
Argentina	530	Brazil	528	Colombia	526	Colombia	512
Peru	527	Argentina	519	Brazil	524	Uruguay	509
Brazil	520	Peru	516	Argentina	509	Guatemala	497
Colombia	515	Colombia	512	Peru	505	Honduras	489
Ecuador	513	Ecuador	507	Ecuador	491	Argentina	485
Guatemala	488	Guatemala	506	Ecuador	489	Peru	483
Honduras	480	Honduras	500	Panama	483	Paraguay	481
Nicaragua	462	Nicaragua	472	Honduras	479	Nicaragua	478
Panama	461	Paraguay	471	Nicaragua	479	Panama	476
Paraguay	456	Panama	465	Paraguay	469	Ecuador	474
Dominican Republic	437	Dominican Republic	440	Dominican Republic	456	Dominican Republic	446

Source: UNESCO TERCE microdata, 2014. These data were made available to the author by request from UNESCO LLECE. Also available from http://gaml.uis.unesco.org/learning-data/. Accessed April 12, 2021.

Note: Adjusted scores are adjusted to Latin American SERCE sample means of mother's education, books in home, age in grade, Indigenous, urban/rural, and private/public school.

The Quality of Education Among Latin American Countries

If I were to compare the quality of the systems in the seven countries in Figure 2.1 based on PISA scores, I would have to argue that the Chilean and Uruguayan systems are probably the best because their advantaged students do so much better on this test than advantaged students in the other five countries, including Argentina, where advantaged students have lost ground to advantaged students in neighboring Chile and Uruguay. I believe that the academic achievement of socially *advantaged* students in each country is especially appropriate for judging the capacity of the educational system in that country to be "high quality." I mean that if the most socially advantaged students in the country are performing at a high level in their schools— no matter whether they are public or private—at least we can say that the national educational system can produce high-quality schooling for *some* students, even if it is a socially advantaged minority. In most

Latin American countries, however, the performance of advantaged students on the PISA is not very high even when compared with Spain or Portugal, especially in mathematics. In the TERCE, advantaged students in the sixth grade in my country, Peru, scored about one-half a standard deviation lower than advantaged students in Chile. Advantaged students in Panama scored much lower than students in Peru (and neighboring Costa Rica) and more than one SD lower than advantaged students in Chile.

This may seem like a strange way to evaluate educational quality in a country, but if you think about it, it is logical. If the highest social class students, with all their family resources and the opportunities that go along with that, are not achieving at high levels, it is a good indicator that the schools in a country must be wanting. So, the way I see it, countries such as Chile and Uruguay, where advantaged students do well, have at least a somewhat better capacity to produce decent schooling.

Conversely, as I also argued earlier, comparing disadvantaged students' school performance, both in absolute terms across countries and compared to advantaged students in the same country, tells us about how the educational system does with its least academically prepared students and how equitable the educational system is in dealing with students from different socioeconomic backgrounds. I could also make the argument that in countries such as Costa Rica and Colombia, where sixth grade disadvantaged students did particularly well relative to advantaged students, and Mexico and Colombia, where the very disadvantaged fifteen-year-olds score high on the PISA relative to advantaged students, those systems are more equitable. Thus, if I were to judge the systems by how *equitable* they are, I would hand the prize to Mexico, Costa Rica, and Colombia.

Adjusting the test score for the students' family resources in each country compared to the Latin American average therefore gives us a more accurate picture of the relative "quality" of the educational systems than the raw scores published by the OECD and UNESCO. The adjusted scores also help us better choose which countries to look at when we search for educational policies that work in the region.

The other important takeaway from Figure 2.1 is that some countries, such as Peru, Brazil, Chile, Mexico, and Colombia, are making gains on the PISA test, and the gains are either fairly equal across all family academic resource groups of students (Brazil, Peru, Colombia), are stronger for the very disadvantaged and disadvantaged (Mexico and Chile), or only for one group, the disadvantaged (Argentina). Thus, in five of the seven countries, the gap between low family resource and high family resource students is gradually closing, at least in mathematics test scores in this test. This means greater equity can and is being achieved. I will talk a lot about ways to close the gap and to raise the overall level of achievement among students. The Chilean case, despite its big achievement gap, has made gains for advantaged students, and in the same period (2000–2018) closed the gap by almost 20 points between very disadvantaged and advantaged students.

I was especially pleased to see how much Peruvian scores increased after my country's very poor performance on the PISA in 2000. The low scores in 2000 may have been due to it being the first time that students were taking this type of test. When Peru participated again in 2009, the scores were much higher, and they have continued to rise for all three groups. I will have a chance to talk about some of the reasons that I think this happened. I doubled teacher salaries from extremely low levels during the five years of my presidency, and I think that this had a major effect on improving teacher morale. Probably the conditional cash transfers I introduced for families in extreme poverty also helped, since one of the conditions was school attendance for all school age children in the families receiving cash transfers and another condition was regular health checkups for children. Since my presidency, many other reforms have been introduced, and these probably have had substantial impact on student achievement.

One country I had to leave out of the analysis because it did not participate in the TERCE was Cuba. Cuba is not a well-off country, but on the SERCE, both its disadvantaged and advantaged students score higher than in any other country, and that is true in sixth and third grade, and it is true both in math and reading. The closest any students come to the performance of Cuban students is sixth grade advantaged students in Uruguay, who come within 16–17 points of advantaged students in Cuba in reading and math, and sixth grade students in Costa Rica, who come within 16 points of sixth grade students in Cuba in reading. Furthermore, the difference in test score between disadvantaged and advantaged students in Cuba is among the lowest of all the countries (about 25–40 points) even though advantaged students in Cuba outperform advantaged students in any other country. Thus, Cuba can apparently reach high levels of achievement with greater equality of results between students bringing very different amounts of social capital from home.

We should be able to draw lessons from the Cuban educational experience (Carnoy et al., 2007). Of course, Cuba is an authoritarian state that puts dissidents in prison, and in drawing from the Cuban experience, we always need to keep in mind that democratic governments, which make social and educational reforms under the harsh spotlights of opposition criticism and a free press, cannot simply command institutions to do what they are told, as in Cuba. Yet, even if Cuban schools are the product of a command society, the results speak for themselves. At least at the elementary level (we don't have any international measures of student performance in Cuban middle or high schools), Cuban students perform above students in much richer countries such as Uruguay or Chile, and even outperform the most advantaged students in those countries. And disadvantaged students in Cuban third and sixth grades scored about a standard deviation higher in math and more than 0.5 SD higher in reading on the SERCE than disadvantaged students in Costa Rica and Uruguay, the next highest scoring countries. In my view, Cuban primary schools must be doing something right, and the rest of Latin America needs to figure out what that is and especially whether any of it is transportable into democratic societies.

We can also learn lessons from Costa Rica, and perhaps some other countries and regions of countries, concerning how these performance results may reflect quite different public educational objectives in each country or region. Later in the book, as a way of making these lessons more concrete, I will discuss long-term educational reform policies in Chile and in the state of Ceará, Brazil.

The Inequality of Educational Delivery

I don't think the data I am presenting in this chapter should surprise anyone. There are few, if any, places in the world where the children of poor people get as much schooling or perform as well in school as children of the rich. My experiences tell me that this is the case because governments around the world, including in Latin America, shortchange the poor by providing fewer high schools in rural areas and sending their least experienced and least trained teachers to rural and low-income urban schools.

Yet, the issue is complicated. For example, do the children of Latin America's rural and low-income urban families get less schooling because they come into schools with fewer family academic resources, so have low levels of initial achievement, and so do not continue with their schooling? It is hard to motivate teachers and students when the students have difficulty learning. In turn, these low-income students have difficulty learning because they enter school with poorer health, lack proper nutrition, have had little exposure as young children to reading materials, are less likely to have had multiple years of early childhood education in a quality preschool, and have families with little knowledge of how to navigate the schooling process. In some countries, a fraction of these students are Indigenous and don't speak the national language well.

My point is that just because rural and low-income students do not do well in school and take fewer years of schooling, does not mean that the education system is shortchanging them. They may get less education and do poorly on school knowledge tests because of factors that have little do with the national educational system. I agree fully with this idea. It would be impossible to improve Latin American education for the children of the almost 21 percent of Latin Americans who lived in poverty or extreme poverty in 2014 (see Chapter 1) without doing something about their poverty and the direct effect it has on children's learning once they enter school. It makes an enormous difference to the general conditions of educational delivery in a country when the total percentage of the population in extreme poverty and poverty is 5.7 percent as in Chile in 2014, or 19 percent, as it was in Peru, or 46 percent, as it was in Guatemala. I discussed this in the first chapter, but it bears repeating: beyond the effects of individual social class, the impact of extensive poverty in the population is also important, because it makes fewer family and government resources available to the school system as a whole and depresses the overall expectations for students in the system.

One reason why educational access and student performance increased in Latin America in the 2000s—especially for low-income students—is undoubtedly the result of a sustained period of economic growth in the region since 2000, accompanied in most countries by a sharp reduction of poverty (see Chapter 1). That is also why it is imperative for Latin America to get its act together to reestablish the economic growth process. Without doing that, it will be difficult to provide high-quality education for all and to enable all children to grow up in the healthy, secure conditions that stimulate learning in early childhood and in school.

What We Need to Know to Move Latin American Education Forward

Of course, sustained economic growth does not guarantee that a country will provide services to the poor—including more and higher quality schooling—that are needed to equalize opportunity across social classes. The usefulness of the inter-country Latin American comparisons of rural-urban attainment differences and test scores of disadvantaged and advantaged children shown in this chapter is that they demonstrate that some countries in the region are doing a better job than others of delivering schooling to rural areas and increasing academic achievement among the disadvantaged. I have drawn attention to countries such as Mexico, where the difference in the number of years of education in the urban and rural population is among the lower figures in Latin America, and students not only average among the highest in the region on the PISA and the TERCE when we adjust for student socioeconomic background, but disadvantaged students do especially well when compared to students in other countries. The same is true for Costa Rica on the SERCE and TERCE. Thus, when we argue that it is possible for national educational systems in Latin America to deliver "better education" to the poor, these comparisons indicate that there are countries that seem to have done that more effectively than others, and that there are examples even in Latin America that we can look at to figure out why.

It is interesting that, in contrast, advantaged students in neither Mexico nor Costa Rica do as well as in other high scoring countries, such as Chile or Uruguay. I have argued in this chapter that how well advantaged students do on these tests is a good indicator of the excellence of the educational system. If advantaged students can do rather well, maybe close to how well at least average students perform on an international test in developed countries, this suggests that there are at least a certain percentage of schools that can produce developed country quality education. If that is the case, we could think it possible that models of high-quality educational "technology" exist in that country and could serve to bring up the majority of teachers and schools. I like soccer analogies, both because I was a player (at the University of San Francisco) and because I love the game. What I am saying is that if you have at least a few good teams in a country that are able to compete with even average teams in the better soccer nations, you can have some confidence that you have at least some player talent and at least some good coaches who could be models for the rest of the nation's teams.

Chile and Uruguay seem to fall into that category, according to PISA results. And if we had PISA results for Cuba, we would certainly find that advantaged students in Cuba would perform on the PISA up there with advantaged students in the developed countries. Now, the common characteristic of all three of these countries is the very low rate of poverty compared to the rest of Latin America. In

Chile and Uruguay, the overall poverty rates in 2014 were 5.7 and 2.4 percent. Even a decade earlier, the poverty rate in the two countries was about 12–13 percent, compared to Latin America's average 30 percent. We do not have comparable statistics for Cuba, but we do know that despite its relatively low average GDP, everyone in Cuba is guaranteed the basic necessities of life. This means that many Cubans are "poor" materially, but they have excellent health care, access to schools, basic nutrition and housing, potable water and sewer systems, and guaranteed work. There is also very little violence in their communities and schools, and children are not allowed to be employed or work outside the home. Therefore, even low-income and rural children grow up in environments with characteristics that are not associated with poverty. I think that this relative absence of poverty helps these countries develop good education. The difference is that Cuba has been able to provide good education for children at all levels of family resources, whereas Chile and Uruguay do a lot less well with their disadvantaged students than do countries with higher levels of poverty, such as Mexico and Costa Rica.

I stressed the idea in *The Shared Society* that for Latin American countries to "develop" into more democratic and economically sustainable societies over the next three decades they need to continue to grow economically and to become more equal socially. To achieve those goals, I believe that they need to reach high levels of excellence in education—to model in each country and across countries what good schooling is (with correspondingly high levels of student performance)—and to deliver much greater access and higher quality education to students now marginalized because they live in rural areas or are part of the urban poor. In this chapter I have tried to show that we have examples of countries that seem to have found ways to progress either on the excellence front or more on the equity front. We are going to continue to try to unravel how to make all this happen, always keeping in mind that we cannot separate the achievement of either of these goals and certainly not both of them at once without continued (and more sustainable) economic growth and the political will to invest more in the economic and social well-being of the lowest 40 percent income families.

This last point is the horse that will pull the education cart. Before focusing on delivering more and better education, I want to focus on the political economic context that is needed to make that happen.

3

Building the Foundation for Better Education

It may surprise you that the lesson I have taken away from my own life trajectory is not that anyone can make it if he or she works hard and takes advantage of educational opportunities. This is the typical message delivered by many who come from humble backgrounds and succeed, usually in terms of making a lot of money. To the contrary, the lesson I learned from my life was that I was a statistical anomaly. I was, to be honest, simply lucky. True, I had parents who were always supportive, and I had some wonderful teachers who inspired me. All that made a big difference in helping me make it. Yet, I realized a long time ago that even with such support we cannot expect that children who spend their early childhood poor and hungry and often sick, are likely to be able to "work hard" and "take advantage of educational opportunities." Nor is it likely that making very poor children's schools better will have large effects on their learning unless we simultaneously remove the enormous barriers to learning posed by ill health, hunger, and community violence.

Thus, before turning to an analysis of how we can improve Latin America's schools, especially for the majority of students that now receive low-quality education, I want to discuss the sustained "preinvestment" needed to eliminate the conditions of child poverty so detrimental to learning. I realize that it is unusual to begin a treatise about educational policy by focusing on the social context of the educational system—on the conditions in which children develop before they get to school and while they are in school. But having lived in

43

these conditions myself, I am acutely aware of their fundamental importance to the whole educational project. They simply cannot be ignored, and we cannot start from the premise that more and better education alone will resolve poverty or the conditions of poverty— that just providing decent schooling will, in some miraculous way, lift children who are now in poverty out of a state of poverty. From my experience, this happens in cases like mine of statistical anomalies, but not on a mass scale. A lot more has to be done to assure that poor children can reach school age ready to learn and can take advantage of better schools once in them.

In my book, *The Shared Society* (2015), I laid out an ambitious agenda for reducing poverty in Latin America, thus laying the foundation for sustained development and deepened democracy. That agenda began with the importance of continued economic growth in the region. Steady economic growth, I argued, is fundamentally important to reaching the long-term objectives associated with creating a developed society. However, I also argued that economic growth is not the end, but rather the *means*, to development. Economic growth can improve peoples' lives by providing them more income and access to more goods. It obviously can help reduce poverty by increasing the purchasing power of the poor. It also provides a greater income base from which to draw resources to invest in society and to achieve greater social well-being.

At the same time, I stressed that while economic growth is an essential part of addressing poverty, economic growth is not sufficient to reduce poverty. I claim that it is crucial to also focus on reducing income and wealth inequality in Latin American societies if we are to attack the roots of poverty.

> The real question is: who receives the benefits of economic growth? In part, this depends on levels of inequality. Inequality and poverty are intricately related, and it turns out that initial levels of inequality have been shown to have a double effect on poverty. They may slow economic growth (making the benefits "pot" smaller than it could be), while also reducing the portion or share of the economic growth that poorer people receive. This connection with poverty means that inequality should be particularly important to all policymakers and leaders who are interested in reducing national or global levels of poverty. So, reducing poverty and inequality can also be a means to achieving the more traditional measure of development: economic growth. (Toledo, 2015: 90–91)

In the sections below, I draw on my discussion in *The Shared Society* that deals with eliminating the correlates of poverty. I consider such efforts key to improving peoples' lives in today's Latin America. As important, they are also key to improving students' learning—they are the "partners" of investing in the educational system itself. Healthier, well-nourished children whose eyesight and hearing have been tested and corrected, and who are able to focus in class because they are adequately fed and are not suffering from chronic illnesses, are going to be able to learn when they have good teachers and attend well-resourced schools. Without these "pre-investments," even better educational resources will have much lower impact on a significant fraction of children in today's Latin America.

Reducing Child Poverty

When it comes to understanding access to and the quality of education in Latin America, it is essential to understand child poverty. Children do not get a second chance at receiving a healthy start in life, and they rarely get another opportunity to access quality basic education. This means that childhood poverty almost guarantees the intergenerational transmission of poverty and inequality.

If today's children do not have the opportunity to develop their minds and bodies, they will grow up to be adults who have limited opportunities. Amartya Sen has written that these poor children's *capabilities* are stunted because of factors outside of their control. In terms of reducing intergenerational poverty in the long term, we need to focus on the welfare and well-being of today's generation of children (Sen, 1999a; 1999b).

A recent Economic Commission for Latin America and the Caribbean (ECLAC) and UNICEF study used a multidimensional framework to estimate child poverty in Latin America. The dimensions included children's nutrition, access to drinking water, quality of housing, and school attendance. Estimating child poverty this way, nearly half (45 percent) of Latin America's children are affected by at least one "moderate to severe deprivation" (UNICEF and ECLAC, 2010). One interpretation of this figure is that the opportunity to develop to their full potential is at least partly compromised for close to 80 million Latin American children.

Of course, Latin America is as diverse in this aspect as it is in others. As with other measures of poverty, this measure shows some countries, such as Chile, Costa Rica, and Uruguay, have less than one-quarter of their children living in poverty, while others, such as Bolivia, El Salvador, Guatemala, Honduras, and Peru, have about three-fourths of their children living in poverty. Figure 3.1 shows the distribution of child poverty as estimated across the region by ECLAC for the first decade of the 2000s.

Sustaining economic growth and taking direct steps to reduce income inequality, such as conditional cash transfers (CCTs) and other direct measures that reduce income inequality, are the surest route to reducing child poverty in Latin America. In a report for the World Bank, Nora Lustig, Luis Lopez-Calva, and Eduardo Ortiz-Juarez (2016) estimated that the sizable decline in Latin America's income inequality during the first decade of the 2000s was responsi-ble, on average, for about 40 percent of the reduction in poverty dur-

Figure 3.1   **Child Extreme Poverty and Child Poverty, by Country, 2005–2011 (percent of child population 0–17 years old)**

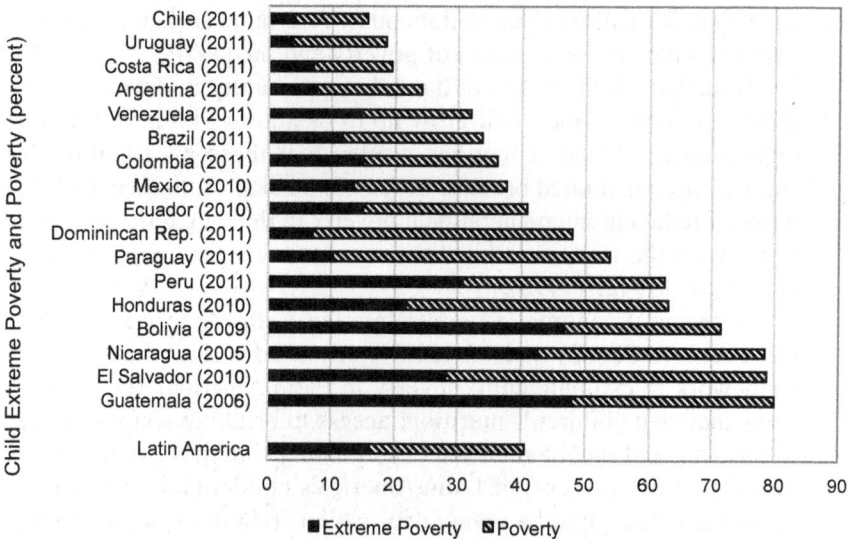

Source: CEPAL, Panorama Social de America Latina 2013, Chapter II. Data from household surveys.

ing that time period, and, in some countries, the percentage was higher.

Yet, there are additional, indirect ways to reduce poverty by attacking the correlates of poverty, including poor health, malnutrition, crime and violence, and, of course, as I argued in the previous chapter, poor education. These are, for me, the most important elements associated with poverty that affect children's performance in school and their social mobility. Since improving access to good education for the poor and everyone else is the theme of the rest of this book, I will focus here mainly on improving health and security.

Access to health care, adequate early nutrition, and physical security are included in most of the new measures of poverty, and there is a rich empirical literature in the academic and development fields that shows that without access to these basic services, the chances a person has to develop a productive life are low to none, even when they get access to basic education. If governments are going to succeed in improving education and the general welfare of their citizens, they will need to address these areas.

Why not just wait for economic growth to gradually erase poverty? Here are several reasons, which are all related to the idea that reducing poverty more quickly than would occur under normal economic growth rates would make the whole society better off. The first is that poverty itself may be an important drag on economic growth, since it may produce costly side effects, such as crime, violence, and political instability. Second, if reducing the correlates of poverty contributes to children becoming better students and more productive adults, it could lift all boats, not just those of the poor. Third, it may be much more inexpensive to reduce poverty through direct means such as conditional cash transfers, or indirectly, through providing health services and improved nutrition to the poor, than to face the social consequences of poverty over the long period required to reduce poverty through "normal" growth rates, especially in economies where income distribution is very unequal. So, reducing poverty directly through transfers or reducing the effects of poverty on human well-being can possibly speed up economic growth and reduce poverty even further—a virtuous circle of economic and social development. And just in terms of helping to improve children's capacity to learn, there is no doubt that when government acts to make children healthier, well fed, and secure physically, the educational system itself becomes a lot more productive.

Access to Basic Health Services

Basic health services have become much better in Latin America in the past generation, and the most common indicators of poor health have declined. But a relatively significant proportion of the child and youth population still lacks access to nutritious food and basic health care.

Life expectancy is a key measure of overall access to health care, and life expectancy is slowly increasing in the region. In 1990, average expected lifespan was 68.3 years, in 2003, 72.3 years, and in 2018, it was 75.4 years. Developed areas such as the United States and Europe have higher life expectancies of 78.5 and 81.2 years, respectively, while a relatively underdeveloped region such as South Asia (India and Pakistan) has a life expectancy of 69.4 years (World Development Indicators). At first sight, Latin Americans' life expectancy is rather close to the United States and Europe.

However, the health-adjusted life expectancy index of the UN Development Programme (UNDP) paints a different picture: the adjusted index shows Latin America's life expectancy as about 65.0 years in 2015, suggesting that many of the years people lived by Latin Americans are in ill health. The biggest killers and causes of health problems in the region are chronic (treatable) diseases of the poor, such as infection and parasitic diseases. Another example is tuberculosis. While declining, it is still one of the main causes of death in our region. Countries with large Indigenous or rural populations, which tend to remain more excluded from access to basic services, still suffer the highest rates of death from this generally treatable and preventable disease.

More directly relevant to a major theme of this book—improving the social mobility of poorer Latin Americans through education—is the access women have to basic health services during pregnancy. It can determine the weight of the child at birth, a key indicator of child health, child survival, and child potential to learn later in life. Carrying a child, and the birth itself, can be dangerous for the health of both mother and child. Women's access to prenatal care, to a skilled medical attendant at their birth, and how many women die while giving birth gives a good indication of the extent of access to health care in a region.

In Latin America, approximately 74 women in 100,000 lose their lives while giving birth. This compares well with less-developed regions like Eastern and Southern Africa, where about 400 per 100,000 women die during childbirth, but still three times the 24 per 100,000 who die in the United States (CEPALSTAT, 2021; World

Bank, 2021). It is interesting that the mortality rate is so much higher than in the United States and Europe, when all three have approximately the same percentage of births attended by skilled health staff—about 90 percent (Vega, Barros, Chanduvi, and Giugale, 2012). This raises issues about the quality aspect of healthcare services in the region rather than access alone.

Young children remain more vulnerable to disease and the effects of malnutrition than older children or adults. How many children die before they reach five years of age is an important indicator of the quality of a country's healthcare and nutrition system. In Latin America in 2018, about 1.6 percent of children died before they reached five years of age (16.4 out of 1,000 births). This is a great improvement over the 53 children per 1,000 who died in 1990 in the region (Vega et al., 2012). All countries have made great progress in child mortality rates, but in Bolivia, Guatemala, and Nicaragua, in 2018, about 2.7 percent of children died before they were five years old. This compared with very low child mortality rates in Cuba, Chile, and Uruguay of less than 1 percent (CEPALSTAT, 2021).

Child Malnutrition

The high child mortality rates in countries with high levels of poverty are associated with high levels of child malnutrition. Malnutrition is one of those correlates of poverty that can easily be eliminated at relatively low cost in the entire low-income population. It is one of the main causes of poor health in Latin America, and there is no reason why anyone, particularly children, in Latin America should be suffering from malnutrition in today's level of economic development. Obviously, it is more difficult for a poorer country such as Guatemala to solve its child malnutrition problem than a country such as Peru. Solving malnutrition as a public health problem in the region, especially as it relates to the effects it has on children—anemia, growth delay, being underweight, and more—needs to be at the top of the list of objectives for every country if we are to improve Latin America's education. Figure 3.2 shows how the main indicators of child malnutrition and acute malnutrition vary across the region.

We can draw some insights into the causes of malnutrition among the poor from the rise in commodity prices during the first decade of the twenty-first century. The Economic Commission for Latin America and the Caribbean estimated that the food price crisis

Figure 3.2   Chronic Child Malnutrition (children under five who are under height) and Acute Child Malnutrition (children under five who are underweight), by Country, 2007–2016 (latest year, varies by country) (percent)

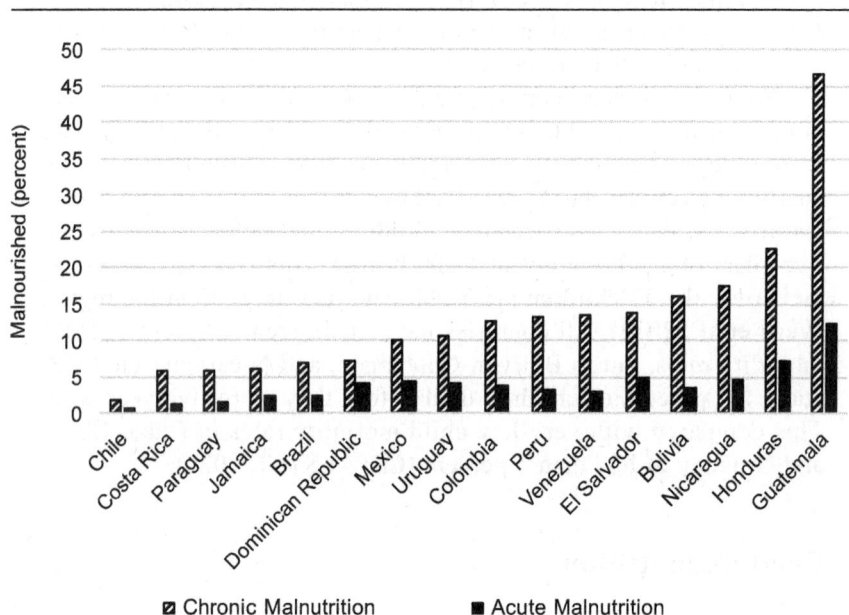

Source: World Bank, 2021.

of 2006–2008 added 10 million people to the ranks of the extremely poor and 10 million more to the moderately poor. Another study of nineteen Latin American countries found that poverty had increased by 4.3 percentage points, or by 21 million additional poor people (Robles et al., 2010; UN, 2011). The poor are hit especially hard by food price increases because poor households can be expected to spend 50–80 percent of their income on food (UN, 2011). This means that when prices increase dramatically, but incomes stay the same, households are forced to cut food consumption: first they generally cut down on the more nourishing (more expensive) foods, and then they tend to reduce the quantity and frequency of meals.

Chronic malnutrition in children is especially high among children in Indigenous and rural communities. For instance, in Bolivia, Ecuador, and Peru, chronic malnutrition among non-Indigenous children under five years old is a high 20 percent, 22 percent, and 20 percent, respectively. But among Indigenous children this rises to a shocking 40 percent, 50 percent, and 45 percent (UN, 2011).

This is not "simply" a health issue, as, for example, for a child that suffers from repeated colds or ear infections but grows out of these maladies when older. Malnutrition in the early years has long lasting, likely lifetime, effects on overall health as well as on children's cognitive and physical development. It is estimated that undernourishment and malnutrition contributes to nearly 11 percent of the total global disease burden and 35 percent of that among children under the age of five (cited in UN, 2011). Undernourishment is particularly hard on children younger than two years old and can have life long physical and cognitive development consequences. A recent study in Peru found that the global food price crisis in Peru between 2006–2008 had significant subsequent cognitive costs on children who were born during or shortly before that time (Outes Leon et al., 2011).

Improving Access to Health Care

As in most other Latin American countries, Peru established a system of conditional cash transfers (CCTs) in 2005, known as JUNTOS, to attack extreme poverty by giving cash to those families that had such low income that they qualified. One of the conditions for getting this cash—again, similar to CCT programs in other countries—was that pregnant mothers and mothers of young children had to show up at clinics on a regular basis to be examined, have their children examined, and to be instructed in proper diet while pregnant and proper diet for and care of young children. Of course, clinics in rural areas had to be built to accommodate this newly created "demand" for additional health services. And this is the point. By increasing health services in rural areas and promoting the use of these services through incentives, many of the chronic illnesses that affect the poor are greatly reduced. This seems like such a simple action for Latin American governments to take: try to make all members of society as healthy as possible by investing in primary care that can identify treatable diseases early and prevent the most common health hazards by providing vaccinations, dysentery kits, and instructions for how to use existing food resources most effectively and to identify child illnesses that require a doctor's care.

As I implied above, one of the most important roles that greater access to primary care can play is in helping pregnant women stay healthy and making sure their fetuses are developing properly. Providing access to medical care for the birth is also crucial and so is postnatal care. It may seem disingenuous to argue that providing all these health services can be done easily—after all, Latin America does not produce enough doctors, and those it does produce do not want to serve in isolated rural areas (for example, against the wishes of the medical establishment, Brazil brought 5,000 doctors from Cuba to serve in more isolated areas). So these are issues to solve, but they are soluble with a bit of political will, and the payoff in greater current and future productivity is high for such investments.

There are other simple healthcare actions that governments can take that improve poor children's ability to do well in school. Two of these are eyesight and hearing examinations for early primary school children. If children have trouble reading and hearing the teacher, how can they learn? Eyeglasses programs in primary schools have been very successful where they have been implemented. Although more expensive, providing dental health programs (including fluoride treatments) in low-income primary schools and teaching parents how to take care of their children's teeth have high overall health benefits for young people. Like other programs that keep people healthy, they have high payoffs, both in school performance and future productivity.

Addressing Hunger and Malnutrition

The evidence is strong that hunger and malnutrition are a major effect and cause of poverty and have significant impacts on children's education and hence on social mobility. When I describe our educational strategy below, I will stress again the important secondary effect that children cannot develop their capabilities in school on empty stomachs or without sufficient nutrients. Improving food security would not magically get rid of poverty, but it would likely go a long way toward reducing the intergenerational transmission of poverty by mitigating the negative effects poverty has on the productivity of adults and the learning capacity of children. In this way, we consider addressing malnutrition as a way to invest in the minds of our people.

Food security relates to both the availability (supply) of food and specific groups' vulnerability to insufficient access to food (demand). We can describe this in terms of chronic food insecurity and transitory food insecurity. Assuming a daily food energy requirement of

2,200 kilocalories per person, by around 1990, Latin America had largely solved the issue of an adequate food supply to feed the entire population. When measured by the average daily requirement per person, the region already had a surplus of food energy in 1990, and this surplus has increased in the first and second decades of the 2000s (Table 3.1).

Even though Latin America had developed an adequate food supply 25 years ago, there are still millions of children and families who suffer from food insecurity and malnutrition. Thus, the main food security problem still facing parts of the population in the region is one of access, not one of enough overall food production. Many low-income children do not receive adequate nutrition even though there is enough food available in Latin America to feed every child adequately.

Some countries already provide models for how to move forward on this agenda. Brazil, for example, has developed a zero-hunger strategy called *Fome Zero*. This has motivated several other countries of the region to adopt similar strategies. Some countries (Argentina, Brazil, Ecuador, Guatemala, and Venezuela) have passed laws regarding food security. While most countries haven't developed a coordinated strategy around food security per se, the issues of supply and demand are being addressed as part of other policy initiatives, including (1) focused efforts on promoting small-scale agriculture and rural development so that low-income rural areas are self-sustaining in food supply; (2) social and food welfare programs that distribute food to low-income communities; (3) nutritional health assistance; and (4) education and training on food and nutrition.

Table 3.1   Food Energy Supply, by Region of the World (kcal/person/day)

Region	1990	2000	2005	2009
World	2,627	2,732	2,787	2,831
Africa	2,278	2,421	2,513	2,560
Americas	2,957	3,173	3,216	3,205
Central America	2,845	2,941	2,989	2,974
South America	2,579	2,782	2,873	2,951
Asia	2,421	2,591	2,635	2,706
Europe	3,378	3,248	3,369	3,362
Australia and New Zealand	3,190	3,037	3,137	3,246

Source: Food and Agriculture Organization of the United Nations, 2013. FAOSTAT. http://www.fao.org/faostat/en/#home.

Note: Average daily requirement = 2,200 kcal.

Access to Basic Services

Poor health is synonymous with poverty not only because of lack of access to health care and because of malnutrition. The poor are more likely to pick up disease because they are much less likely to have access to safe drinking water and basic sanitation. That said, Latin America had managed to reach over 90 percent of its population with piped, on premises, water by 2017—up from 73 percent in 1990 (UNICEF, 2012; Queiroz, Carvalho, and Heller, 2020). However, latest figures suggest that only 65 percent of the population in the region have access to safely managed drinking water. Most of the population that does not have access to piped, safe water in Latin America is concentrated in the rural areas of the region, and in some countries the proportion of those living in rural areas without safe water is 30 percent or more (Figure 3.3). Unfortunately, Peru is one of those countries, along with Bolivia, Colombia, and Nicaragua. But even in Costa Rica and Chile, normally thought of as very socially advanced, 10 percent of the rural population is without clean drinking water.

The Human Opportunity Index (HOI) goes beyond overall coverage to take into account the inequality of distribution of these services. The HOI is a percentage of coverage discounted by inequalities in coverage: it runs from 0 to 100 and a society that has achieved universal coverage of all services would score at 100. When equity of access—how access is distributed across the population—is considered for Latin America, access to clean water and sanitation is worse. The HOI measurements show that "at least one-third of the region's children do not have equitable access to water and sanitation opportunities" (Vega et al., 2012, p. 54).

Decent Housing

Living in decent housing is a fundamental part of access to safe and sanitary living conditions. Through decent housing, communities have greater safety, less drug use, less crime, and a more participative civil society. For children growing up and trying to learn in school, living in adequate housing can provide an environment that encourages study rather than making it extremely difficult to focus and do well in school.

Access to decent housing can be measured best through proxies such as access to sanitation and potable water and via measures of

Figure 3.3   Rural Population with Access to Improved Piped Water, by Country, 2011 (percent)

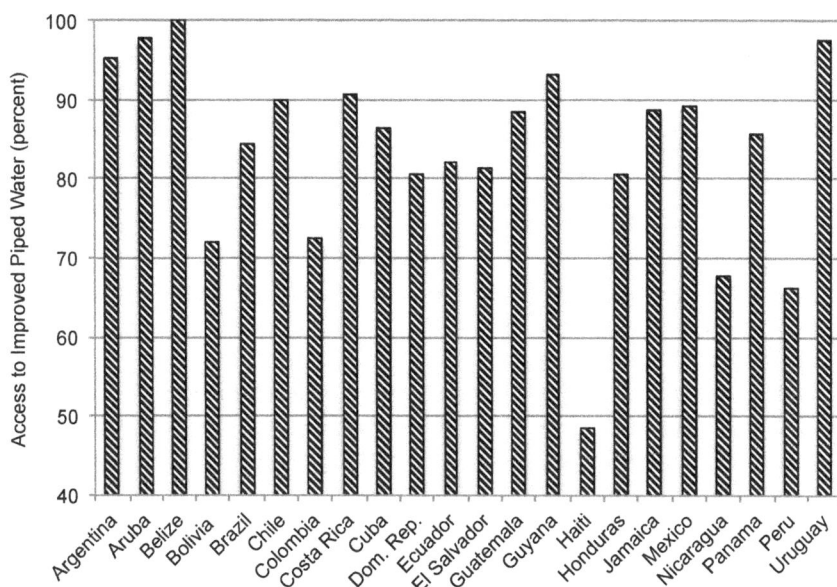

Source: WHO/UNICEF joint monitoring program.

severe overcrowding. Severe overcrowding is useful because it is strongly linked to a number of issues we care about, including the likelihood of being exposed to unhygienic conditions, poor mental health, strained relationships between parents and children, lower educational attainment, and more.

Most of Latin America still has a long way to go when it comes to equitable access to uncrowded housing. Other than Brazil, Chile, and Costa Rica, all countries were more than ten points below the mean for European countries. They ranged from 7–8 percent in Guatemala and Nicaragua, to 87 percent in Peru. In Peru, only 31 percent of the opportunities to access uncrowded housing are equitably distributed. In this measure, the large HOI gap between Latin America and Europe is almost fully attributable to inequality of opportunity levels that are nearly twice as high in the Latin American region (Molinas Vega et al., 2011).

Migration from rural areas to the outskirts of urban areas is a major challenge when it comes to ensuring access to decent housing.

Migrants almost universally locate in the outlying areas of large cities, where there is often little infrastructure for decent shelter, health care, schooling, recreational areas, or other services that are basic for inclusion and participation in society. Normally, one does not think about housing policies as an important factor in improving education. But decent housing is a crucial context for children to be able to feel safe and live in conditions that promote learning.

Almost all Latin American countries have implemented programs that try to ease the situation for migrants. Solutions attempted have included what has been termed *low-cost urbanization*, providing minimal basics (e.g., streets, electricity, water, sanitation) and then letting migrants build their own houses. Despite these efforts, there is still not equitable or adequate access to decent housing for a large percentage of Latin Americans. Improving and building decent housing for all, including the poor, can have a major benefit for our societies and could contribute significantly to improved educational outcomes. If planned and financed prudently, building housing can create decent employment and increase skills in the low-income, lower-skilled labor force—precisely the population the programs are designed to help. To do this, there is room for strengthened partnerships between government, private builders, banks, and the poor to increase the supply of affordable, safe, and sanitary housing.

In addition, we should consider the impact on schooling of segregating the poor into the low-income barrios of Latin American cities. Latin American urban schools are highly class-segregated, for various reasons. First, in urban areas, a high fraction of students attend privately run schools, many charging significant tuition. These schools cater largely to middle, upper middle, and higher social class students. Second, lower middle and lower social class students attend public schools, and even these are class segregated, largely because of residential segregation. Not surprisingly, as we have already pointed out, the best trained teachers tend not to teach in the lowest income areas of cities, which are also far away from where most teachers live (Rosa, 2019). Concentrating low-income students into schools with other low-income students tends to reinforce low expectations from school personnel, and from students themselves. Almost all studies of student performance that include a variable for average social class of the school shows a very large, positive, statistically significant coefficient for average student social class (Carnoy and Garcia, 2017).

It is one thing to build decent housing and another to create neighborhoods based on social diversity by providing affordable housing alongside more expensive, middle class housing. Some local governments have experimented with housing vouchers to create more diverse neighborhoods. Some Italian cities, such as Bologna, socially engineered diverse neighborhoods by building different types of housing within specific areas of the city. There are models for such efforts, and Latin America should begin a process of urban planning that could create mixed housing neighborhoods with the objective of developing more socially diverse public schools. There is some evidence suggesting that these efforts benefit lower income students educationally without a significant negative effect on higher income students (Chetty, Hendren, and Katz, 2016).

Reducing Violence

Another important correlate of poverty is violence. In much of Latin America, the violence associated with poverty is associated with drugs and turf wars among rival gangs. Gangs are hardly a recent phenomenon in poor communities, and they are just as prevalent in developed as in developing countries. Since they offer themselves as an "alternative" to the barriers to social mobility for young people living in urban poverty, they and the violence they perpetrate exacerbate these barriers, both for those who accept this alternative and for the vast majority of young people who do not.

Children growing up in poverty are more likely than other children to face other forms of violence, including domestic violence and child abuse. These, too, have enormous impact on the capacity of poor children to move out of poverty even if they are able to attend reasonably good schools.

I have talked to many teachers teaching in (especially urban) poor communities, and almost universally they discuss the impact of the violence that is part of their students' everyday lives. In middle and secondary schools, this violence also can spill over into the schools. Student- and teacher-reported violence in schools is an important correlate of school social class, and, in turn, is significantly (negatively) correlated with student performance in school (Carnoy et al., 2007).

Of the many barriers poor children in Latin America face in taking advantage of increasing educational access, community violence may be the most difficult for governments to solve. Much of the violence in poor communities stems from economic incentives—particularly drug trafficking—but it is also rooted in a not incorrect view held by young people in these communities that their prospects of "making it" in the formal economy and into middle class society are pretty slim. This view of their own marginality is reinforced by the conditions that they see in their environment, including the poor public services available to them, and often the corruption of the police and other public officials they encounter. This turns into a culture of low expectations (Willis, 1977) that can feed the violent alternative culture offered up by gangs.

Nevertheless, there are direct interventions that can help, such as comprehensive after-school programs for middle and high school youth; well-developed sports programs and after-school arts and crafts programs for boys and girls that create more positively oriented sub-communities, such as clubs and student newspapers, for example. These are not inexpensive solutions to violence and crime, but if they work, they avoid costs that are much, much higher, including the expense of prisons and the costs of criminality itself. Put another way, investing in the youth of poor communities can have large positive benefits for society at large, in addition to the payoff to low-income youth. Any rational system would make that investment.

Summing Up

Health, education, and poverty are not only interrelated, they are essential and self-reinforcing components. Children who are healthy and properly fed, live in decent housing, and do not face violence as a regular part of their lives are more able to attend school, learn, and attain high levels of education. We know that people who are healthy and educated are more likely to be economically successful. They are also more likely to be involved actively in their country's political process, which contributes to the construction of vibrant, functioning democracies that work for the mutual progress of all.

We also know that improving the health of young women leads to better health not only for themselves but also for their children. It is often women who are responsible for the welfare of children, including their nutrition and how often they see a healthcare provider. We can create a virtuous circle by investing in young women's health care and education. Above and beyond whether and how often they access health care, a woman who is educated is more likely to understand when treatment is necessary, seek the treatment, and then feel empowered in her interactions with health service providers (Sperling, 2005; Watkins, 2000). This can enable her to demand better treatment by her healthcare providers.

Health also plays a key role in schooling. Children's health affects their capacity to learn and therefore the likelihood of acquiring key skills and knowledge from the education they receive. Malnutrition and hunger diminish the brain's ability to process the information it receives and to perform complex tasks. Malnutrition also decreases children's ability to concentrate on their lessons or reading and suppresses energy levels (Del Rosso, 1999; Dercon and Lives, 2011; Outes-Leon et al., 2011). From these effects, it seems obvious why malnourished children are more likely to drop out of school than healthy children, and more likely to miss class regularly if they are enrolled.

At the beginning of this chapter, I stated that sustained economic growth is fundamental to eradicating poverty, but economic growth itself does not eradicate the conditions of poverty. The United States is a rich country that has had enormous economic growth in the past seventy years, but it has not eradicated poverty and certainly has not eradicated the many correlates of poverty. According to UNICEF, more than 20 percent of US children grow up in poverty, the highest figure in the developed world. Latin America could reach the income per capita levels of the United States and still have tens of millions of children living in poverty and facing the conditions of poverty. But this does not have to be the case. There are many countries with lower income per capita than the United States and with low levels of child poverty. In addition, there are many interventions available that can reduce the correlates of poverty, such as children's poor health, lack of clean water, and malnutrition, even while people's incomes remain relatively low.

Latin American countries have made progress on all these fronts, but we have a long way to go. How quickly we act to reduce the correlates of poverty will have an important impact on how quickly we can improve the quality of educational outcomes in the region. It is crucial to keep this in mind in the following chapters that focus on improving the educational systems themselves.

4

The Imperative of Early Childhood Education

A primary objective for anyone who wants to promote social well-being in the future should be to improve the childhood experiences and opportunities of today's children. We need to help them survive the first years of life, improve their childhood health, and keep them from violence. These are obviously fundamental to becoming healthy adults. I lived the reality of a Latin America in which healthcare supports were limited. Seven of my siblings died before they were five years old. But we have to do more than just help children be healthy. Beyond health, the most important thing we can do for them is to invest in their early childhood education. Poor children deserve special attention from the public sector in providing early educational experiences because their families are least likely to be able to provide access to it without public intervention.

I like to quote Amartya Sen, because he describes development issues so clearly and so humanely. In an address he made to an Inter-American Development Bank seminar more than two decades ago, Sen laid out the case for investing in children as a fundamental element of a social and economic development policy. He argues that "the success of an economy and of a society cannot be separated from the lives that members of the society are able to lead. Since we not only value living well and satisfactorily, but also appreciate having control over our own lives, the quality of lives has to be judged not only by the way we end up living, but also by the substantive alternatives we have" (Sen, 1999: 1). He went on to argue that adult capabilities and possibilities are profoundly conditional on their childhood experiences, and that enhancing these experiences through investments in childhood opportunities can improve those adult capabilities in four important ways:

- First, it can directly make adult lives richer and less problematic since a securely preparatory childhood can augment our skill in living a good life.
- Second, in addition to that "direct effect" in the capability to live a good life, childhood preparations and confidence also contribute to the ability of adult human beings to earn a living and to be economically productive. Through these earnings and economic rewards, the lives of the adults are enriched . . . that in turn influences the lives of their children and their future adult lives. . . . This connection is important in general, but it is especially serious in the specific context of female-headed households and female maintained families.
- The third connection . . . relates to social linkages, which can extend beyond purely economic ones. Our ability to live with others, to participate in social activities, and to avoid social disasters, is also deeply influenced by the skills we form as children.
- There is also a fourth—a political—connection. The success of a democracy depends on the participation of citizens, and this is not a matter of just "gut reaction" but also of systematic preparation for living as active and deliberative citizens. (Sen, 1999: 4–5)

Sen is not the only Nobel Prize winner in economics to advocate strongly for early childhood education. James Heckman, a University of Chicago Nobel economist, has done a lot of research showing a high economic and social payoff to investing in preschool, especially for poor children (Heckman, 2000, 2006; Cunha and Heckman, 2007). For me, the main takeaways from both Sen and Heckman are (1) that early childhood education should be part of a larger program of early childhood development that includes nutrition and health care, and (2) that investment in early childhood development is an essential part of increasing adult productivity and life possibilities. I totally agree with their conclusions. Early childhood education is key to increasing learning in Latin American schools, and it is especially important as a way to help low-income children catch up to those who are more advantaged.

As I showed in Chapter 3, sustained economic growth and the spread of conditional cash transfers (CCTs) in Latin America have had a big impact on reducing poverty and improving children's health in the region, including decreases in child mortality and common childhood illnesses. There have also been rapid increases in the fraction of pupils four to five years old in preschool. However, as Marcela Pardo and Cynthia Adlerstein (2016) show in their comprehensive review of early childhood education in the region, the variation in access to preschooling remains a major problem, both across and within countries. More important, the *quality* of preschooling varies greatly, even when it is more widely available. A main feature of this variation is the preparation preschool teachers receive in different countries—there is generally a lack of standards regarding what preschool teachers should know and how they should be certified (Pardo and Alderstein, 2016).

In this chapter, I review evidence showing that preschool education (or day care) has an important impact on a child's academic achievement, even though there are few studies in Latin America that estimate the link causally between a pupil attending preschool and higher achievement once in regular school. I then turn to assess the problem of access to preschool and speculate on how it is distributed among different groups in the population. I also present the limited information available about the quality of preschool education. By the end of the chapter, I make some recommendations for action, based both on the conclusions reached by researchers who have studied preschooling in developed countries and Latin America and on my own observations and interpretations of the data.

Does Early Childhood Education Improve Students' Primary School Achievement?

My read of the research in the United States indicates that early childhood education makes a significant difference in students' later school academic achievement and high school graduation. Janet Currie, a UCLA economist, reviewed seven randomized control trial evaluations of early childhood interventions for low-income children that ranged from home visits to quality preschools (Currie, 2001). She concludes that "studies of model early intervention programs do not show universally positive results. In particular, studies with nonrandomized designs frequently find insignificant or even wrong-signed effects. However, I believe it is a fair reading of the evidence to say that well-designed studies of intensive educational interventions show that it is possible for intervention to make a positive difference in children's lives" (Currie, 2001: 220).

Currie also reviews the evidence on the academic and later-life impact of Head Start, the largest-scale US federal government–funded preschool program aimed at low-income children. Yet, even though it is the largest program, it only covered about 12.5 percent of four-year-olds and 8 percent of three-year-olds in 2006–2007 (Barnett, 2008). In her own study with Thomas (Currie and Thomas, 1993), they compared children that had been in Head Start with siblings that had not. They found that African American children's "initial gains in vocabulary and reading test scores 'faded out' while the children were still in elementary grades. For white children, in contrast, there were persistent gains in test scores, as well as reductions in grade repetition. It is worth emphasizing that the initial gains in test scores were the same for whites and blacks—thus, the real difference was not in the initial impact of the Head Start program but in what happened to the children after they left" (Currie, 2001: 224–225). The point is that the primary schools that African American Head Start children attended were of such low quality that the Head Start advantage dissipated. Furthermore, Garces, Thomas, and Currie (2000) show that, again comparing Head Start participants to siblings who did not attend, "participation in Head Start is associated with a significantly increased probability of completing high school and attending college among whites, and with decreases in the probability that African-Americans have ever been charged or convicted of a crime" (Currie, 2001: 225).

In 2008, W. Steven Barnett reviewed the effects of early childhood education programs in the United States and concluded that

> Multiple meta-analyses conducted over the past 25 years have found preschool education to produce an average immediate effect of about half a standard deviation [SD] on cognitive development. This is the equivalent of seven or eight points on an IQ test, or a move from the 30th to the 50th percentile for achievement test scores. For the social and emotional domains, estimated effects have been somewhat smaller but still practically meaningful, averaging about .33 standard deviations. To put these things in perspective, it's important to realize that on many measures, . . . the standard deviation is enough to reduce by half the school readiness gap between children in poverty and the national average.
>
> Dozens of studies have examined preschool education's long-term effects, providing information on effect into elemen-

tary school and beyond. Recent meta-analyses of these find that preschool education has significant lasting effects on cognitive abilities, school progress (grade repetition, special education placement, and high school graduation), and social behavior. Estimated effects decline as students move from immediate experience to elementary school, to adolescence, and to adult follow-up. Thus, long-term effect sizes (reported as standard deviation units for each measure) are smaller, and are roughly 0.10 to 0.20 for cognitive abilities, 0.15 for school progress, and 0.15 to 0.20 on social behavior including delinquency and crime.

These effect size estimates are averages across studies that vary widely in regard and program types included. There is also some variation in population served, although most studies have focused on economically disadvantaged populations. The strongest studies, which are randomized trials, and examine programs ranging from intensive "model" programs for children from birth to age 5 to typical head start centers. The largest estimated effects have been reported by these more rigorous studies. Also, programs focused directly on educating the child had greater effect than multipurpose programs delivering a mix of services to children and families. Thus, the average effect sizes across all studies summarized by meta-analysis are significantly smaller than the average effect sizes down from well implemented, intensive educational programs. (Barnett, 2008: 5)

A major conclusion I draw from the US studies is that these programs work to improve children's cognitive achievement and later school success, but the long-term effects are much smaller than in the short term. Furthermore—and this is very important—the type and quality of early childhood programs matter in how large of an effect they have on children's development.

Milagros Nores and Steven Barnett (2010) did a meta-analysis of non-US international evidence on the benefits of early childhood interventions using studies on thirty interventions in twenty-three countries. Although these studies covered cash transfers, nutritional, mixed, as well as educational interventions, the Nores-Barnett analysis is useful for our purposes because it tries to estimate the relative size of the effect of educational interventions alone versus the effect of these other interventions. They conclude that

interventions that were either educational or mixed (e.g. stimulation and nutrition, care and nutrition, pre-K [pre-kindergarten], pre-K and nutrition) evidenced the largest statistically significant effect on cognition, in comparison to interventions that were cash transfers or solely nutritional. The combination of education and nutritional assistance seems to be more powerful for improving child development over nutritional assistance alone. . . . [E]xtrapolating from the results reviewed here—the policies for a broad range of countries where millions do not have access to early education, child care is of poor quality, children are malnourished, and grade repetition and school dropouts are high—is complicated by the vast differences in social and economic conditions across countries. Nevertheless, the potential for large economic benefits of improvements in child development outcomes is large nearly everywhere, and [for] all the major types of early childhood interventions at substantial average effect sizes across a diverse sample of programs in countries. (Nores and Barnett, 2010: 279–280)

Specific to Latin America, some of the studies of preprimary education impacts that approach causal inference estimate quite large effects. Berlinski, Galiani, and Gertler (2009) show that when Argentina implemented a large program to expand the coverage of preprimary education between 1993 and 1999, children who benefited from this expansion in coverage performed better on mathematics and Spanish achievement tests in third grade. One year of preprimary school increased children's test scores by 0.23 standard deviations. Children who attended preprimary school also demonstrated superior participation skills, such as attention, effort, class participation, and discipline, as reported by their teachers.

Although Costa and Carnoy's analysis (2015) of an early literacy program in northeast Brazil did not focus directly on early childhood education effects on a student's later school performance, one of the surprising outcomes of that study of the literacy program was that for all the program's positive impact on math and Portuguese scores in primary school, the early grades literacy program did *not* offset differences in student performance for those students who had participated in early childhood education of any kind and those who had not (Costa and Carnoy, 2015, Figure 4). Even after exposure to the literacy intervention, fifth graders who had participated in early childhood programs had a 0.25–0.30 SD advantage in Portuguese and about a 0.33 SD advantage in math over students who had not had early childhood education.

In an example from another country, a twenty-year follow-up of a randomized experiment in Jamaica, where the mothers of malnourished children were encouraged to play with their nine- to twenty-four-month-olds found that those who received the stimulation intervention eventually had earnings around 25 percent higher than those in the control group.

We made our own estimates of the possible effects of preschool on students' test scores in third and sixth grades, using data from UNESCO's SERCE (2006) and TERCE (2013) surveys. These are not causal estimates, but they strongly support the claim that those third and sixth graders who had participated in early childhood programs of any kind were likely to score higher on math and reading tests than those students who had not, even when we adjusted the outcomes for a series of family academic resources and social class proxies, as well as school fixed effects—that is, the average student and school resources in the school attended by each student. This was the case for every Latin American country for which these data were available, and was the case in both SERCE and TERCE.

Our method was to estimate ordinary least square (OLS) regressions for individual student mathematics and reading performance in each of the countries in the SERCE and TERCE surveys (there was some variation in the countries that had all the available data we needed). The independent variables included individual student characteristics, such as gender and age, plus parents' education and articles in the home, whether the student had participated in early childhood education (ECE), and the school that the student had attended (school fixed effect). The coefficient for the early childhood dummy in SERCE for those students who had three years of ECE estimated the difference in test score between that group and those without ECE, controlling for the other variables and shown in Table 4.1; similarly, in TERCE, the coefficient for the students who had attended one or more years of ECE and those who had attended none, estimated the difference in test score for each country shown in Table 4.2.

The results show that in the 2006 survey, the differences in third grade math and reading scores between students that had taken three years of ECE and those that had not had any ECE varied from lows of 14 to 15 points to highs (Argentina) of 20 to 22 points. In sixth grade, the differences were somewhat lower in math and somewhat higher in reading. These differences represent between 0.11 SDs (Ecuador, sixth grade) and 0.24 SDs (Argentina and Panama, reading). In the 2013 survey (TERCE), the difference between the performance of those students who had any amount of ECE and those that did not is larger than in 2006, increasing from 0.2 to 0.4 SDs.

Table 4.1   Estimated Effect of Three Years of Preprimary Education on Primary School Students' Test Scores, 2007

Country	With No Years Early Childhood Education				With Three Years Early Childhood Education			
	Third Grade		Sixth Grade		Third Grade		Sixth Grade	
	Math	Reading	Math	Reading	Math	Reading	Math	Reading
Argentina	497	492	493	506	520	513	510	530
Brazil	492	488	488	504	513	507	505	525
Chile	505	499	493	506	521	515	509	528
Colombia	491	487	489	502	511	505	504	523
Costa Rica	501	495	496	509	517	510	507	526
Dominican Republic	492	489	490	503	511	504	503	521
Ecuador	501	495	494	507	515	509	505	523
El Salvador	489	484	484	500	505	498	498	520
Guatemala	487	484	483	494	503	499	497	513
Nicaragua	493	489	486	498	508	502	498	516
Panama	504	497	496	510	524	516	513	534
Paraguay	493	489	489	501	510	504	501	518
Peru	498	495	494	506	517	513	509	526
Uruguay	496	491	492	503	516	509	507	526

Sources: UNESCO LLECE (2021). SERCE microdata, author calculations using third and sixth year test scores, SERCE test, by country, adjusting for student SES and school fixed effects.

My purpose is not to analyze these differences among countries or to delve into why the differences varied between the SERCE and the TERCE. Most important for me is that so many studies, including the analyses we did, strongly suggest that academic performance in primary school is influenced positively by participating in early childhood education, and that all signs point to substantial differences in the academic performance in primary school between those children who are exposed to early childhood education and those who are not. This makes it all the more imperative that Latin American governments increase their investment in the early childhood education of children—especially those many children in low-income families that do not have access to ECE. In particular, I will argue later in this chapter that the investment should be mainly in quality center-based ECE with well-trained teachers and sufficient numbers of them so that these children are in small ECE classes and receive lots of attention and exposure to enriched learning experiences (Pardo and Adlerstein, 2016).

Table 4.2   **Estimated Effect of Three Years of Preprimary Education on Primary School Students' Test Scores, 2014**

| Country | With No Years Early Childhood Education | | | | With Three Years Early Childhood Education | | | |
| | Third Grade | | Sixth Grade | | Third Grade | | Sixth Grade | |
	Math	Reading	Math	Reading	Math	Reading	Math	Reading
Argentina	521	503	517	492	550	527	551	523
Brazil	536	518	515	520	558	535	542	546
Chile	569	561	568	538	597	583	598	566
Colombia	522	517	513	523	555	544	550	557
Costa Rica	557	545	538	547	585	569	573	578
Dominican Republic	452	458	414	497	481	482	447	527
Ecuador	520	508	509	487	546	528	539	513
Guatemala	507	504	493	492	539	531	525	522
Honduras	521	513	494	491	555	542	533	526
Mexico	546	518	561	520	575	540	592	549
Nicaragua	491	483	460	479	522	510	496	511
Panama	505	503	472	495	534	526	506	525
Paraguay	495	486	465	475	527	512	503	507
Peru	520	511	510	489	547	532	541	517
Uruguay	503	497	548	506	530	520	581	536

Sources: UNESCO LLECE, 2021. TERCE microdata, author calculations using third and sixth year test scores, TERCE test, by country, adjusting for student SES and school fixed effects.

Current Access to Early Childhood Education

UNESCO publishes two measures that give us some sense of access to early childhood education in Latin America. The first is the percentage of three- to five-year-olds who participated in some type of ECE (child care, early childhood education centers, preschool). This gross enrollment rate in ECE gives a very approximate glimpse of how much exposure children in the various countries are getting to "education" before they enter formal primary school. However, it gives us almost no insight into the quality of that exposure. That aside, there were seven countries in 2015, according to the figures reported to UNESCO, that had 50 percent or higher gross enrollment in ECE, and nine countries with less than 40 percent participation, including Argentina and Mexico (Figure 4.1).

The second measure UNESCO uses is the gross enrollment in preprimary education. I would have thought that preprimary education in Latin America would be almost universal, with almost all children attending at least one year of "pre-escolar" in the same school buildings that house primary school. But, apparently, they do not. As Figure 4.1 shows, in some countries, gross enrollment in preprimary is less than 60 percent, and a few more with less than 70 percent. That means that many children enter first grade with no previous exposure to a school environment. One clue to the quality of education in preprimary is the number of pupils per teacher. Figure 4.2 shows that the ratio is high in many countries, at or above twenty-five pupils per teacher. In my country, Peru, the pupil–teacher rate fell to under twenty by 2010 and continues to fall even as the gross enrollment ratio increased to almost 80 percent. On the other hand, although gross enrollment in Bolivia increased in the 2000s, and the pupil–teacher ratio fell somewhat during the expansion, it remained at almost double the average in Latin America. Colombia, on the other hand, expanded the gross enrollment ratio in preprimary but did so by greatly increasing the average teacher–pupil ratio.

In a recent study done at the Inter-American Development Bank called *The Early Years*, Berlinski and Schady (2015) conducted an extensive review of the various investments in children's health and education, and they, too, found that the quality of child care in Latin America, which broadly defined includes ECE, is low. Most day care in the region is community-based, in which children are provided full-time day care and food in the home of a mother. Studies of the quality of day care programs in Ecuador, Bolivia, Peru, Colombia, Chile, and Brazil, in which caregivers and their interactions with children were assessed and observed, showed that "the quality of daycare in many countries in the region, as measured by direct observation of centers, is very low. This is the case in countries that primarily provide daycare through the community modality (like Colombia and Peru), those that use the institutional modality (like Brazil and Chile), and those where the service is a mixture of both modalities (like Ecuador)" (Berlinski and Schady, 2015: 111).

A number of daycare programs have also been evaluated for their impact on children's development—in Bolivia, Ecuador, and several in Colombia. The programs cost in the range of $400–$500 per child. These evaluations show mixed results. In Bolivia and one program in Colombia, the results were positive, but modest; in Ecuador, the results were not significant, and even tended to be negative, both for children and for mothers who attended day care; another study in Colombia, of providing 2,500 hours of training for caregivers,

Figure 4.1   Latin America: Gross Enrollment in Early Childhood Education and Preprimary Education, by Country, 2015 (percent)

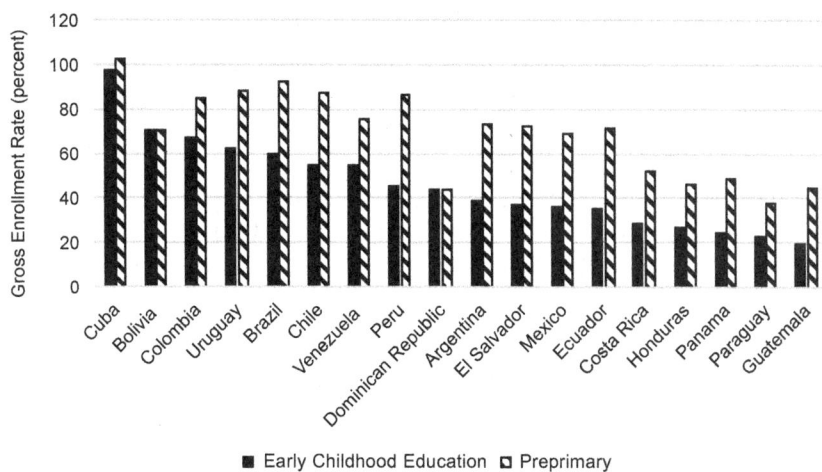

Source: UNESCO Statistical Institute, 2021.

Figure 4.2   Pupil-Teacher Ratio, Preprimary Education, by Country, 2005–2015

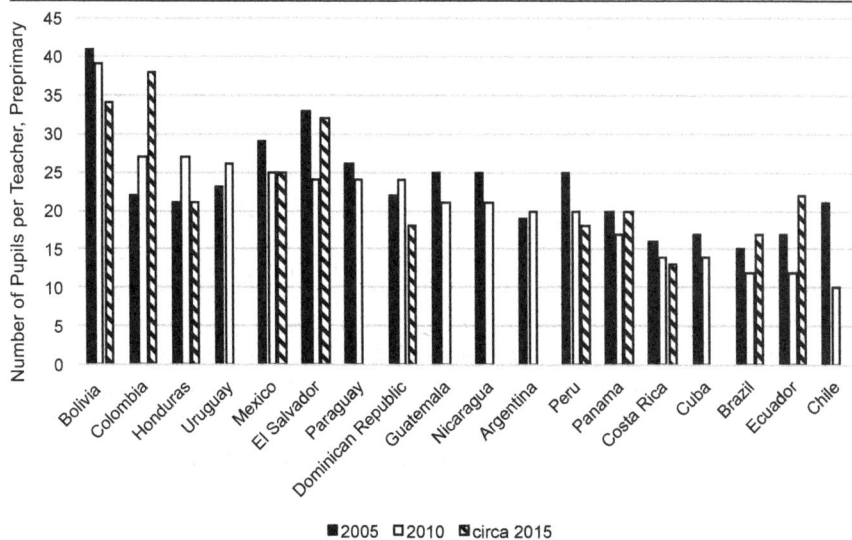

Source: UNESCO Statistical Institute, 2021.

showed some positive effects; and yet another study in Colombia of replacing community home-based child care with large daycare centers, showed very disappointing results, with no improvement over home-based care (Berlinski and Schady, 2015: 113–115). Berlinski and Schady conclude that "the most salient characteristic of the public daycare that is currently available in the region is its very low quality. Seems unlikely that daycare of such low quality would improve child outcomes. The results from a handful of impact evaluations programs in the region confirmed that the benefits of the state care for children are uncertain at best" (p. 115).

In summary, many Latin American countries are reaching high gross enrollment ratios in ECE and preprimary education, but others are still at low enrollment levels, especially in ECE. Perhaps more important, one indicator of quality, the public–teacher ratio in preprimary, and the observations and a few impact evaluations of daycare programs (which include ECE) strongly suggest that in many countries, the quality of preprimary education and ECE is quite low.

How Should Latin American Countries Invest in Early Childhood Education?

Latin America will continue to increase the amount of early childhood education in the form of day care and preschool. Much of this will be publicly run, some will be private but subsidized by the public in various forms, and some will be completely private. The availability of childcare is important to our economies because it releases women to work, but childcare in the region is generally of such poor quality that in many cases, it has no effect or may have a negative effect on young children's development. It would be a big mistake to encourage a system in which we trade off more (women's) labor now for future adults that are worse off cognitively than if they and their mothers had stayed at home. Simply increasing the current quality of childcare, either with publicly provided childcare or public subsidies to families to buy private childcare, is unlikely to make any significant improvements in children's development and learning.

On the other hand, preschool programs for children who are three to five years old seem to have a significant positive impact on their later learning in primary school despite the low average quality of most of those programs. Perhaps preschool teachers are better trained than their daycare counterparts, or perhaps preschools are more likely, especially for four- and five-year-olds, to focus more on academic activities.

We know that childcare and ECE can make a big difference in the development and capacity to learn of Latin America's young people, but we also know that just sticking children at an early age into community homes with untrained caregivers or, later, into preschools with untrained teachers will produce much less impact than if we focus on developing well-organized, well-staffed situations in which these children can improve their motor, cognitive, and affective skills.

I think that there are some obvious directions we can move that will make a difference in both the quantity and quality of ECE in Latin America.

First, regarding childcare, Berlinski and Schady (2015) are certainly right that in rural areas of Latin America, we should probably stick with the community modality of childcare, but give much more training to the mother-caregivers in the community plus enough supervision that they can improve child development significantly.

In urban areas, it makes much more sense to use the center modality or a mixed modality. These also require extensive training and supervision for caregivers. All the expertise on childcare seems to agree that it can have a high payoff but often—or even usually—does not because the usual mode is home-based with untrained caregivers. To make childcare effective, it has to be high quality, and to be high quality, it has to be child-focused, with low caregiver turnover, and low child to caregiver ratios. "As a result, caregivers know the children in their care well, and can establish close, emotionally stable relationships with them. Caregivers are professionals, use rich language, and provide learning opportunities that are cognitively stimulating. In practice, very few children in Latin America and the Caribbean received daycare services with these characteristics" (Berlinski and Schady, 2015: 117).

The problem is that such day care is expensive. According to Berlinski and Schady, a program in Colombia, designed to give high-quality day care to poor children, costs about four times what typical large-scale day care in the community modality costs. If we would focus these more expensive public, center-based programs on the poor in urban areas, while investing in training programs for home-based caregivers in rural areas, other parents would have to turn to private, perhaps partially subsidized, centers for their children's care. I think we should regulate private day care, since most parents have a difficult time judging whether these kinds of services are high quality or not. Of course, in the age of the internet, we could have parents rate day care just like hotels or restaurants, but like restaurants, the public sector should provide minimal protection to consumers against unscrupulous, potentially harmful, or very low-quality providers.

Governments should also consider training professionals, perhaps preschool teachers, to help mothers who do not work—and this includes middle class mothers—how to be more effective in providing an enriched learning environment for their very young children. The Cuban government has had such a program for decades. In Cuba, only working mothers have access to childcare, but the government does send specially trained professionals to homes to train nonworking mothers to become "better" mothers. Some mothers seem to know what to do naturally, but most don't, and home visits are a low-cost way to potentially greatly improve child development in families that do not participate in high-quality collective childcare.

As far as preschool is concerned, the seemingly positive payoff even to not very high-quality preschooling convinces me that mass higher-quality pre-K for three- to five-year-olds has enormous potential for improving the quality of student outcomes in Latin America. Although this does not guarantee that primary and secondary schooling will improve, it should greatly reduce dropout and increase educational attainment just because students will find it easier, on average, to do well academically when they reach middle school and high school, where most dropouts occur.

Steven Barnett is referring to the United States when he says that

> well-designed preschool education programs produce long-term improvements in school success, including higher achievement test scores, lower rates of grade repetition and special education, and higher educational attainment. . . . The strongest evidence suggests that economically disadvantaged children reap long-term benefits from preschool. However, children from all other socioeconomic backgrounds have been found to benefit as well. (Barnett, 2008: 20)

But this also applies to Latin American countries, and so does his observation that "pre-K programs with high standards have been the most effective, and such programs need not be provided by public schools" (Barnett, 2008: 20). We should follow his recommendations to develop preschool programs with reasonably small class sizes and well-educated teachers who are adequately paid. These programs could be attached to regular primary schools, as they already are in many Latin American countries. As Barnett writes, "Because an earlier start and longer duration does appear to produce better results, policies expanding access to children under four should prioritize disadvantaged children who are likely to benefit most" (21).

Pardo and Alderstein (2016) develop a number of recommendations in this same spirit of recruiting and preparing *professional* early childhood educators with well-defined standards of what it means to be a certified preschool teacher, accrediting institutions to train such teachers, providing in-service training to preschool teachers, and raising their pay to professional teacher levels.

In addition, there is now evidence that focusing on academic activities as part of preschool education may produce even greater future academic benefits than just focusing on constructive play. For example, Bruce Fuller and his colleagues showed that, in the United States, children in academic pre-K achieve higher test scores than those attending pre-Ks that concentrate on social skills (Fuller et al., 2017). Similarly, in assessing the effect of Brazil's reform that dropped the entrance age for primary school from seven to six years old and, in effect, converted the last year of preschool into first grade and the preschool social skills curriculum into a first grade reading and arithmetic curriculum, Rosa and his colleagues showed that the additional year of academics increased fifth grade test scores by a significant 0.3 of a standard deviation (Rosa et al., 2019). At the same time, it is important to keep in mind that preschools can play a crucial role in developing the whole child (as should primary and middle schools) by paying a lot of attention to social and emotional development and self-regulation (Barnett, 2008: 21).

I also agree with Barnett, Pardo and Alderstein, and other experts that teachers in preschools should get the same high-quality pre-service training, supervision, and coaching that I will later recommend for teachers in primary and secondary schools. Latin America must focus increasing effort and resources on the quality of teacher pre-service and in-service training at all levels, including preschool. The same goes for supervision.

As I mentioned above, providing high-quality daycare and preschool education will not be cheap, and Latin American governments may face some difficult decisions about investing in quality ECE, perhaps at the risk of not being able to expand these services as quickly as they would like. My bias is to put more public funding into extensive training of child caregivers in rural area community-based care, investing in higher quality childcare centers mainly in low-income urban areas, and investing in high-quality preschools (attached to primary schools) in both rural and low-income urban areas. This would, of course, not be very popular politically with middle class parents, who would largely have to foot the bill for their children, but one way to reduce their opposition would be to invest in the improvement of private childcare and preschool by publicly subsidizing the training of much higher quality caregivers and preschool teachers, many of whom would end up working in privately run centers and preschools. I would also recommend that governments offer generous scholarships to university students who would be willing to train as preschool and primary teachers and teach for five years in return for these scholarships. Many of them would work in private preschools, improving the quality of preschool education for all students.

There are many other steps we could take to both expand and implement quality improvements in early childhood education. They are worth the expense. They will certainly make the rest of our educational systems more effective, and will have a major impact on our societies. I cannot say that they will close the learning gap between the haves and the have nots in our countries, but if we greatly increase the opportunities for rural and low-income urban children to access reasonable quality ECE, they may indeed close the learning gap.

5

Bringing Quality
Education to
Rural Areas

About one-fifth of Latin America's children live in rural areas and attend rural schools. The proportion of the population living in rural areas has steadily declined in Latin America in the past fifty years, from an average of 35.5 percent in 1980 to 24.5 percent in 2000 to 19.1 percent in 2019. Nevertheless, this percentage remains high in many countries—30 percent to 45 percent in Bolivia, Ecuador, El Salvador, Guatemala, Honduras, Nicaragua, Panama, and Paraguay (see Table 2.1). As I wrote in Chapter 2, rural children are likely to complete fewer years of schooling than children in urban areas. In some countries, this means that they complete only about one-half as many years. Even in the most socially "advanced" countries, such as Chile, Costa Rica, and Uruguay, the educational attainment of rural children is only three-quarters of those living in urban areas (Table 2.2).

It is true that rural areas are, on average, poorer than urban areas in Latin America, and that means that they have fewer resources to invest in infrastructure, education, and health services. It is also true that people are more dispersed in rural areas, so bringing social services and infrastructure to the population in these areas can be more expensive than in more densely populated urban areas. Education is a good case in point. Providing teachers to rural schools is costly because, often, a teacher in a rural school has fewer children in the class, so the cost per student in higher than in an urban school.

One of the hidden costs is that it is difficult to get teachers—especially experienced teachers—to teach in rural areas unless they are from that area. Teaching is a highly local profession—a very high percentage of teachers teach in the local region where they themselves went to school. Yet, here is the problem: since the education levels in rural areas are low, many fewer children from rural areas end up going to universities or even teacher training colleges (pedagogical institutes or normal schools). Thus, the "surplus" of trained teachers in urban areas must be "induced" to teach in rural schools. And one more thing: adequate housing for teachers in rural villages is scarce, and therefore teachers choose to live in a larger town rather than in the village itself and travel to the school daily. This tends to increase teacher absences, which in turn increases children's absences. Teacher isolation is also a severe problem for rural teachers.

As education levels have increased, the rural education problem has compounded because of the much greater costs of providing middle and secondary education on a small scale. Middle and secondary schooling traditionally require teachers specialized in mathematics, science, and language. Therefore, as postprimary education has spread out from urban areas, it often does not stretch beyond towns that are "hubs" for a collection of smaller villages around them. To reach secondary schools in these hub towns, children from the rural villages around them have either had to move to the town to live with relatives or travel rather long distances to reach school—this is a major reason for the lower attainment rates in rural areas. Without public school transportation, distance becomes a major barrier to increasing education levels for rural young people.

In addition to the difficulties of supplying quality traditional schooling to rural areas, the Covid-19 pandemic has exposed the low level of access of Latin America's rural populations to internet and computers—the basic infrastructure of distance education. According to a 2020 report sponsored by the Inter-American Institute for Cooperation on Agriculture (IICA), the Inter-American Development Bank (IDB), and Microsoft, *Rural Connectivity in Latin America and the Caribbean—a Bridge to Sustainable Development During a Pandemic* (Ziegler et al., 2020), 77 million Latin Americans in rural areas don't have access to minimally acceptable internet service—this represents 37 percent of those who live in rural areas. Although there is variation in rural access among countries, the overall figure suggests that the second-tier option of providing distance education on a large scale even as an "add-on" to help teachers supplement traditional classroom work will require massive IT infrastructure investment as well as investments in teacher training to effectively use internet resources in their rural classes. In addition to my analysis in this chapter, I discuss the digital divide in greater detail in Chapter 9.

A comprehensive rural education policy in Latin America therefore requires four key elements to successfully improve access to greater quantity and quality of education for rural young people: improved working conditions and special training for teachers serving in rural areas—such training tailored to the student context in rural areas, including multigrade classrooms; investment to build and staff more middle and secondary schools in rural areas or investment in transportation infrastructure to connect villages with middle and secondary schools in local towns; investment in electrical and internet connectivity in rural areas to develop information technology access; and more access to computers and online learning and communication.

In this chapter, I want to talk about how this can be done, and about examples of how it is currently being done in Latin America. Having spent my early years in a very poor rural region of Peru, on the back side of the High Andes, I know what a difference it could make for marginal populations in Latin America if countries would improve the quality of life in rural areas. Certainly, changing the nature of schooling in these areas is one key to unlocking opportunity for the next generation of rural children. And if the next generation in rural areas is to be able to use greater knowledge to realize a better life, we also need a much higher level of investments complementary to schooling. These include better health care, better infrastructure—including electrical power, sanitation, and transportation—and more capital and technical assistance to improve family farms and food security.

Some Evidence of the Low Quality of Rural Education

Before I review some examples of Latin American successes in trying to improve education in rural areas, I want to show some empirical evidence of the depth of the rural education problem, and, further, what may be some of the sources of this problem.

School Infrastructure

First, rural schools in Latin America have much worse infrastructure than urban schools, according to a report for the Inter-American Bank

(Duarte et al., 2011), based on 2007 data from UNESCO's second evaluation of Latin American countries' educational quality (SERCE). According to school principals surveyed, only about 80 percent of rural primary schools (with six grades) had electricity, 70 percent drinking water, less than 15 percent computer labs, and only a few percent a science laboratory (Duarte et al., 2011: Figure 2)—all much lower percentages than in urban public schools and especially lower than in urban private schools. Our estimates from UNESCO's third evaluation in 2014 (TERCE) are shown in Table 5.1. The percentages have risen in the seven years between surveys, but rural schools remain at a distinct disadvantage in every category of school infrastructure. Furthermore, these are averages for all the countries in the sample. As in Duarte et al.'s (2011) study using the 2007 data, rural schools in my home country, Peru, and those in Guatemala and Honduras, for example, are less likely to have electricity, drinking water, an internet connection, a telephone, a library, a science lab, and these other elements of school infrastructure than in the other countries surveyed.

Decent infrastructure is an essential element of providing adequate education. If a rural school does not have the basic elements required to support the educational functions of a school, it is that much more difficult for rural teachers, principals, and students to

Table 5.1   **Latin America: School Infrastructure, by Type of Service and Type of School, 2014 (in percent)**

Type of Service	Urban Private Schools	Urban Public Schools	Rural Schools
Electric light	99.3	98.6	86.4
Drinking water	97.4	94.6	71.6
Drainage system	92.0	81.8	38.3
Principal's office	97.3	90.4	61.0
Sports field	76.3	67.6	58.1
Garbage collection	96.6	91.3	50.5
Bathrooms	98.6	79.4	65.2
School library	77.7	66.4	46.3
Telephone	95.7	79.8	31.2
Internet	88.3	77.4	34.4
Computer room	88.6	59.3	37.6
Infirmary	40.6	08.6	4.7
Science lab	53.2	17.1	8.7
School transport	49.1	25.4	18.0

Sources: UNESCO LLECE, 2021. TERCE microdata.

deliver decent schooling. In modern society, what a school "has" does a lot to define what it represents in the minds of its teachers and students and students' parents. In the information society—whether they make a difference in students' learning or not—computers, internet connectivity, and science labs are an important part of that definition. I would even say that computers and connectivity are more important for rural schools than for urban because children in rural areas are much less likely to have internet access or a computer at home than students in urban areas. Yet, according to principals' responses on the TERCE questionnaire, the average number of computers with internet connectivity in rural schools in the fifteen countries surveyed was 9.5, but about 65 percent of rural schools had no computers with connectivity. In urban public schools, the average was eighteen computers, and in urban private schools, twenty-six computers. Even in urban areas of Latin America, about one-fourth of public schools reported no connectivity. And in Peru, although the number of computers in urban schools was about average for TERCE countries, almost no rural schools had computers with connectivity. This was also true in many other countries, such as Mexico, Nicaragua, Guatemala, and Honduras, where about 85 percent of rural schools reported no connectivity.

A second source of information on internet access is the study we mentioned above, *Rural Connectivity in Latin America and the Caribbean* (Ziegler et al., 2020). That study uses a "significant connectivity index," a simple average of four indicators: internet access, equipment, broadband services, and 4G coverage technologies. In seven countries for which data are available for rural and urban areas—Bolivia, Brazil, Costa Rica, Ecuador, Honduras, Paraguay, and Peru—in 2017, the 0 to 1 index varied from about 0.2 in Bolivia, Honduras, and Peru to about 0.45 in Brazil and Costa Rica, and the gap with urban areas in each country was about 0.3 in most of the seven countries, but somewhat smaller (0.26–0.27) in Honduras and Paraguay (Ziegler et al., 2020: Table 1). The point is that rural areas have about one-half the access to connectivity as urban areas in these seven countries. This represents a major obstacle to any attempts to use technology in rural areas to improve education.

Student Achievement in Rural Schools

With this relatively large difference in the quality of infrastructure in rural schools, and what I have pointed out about the much weaker preparation of teachers who end up teaching in Latin America's rural schools, I don't think it should be surprising that student achievement in these schools is much lower than in urban schools—and this is true even when we control for students' parents' socioeconomic background and other student characteristics. We analyzed the SERCE and TERCE data and found that sixth grade rural students scored, on average, about 20 points lower in mathematics than urban students when these other factors were controlled for. Twenty points is equivalent to 0.2 standard deviations in test score—about two-thirds of a year of schooling (Table 5.2).

Although this difference varies among Latin American countries, it is generally the case across all countries that rural students underperform their urban counterparts on the SERCE and TERCE, even controlling for student social class differences. Our analysis using SERCE and TERCE data show a few exceptions in sixth grade, such as the case that rural Costa Rican students score higher on math than their urban counterparts (in SERCE but not in TERCE), and rural Chilean students score higher than their urban counterparts in math (in TERCE, but not in SERCE).

The reasons are many for fewer resources and less prepared teachers in rural schools, but the most obvious is that rural areas have less political power and that individuals from rural areas are much less likely to attain higher education, hence much less likely to become trained as teachers. The shortage of teachers in rural areas

Table 5.2   Latin America: Rural Education Deficit, 2007 and 2014

| | SERCE (2007) | | | |
	Third Grade Reading	Third Grade Math	Sixth Grade Reading	Sixth Grade Math
Rural	−30.4	−22.6	−25.1	−20

| | TERCE (2014) | | | |
	Third Grade Reading	Third Grade Math	Sixth Grade Reading	Sixth Grade Math
Rural	−11.3	−10.5	−20.7	−17

Sources: UNESCO LLECE, 2021. SERCE and TERCE microdata.
Note: Data controlled for student characteristics and by country.

means that they need to be brought from urban areas. More experienced, better trained teachers prefer to work close to home in urban areas—even more likely, in higher income urban areas.

Thus, the main barriers to improving rural education are both political and structural—that is, the unequal distribution of high level human capital in Latin America's rural regions. Ultimately, politics must change and more resources must flow to these regions, mainly to create the conditions in which higher quality teachers are available and willing to come from urban areas to work with rural children, but also to provide greater access to online digital learning opportunities. The examples I describe below have succeeded in equalizing rural education to improve conditions and teaching in rural schools.

Colombia: Escuela Nueva

Perhaps the best-known rural education initiative in Latin America is the Escuela Nueva, developed by my fellow student at Stanford, Vicky Colbert, when she became the vice minister of education in Colombia in the mid-1970s (Schiefelbein, 1992; McEwan and Benveniste, 2001; Villar, 2010). Colbert based her rural education reform on the cooperative education model she studied at Stanford with her mentor, Elizabeth Cohen. Cooperative education combines a well-developed theory of how children learn with powerful practices of teaching tested in classrooms. In addition, Colbert tailored cooperative education to a rural setting: she took into account the multigrade conditions in which most rural teachers in Colombia were teaching as well as their isolation from other teachers. She designed the Escuela Nueva system to make teachers more effective in multigrade classrooms and to have regular encounters with other rural teachers in professional development workshops.

Thus, Escuela Nueva was rooted in a high-quality teaching model using inclusive techniques that were designed to engage all students in classroom learning, to professionalize rural teaching, and to simultaneously improve rural teachers' conditions of work. While Colbert was in the government, the program was adopted as a national policy whose main objective was to achieve universal access to rural primary schools and to greatly improve the quality of that schooling. Thus, from the beginning, it overcame both the political barrier to moving more and higher quality resources into rural education and improved the human capital in rural schools.

This rural education initiative integrates curricular and communal strategies, training, follow-up, and management. One of the key aspects of Escuela Nueva is the integration of all these aspects into one single package that has been successfully implemented at large scale. Yet, the importance of paying attention to all elements of the Escuela Nueva package cannot be underestimated. Countries such as Honduras, Venezuela, Ecuador, and Bolivia tried to implement the same experience but apparently with much less success than in Colombia. Schiefelbein (1992) argues that their failure was likely the result of not implementing all the elements of the Escuela Nueva model.

The program promotes students' active learning by implementing a new curriculum, adaptable to the sociocultural characteristics of each region in the country, and by providing students with opportunities to follow their own pace (individualized instruction). Another feature of Escuela Nueva is its use of peer instruction (mastery learning), where older students coach and support younger ones (Psacharopoulos et al., 1993). It also promotes a strong relationship between the school and community, getting parents involved in school life and engaging students to apply what they learn within their own environments and culture (Villar, 2010).

Given that the program was designed to target multigrade schools, it developed auto-instructional materials (learning guides) for students from second to fifth grade in the four basic subjects (natural sciences, social sciences, mathematics, and language arts). Students are assessed and promoted according to their completion of certain "units." Escuela Nueva thus eliminates the concept of "grades." This flexible mechanism of promotion allows students to study at their own pace and to keep up with their units when they come back to school after leaving to help their parents during the harvesting season, for example. It is ideal for multigrade schools.

Additionally, Escuela Nueva implemented school innovations such as activity centers or learning areas (*rincon escolar*) and school or classroom libraries where the students can complement their activities with different experimental and observational materials. Also, Escuela Nueva organized a student council to foster students' democratic values and to promote civic attitudes such as participation, mutual respect, and collective work (Villar, 2010). Students, teachers, and parents were encouraged to actively participate in school activities, including its direction and organization (Psacharopoulos et al., 1993).

A crucial element of Escuela Nueva is extensive and systematic teacher training. The teaching-learning model requires specially trained teachers in two areas: (1) subject matter and (2) the application of the different educational materials of the program (Pscharopoulus et al., 1993). The ongoing training aims to make teachers the guides and facilitators of students' active learning (Schiefelbein, 1992). The training includes "demonstration schools," training the teachers into their new roles, three one-week training seminars, and a monthly micro-center workshop. The micro-center meetings analyze problems and discuss results along with other teachers. The meetings usually take place in nearby demonstration schools once a month (Schiefelbein, 1992). The micro-center meetings are not just about training; they also serve the very important function of social interaction between teachers, many of them isolated in one or two teacher multigrade schools in small villages. The meetings give teachers the opportunity to share experiences and just to socialize with fellow professionals, in addition to developing their skills in a cooperative fashion with other teachers who are working in similar environments.

Escuela Nueva was subjected to two impact evaluations in the late 1980s and early 1990s. In 1987, Psacharopoulos, Rojas, and Velez (1993) used a quasi-experimental design to compare a sample of more than 3,000 third and fifth graders from 168 Escuela Nueva and 60 traditional schools (a control group) in rural areas of twelve regions of Colombia that had experienced Escuela Nueva. They estimated a school production function for all schools in the sample and found that the dummy indicator for Escuela Nueva was positive and significant for the cognitive tests of Spanish and math in third grade, Spanish in fifth grade, and for civics. They also found that Escuela Nueva had increased student and community participation and decreased dropout rates. "The mean scores of the cognitive tests revealed that *Escuela Nueva* students scored higher than traditional school students, except in the math test among fifth graders. Regarding the non-cognitive tests, the mean scores again were higher for *Escuela Nueva* students, especially among third graders" (Psacharapoulos et al., 1993: 8).

In a second evaluation, McEwan (1998) replicated the previous evaluations regarding Escuela Nueva's effectiveness for raising student achievement. Escuela Nueva focuses on a number of broad student outcome objectives, including inculcating students with democratic values, the promotion of creativity and leadership among students, and the improvement of students' self-image, but it is also responsible for delivering "good" outcomes in traditional academic subjects such as mathematics and Spanish language.

McEwan found that students in the Escuela Nueva multigrade schools had positive and statistically significantly higher Spanish and mathematics achievement in third grade and Spanish achievement in fifth grade than students in traditional rural schools. These estimates controlled for a number of student and student family characteristics, as well as teacher and school variables. The differences in test results for students attending Escuela Nueva were large. In third grade Spanish, it was 3.82 points, or almost 0.4 standard deviations; in third grade math, it was 4.98 points, or 0.5 standard deviations. In fifth grade Spanish, the significant difference was 0.24 standard deviations. There was no significant difference in fifth grade math. One reason for the fifth grade differences in student performance in math may have been fade out, as McEwan argues, but it could also reflect lower primary school dropout rates in Escuela Nueva than in regular rural schools. Assuming that it is lower scoring students who drop out, regular schools would have lost many lower scoring students by fifth grade.

Peru

My own country, Peru, has also implemented several rural education initiatives designed to improve basic and secondary education in rural areas. These started later than in Colombia—the first project in Peru began in 2004, then larger projects were initiated by the national Ministry of Education in 2009 and 2015. The programs all have one thing in common: they focus largely on improving teacher capacity to teach in rural areas.

The first of these is the Programa de Mejoramiento de la Educación Básica (PROMEB), which was implemented in the province of Piura in 2004, and was mainly a professional development program for in-service rural teachers in a set of rural schools targeted for improvement (Cordero et al., 2005). Its aim was to get students in those schools to complete their primary education by improving the pedagogical efficiency of key educational actors and the educational management systems in each school and in the network of rural schools subjected to the intervention.

PROMEB's strategy was organized in three basic programs: early stimulation (*estimulación temprana*), pedagogical and institutional management (*gestión pedagógica e institucional*), and strengthening capacity (*fortalecimiento de capacidades*). As part of the capacity-strengthening activities, PROMEB developed a certification course (*diplomado*) in rural education for teachers and school principals. In addition, PROMEB implemented two centers of educational resources (*centros de recursos didácticos*) that included computers, videos, internet, satellite TV, and a library for teachers. Thus, PROMEB's package included additional training for teachers (and managers) and additional education resources, filling the most important gaps in rural education.

The second program I want to feature is the coaching program called Accompañamiento Pedagógico, which was started in 2009 and is an in-service training strategy for multigrade and bilingual teachers in preschool and primary-level rural public schools implemented by the Peruvian Ministry of Education (MINEDU, 2014; Rodríguez, Sanz, and Soltau, 2013). Its main goal is to improve students' learning outcomes by enhancing teachers' pedagogical practices via in-school support and orientation given by coaches (MINEDU, 2014). A distinctive aspect of this strategy is its decentralized arrangement, in which regional governments are in charge of implementing the program according to the guidelines defined by the central ministry.

Since the intervention was piloted in 2009, it has had two main phases. Following a redesign in 2012, in 2013 the program switched its target population from individual teachers to the entire school (during the first phase of the program, only teachers from first and second grade were targeted in primary schools) and focused on rural and multigrade schools, prioritizing those with the lowest socioeconomic class students and with the lowest levels of student performance (Rodríguez, Sanz, and Soltau, 2013).

This intervention provides feedback and technical support to teachers through three main strategies: classroom visits, small-group workshops led by coaches, and large-group professional development workshops led by teacher trainers (MINEDU, 2014). Classroom visits are held once a month throughout the academic year (March to December). They consist of participatory classroom observations, in which the coach can carry out demonstrative or shared lessons, and personalized support sessions in which the teacher and coach reflect together about the teacher's teaching practice. The coach holds small-group workshops and meetings with the group of teachers he or she is coaching. In these spaces teachers can share their classroom experiences, discuss strengths and weaknesses identified during classroom visits, and more deeply explore specific multigrade teaching topics, in accordance with their needs (MINEDU, 2014).

Acompañamiento Pedagógico (AP) has been evaluated by several different researchers. The studies show that the intervention has been effective in improving student achievement, as measured by the mean Rasch scores[1] in mathematics and reading and in the percentage of students in each proficiency level in Peru's national evaluation test (Sempé, 2015; Majerowicz, 2016; Rodríguez et al., 2016). A study on the first phase of AP (2011–2012) found an increase of 0.2 and 0.1 standard deviations in mathematics and reading, respectively. A second study that took advantage of the program's redesign in 2012 also found an increase of 0.2 and 0.1 standard deviations in mathematics and reading in the year 2013 (Rodríguez et al., 2016). Using mixed-designed ANOVA tests, Sempé (2015) also found statistically significant differences in test scores between coached and noncoached schools after three years of implementing the program (2011–2013). Following that study, other researchers have measured the causal impact of AP on student learning using a difference-in-differences approach complemented with fixed effects analysis and matching methods. Finally, an unpublished in-house impact evaluation conducted by MINEDU for 2013 and 2014 (Peruvian MINEDU, 2014) found that the program improved mathematics and reading test scores even more, by 0.28 and 0.25 standard deviations, respectively (see also Majerowicz, 2016).

In addition to the overall impact of the program on student learning, these studies present other interesting findings. Using a multivariate analysis, Rodríguez and others (2016) found that coaches' having a university degree and more experience in multigrade classrooms contributed to a larger program impact in 2013. Further, Majerowicz (2016) measured the effect of "losing" the program from the first to the second phase, concluding that previously coached schools not only stop improving but also lost the progress they had made with respect to noncoached schools.

The last rural education intervention in Peru I want to discuss is the Soporte Pedagógico para la Secundaria Rural. This intervention, implemented by the Secondary Education Directorate of the Peruvian Ministry of Education, aims to improve the quality of education for students in rural secondary schools. Its main objective is "to achieve meaningful learning in adolescents through a contextualized quality service, with teachers strengthened in their skills and professional practices, and with a school climate that prevents and reduces social risk factors, incorporating the educational institution with community" (author's translation; see Peruvian MINEDU, n.d.).

Soporte follows a "competencies approach" (*enfoque por competencias*) that seeks to generate learning based on challenging situations that allow students to show their performances in relevant tasks while providing solutions that allow them to reach higher levels of accomplishments throughout their schooling, and ultimately, their life (see Peruvian MINEDU, n.d.). One of the components of this intervention entails strengthening teachers and school principals' capacities. In this way, coaches (*acompañantes pedagógicos*) provide support and personalized guidance to teachers and principals in subjects such as mathematics and language arts, and in management and pedagogical leadership. Additionally, Soporte links the work of the school with parents and the community by developing structures such as the classroom committee. To this end, the program organizes workshops, coordination meetings, campaigns and other strategies to prevent and address the problems of dropouts and school violence that strongly affect individual and group well-being within the school and impact on student learning and community well-being (Peruvian MINEDU, n.d.).

Mexico

Mexico has initiated a lot of educational reforms over the years, most recently coming to agreements with the powerful teachers' union to professionalize teaching and turn to a more merit-based system of teacher hiring, incentives, and assignment (for earlier efforts, see López-Acevedo, 2002). This could have an major impact on rural education, which, as in other Latin American countries, has been greatly affected by the political nature of teacher assignment. One intervention that I consider important is representative of a series of World Bank attempts to improve rural education—especially in Central America—by promoting greater parental participation in influencing spending on education (even hiring teachers, as in the Education with Community Participation [EDUCO] project in El Salvador; see Meza et al., 2004). This intervention was called Apoyo a la Gestión Escolar (AGE) (see Gertler et al., 2006).

AGE is part of the Compensatory Program, a broader school reform designed to improve the supply and quality of education in schools in highly disadvantaged communities. The Compensatory Program also includes infrastructure improvements, provision of school equipment and materials for students (notebooks, pens, etc.), pedagogical training, and performance-based monetary incentives for teachers. AGE provides small monetary grants to parent associations that they can use to invest in infrastructure or in materials they deem important for their schools. Parents also receive training in the management of these funds and in participatory skills to increase their involvement in school activities.

AGE creates both a need and a right for parents to have access to schools to decide on the allocation of the grant, manage the funds (establish a feasible budget, record expenses, etc.), and participate in infrastructure works directly. AGE was the first program that gave parents any authority over school matters in Mexico. Qualitative interviews with parents and school principals revealed that they perceived AGE had increased parental participation in school, made parents more demanding in terms of attention to their children's learning needs and teacher effort, and increased parental involvement with homework.

An impact evaluation conducted by Gertler et al. (2006) using difference-in-differences methodology suggested that AGE decreased the proportion of students failing and repeating a grade in the school by about 5 percent. They found larger impacts during the first three grades of primary school, where failure and repetition are also more frequent. For these grades, they observe a 7.5 percent decrease in grade failure and a 5.4 percent decrease in grade repetition. Their results suggest that parental participation in school decisions in rural areas can influence student outcomes, perhaps because their participation makes parents more directly committed and involved in their children's school behavior—for example, attendance and attention to schoolwork. It may also be the case that more parental involvement in small, rural schools may increase effort by teachers, as shown by the EDUCO evaluations in El Salvador (Meza et al., 2004). Although probably not nearly as impactful as improving the capacity of teachers to teach and the interventions provided by educational packages such as Escuela Nueva, parental participation reforms are important to consider in rural education, where community and school are closely intertwined.

Brazil

In the late 1990s, the Brazilian government implemented several important initiatives to improve public primary education, including in rural areas. FUNDESCOLA II was one of the largest of these. FUNDESCOLA II targeted school improvement efforts in poorer, often rural areas, emphasizing teacher training. The teacher training subcomponent was implemented in more than 5,000 rural schools (Shin, Iyengar, and Bajaj, 2013). The models of teacher training used were called GESTAR and PRALER.

GESTAR (Management of School Learning) was a distance-learning component of the school improvement program. It provided continuous pedagogical training in mathematics and Portuguese language for first through fourth grade teachers. The prerequisite to this training was submitting a school development plan (PDE) to express the need for this intervention. The program was piloted, evaluated, and disseminated under FUNDESCOLA II to schools in states and municipalities that were undergoing the Strategic Plan for the Secretariat (PES) program.

PRALER (Program for Reading and Writing Assistance) was developed in 2003 to focus on improving pedagogical techniques around literacy for first and second grade teachers who had finished the abovementioned GESTAR training. According to the pilot in four states—Bahia, Roraima, Goias, and Mato Grosso—PRALER had a positive impact on the professional development of teachers (Shin, Iyengar, and Bajaj, 2013: 26).

Starting in 1997, and with the help of the World Bank, Brazil got its own version of the Escuela Nueva, called Escola Ativa (Knijik and Wanderer, 2015; Tarlau, 2017). Like its counterpart in Colombia, Escola Ativa sought to improve the quality of instruction and learning in rural, multigrade schools in poorer Brazilian regions in the north, northeast, and center-west (specifically, the states of Bahia, Ceará, Maranhão, Paraíba, Pernambuco, Piauí, and Rio Grande do Norte). Also, the program was developed to fight student dropouts in rural schools. And, like Escuela Nueva, the program in Brazil used modules for self-paced student progress and implemented various strategies suitable for multigrade classrooms, such as self-learning and group work, and teaching using pedagogical materials (learning guides). It also aimed to engage communities to participate.

In the next ten years (1997–2007), supported by World Bank funding, the program spread to nineteen states and several thousand schools (Tarlau, 2017). In 2008, with the end of World Bank funding, Brazil's Ministry of Education in the Worker Party government "universalized the program to serve 40,000 multigrade schools across all 26 Brazilian states, with a new curriculum that embraced rural social movements—including the controversial Brazilian Landless Workers Movement (MST)" (Tarlau, 2017: 675). Yet, the MST organized against the Escola Ativa, which it saw as an "imported" educational reform that competed with the MST's rural education program based on government schools run by MST educators and closely tied to the MST's land reform program. In 2010, the Ministry of Education compromised with the MST by allowing the MST to revise the Escola Ativa curriculum toward a more social movement orientation. By 2012, the government ended funding to Escola Ativa, and the program was effectively terminated. In its place, the ministry created Escola da Terra, whose main role was to continue to train multigrade teachers—in universities (Tarlau, 2017).

Politics and Rural Educational Reform

These examples of rural educational programs and the evaluations show that some can be effective in improving rural students' academic achievement and reducing repetition and the number of dropouts. The programs suggest that, although the problems of rural education are deeply rooted in the socioeconomic conditions of Latin America's rural areas and, in some countries, that the population is *Indigena* (see Chapter 6), we know at least some programs that will work to make rural education much better. The core of all these programs are an improved curriculum and teacher training—training specifically oriented to rural conditions, including adaptations to multigrade classrooms.

At the same time, these examples also tell another story. I argued earlier that moving resources and education improvement into rural areas require effective "technical" reforms, but also the right political conditions. The life and death of Escola Ativa in Brazil is a good example of how politics plays such an important role in the process of educational reform. Rebecca Tarlau claims that the World Bank could convince the Cardoso government in the late 1990s to implement the Escuela Nueva model in Brazil because the land occupation activities of the MST in rural areas had created a political problem for which effective rural education seemed to serve as a reasonable response (Tarlau, 2017). Later, the Lula government—much more sympathetic to rural reform, including land reform—logically expanded the Escola Ativa nationwide, but Escola Ativa was opposed from the left because it competed with another rural education reform. Yet, today with conservatives at the helm in Brazil, financial support for any rural education efforts has dropped precipitously.

A similar case can be made that once social strife declined in rural Colombia, government support for Escuela Nueva waned. Tarlau contends that a main reason Escuela Nueva was so broadly implemented in Colombia in the late 1970s and into the 1980s was as a government response to social unrest in Colombia's rural areas— this was a period of major guerrilla operations in rural Colombia. Vicky Colbert was very effective in garnering international support and the support of local teachers, but Tarlau argues that "her effectiveness was within a particular political context that made the state more open to these initiatives" (Tarlau, 2017: 683).

> Paradoxically, it was in the late 1980s and 1990s, *after* a series of studies were published about Escuela Nueva effectiveness (Psacharopoulos et al., 1993; Schiefelbein 1991; McEwan 1998), that the program began to lose momentum . . . the Colombian state had embraced the Unitary Schools program and *Escuela Nueva* in the late 1960s and 1970s, when violence in rural regions was at a peak and there was an urgent need to incorporate farmers into the political process. However, in the 1980s, rural violence was more isolated, and "thus, the importance of 'incorporating' rural denizens into the political process gradually lost importance" (McEwan and Benveniste 2001: 556). The early 1990s brought other changes, including the decentralization of education to municipal governments and privatization policies. Under a new hegemonic bloc, which had less concern with rural development, support for Escuela Nueva declined. (Tarlau, 2017: 683–684)

Thus, although we still need to keep researching and experimenting with new ways to close the rural-urban education gap, we have already gained important insights into increasing the quality of education for rural children. Yet, all that said, whether these investments are made depends on the political importance that governments in Latin America give to incorporating rural peoples into the national project. Therein lies an important lesson of these reforms. Yes, the problem is partly technical, and implementing reforms effectively is also not a simple matter. But the problem is also very political. How do we convince Latin American governments that equalizing opportunities in rural areas should be part of their political project even when there are no uprisings or conflictive social movements in rural areas? This is not an easy task, especially with the ongoing problems Latin America has in much more politically vocal urban areas—particularly the crime and violence spilling over into middle class residential zones. Yet, it is up to both the political class and social movements to draw attention to the "unseen" rural poor, who are the farthest behind in Latin American societies. Rural education initiatives combined with other investments can have big effects in rural areas, as the cases we have featured exemplify. There is no reason why these educational reforms cannot be intensified everywhere in the region immediately. Down the line, the payoffs to such investments would be high.

Notes

1. The Rasch model scores the responses of individual students to questions of different levels of difficulty. Thus, it measures a student's performance on a test of items of lower and higher levels of difficulty. As long as tests are designed with various items with comparable levels of difficulty, a student's performance can be compared based on different tests with different items.

6

Education Policy for Indigenous Populations

According to various sources (López, 2010; World Bank Group, 2015; Hoffay and Rivas, 2016), there are now about 30–45 million Indigenous peoples in Latin America—about 6–8 percent of the total population. It is not easy to estimate this number. A main identifier of Indigenousness—Indigenous language spoken—has declined from generation to generation as increasing numbers of Indigenous peoples move into urban areas and become more educated. Furthermore, even when the language is retained, many who should be classified as Indigenous speak an Indigenous language only second to their main language, Spanish or Portuguese.

With that caveat, and to the degree that Indigenous peoples can be identified, there are sixteen Latin American countries with some Indigenous peoples, often speaking many different languages and representing different ethnic groups. Five or six countries had more than one million Indigenous peoples in 2010—Mexico, Peru, Guatemala, Bolivia, Colombia, and probably Ecuador, and seven countries had Indigenous populations that were more than 7 percent of their total population—Bolivia, Guatemala, Peru, Mexico, Panama, Honduras, and Ecuador.

Why is it important to discuss educational policy and more general social policies for Indigenous peoples if they represent a relatively small percentage of the total population in Latin America? For one, in some countries they are a relatively large percentage; second, they are poorer and less educated than the non-Indigenous populations; third, they are highly unrepresented politically in the political system of the region; and fourth, they are discriminated against economically and socially—they have fewer opportunities, less access to public services, and lower incomes than the non-Indigenous population with the same education, of the same age, and of the same gender. Finally, given that Indigenous peoples have distinct cultures—cultures that preceded and differ considerably from these nations' dominant European culture—crucial questions arise whether it is important to preserve distinct Indigenous cultures as part of the national project, how to preserve them while building coherent and unified nations, and how to reduce discrimination in the region against nondominant groups as part of developing democracy based on social inclusion.

I have a special interest in these questions, since I was the first Indigenous president to be elected in Peru. By chance, and with a lot of luck to be in the right place at the right time before I became president, I was able to get a world-class education, work for international agencies, and become a university professor in Peru. This is far from the usual trajectory for someone of Indigenous origin in my country. Further, in some definitions of Indigenousness, I don't fit the classification because I barely speak Quechua, the language of my Indigenous people. Like almost all my friends in Chimbote, a city in the north of Peru, where my family moved from the Sierra when I was five years old, I was "assimilated."

At the same time, because of my unmistakably Indigenous appearance, in many ways I was and still am treated in my own country as the "other." That otherness carries with it a distinct "second-class status" rooted in dominant European views of the inferiority and primitiveness of Indigenous culture. Every person who looks Indigenous in Latin America, even if they do not speak an Indigenous language, understands the everyday meaning of being viewed in that way. Worse, Latin American states have legitimized those views into unequal treatment—unlike my experience, Indigenous peoples average much lower educational attainment and lower quality education than the non-Indigenous. Indigenous peoples are more likely to be poor, are underrepresented politically, and are discriminated against socially. All this has put the Indigenous citizens of our countries at the end of the opportunity queue. In many estimates, a significant part of Indigenous peoples' higher poverty rates and lower earnings is due to lower quantity and quality of schooling and other educational opportunities. Also by not explicitly recognizing it for what it is, Latin American governments legitimize discrimination against

Indigenous peoples in labor markets and the court system, even for those with the same education as the non-Indigenous.

I cannot and will not ignore the larger issues of discrimination, but because this book is about education, here I want to focus on what education can do to reduce inequality. What should be the educational strategy that best serves the advancement of Indigenous peoples, helping them to preserve their culture, to substantially increase their earnings and at the same time furthering democracy and economic development in the region?

The Condition of Indigenous Peoples in Latin America

The condition of Indigenous peoples in Latin America changed considerably in the twentieth century as many moved out of very poor rural areas largely inhabited by Indigenous peoples to more ethnically diverse and less poor urban areas. On average, they reached higher levels of education, high levels of poverty declined in absolute terms as the region's economies progressed, and a higher fraction of Indigenous peoples became bilingual and were assimilated. Nevertheless, at the end of the century they remained at a distinct economic and social disadvantage compared to the non-Indigenous population, and throughout the region continued to face oppressive economic and social barriers to further advancement.

On January 1, 1994, the Zapatista Army of National Liberation (EZLN) gained international attention for the plight of Indigenous peoples by coordinating a twelve-day revolt in the Mexican state of Chiapas. The immediate issue was a protest against the signing of the North American Free Trade Agreement (NAFTA) with the United States, but the underlying catalyst for the revolt was the 1991 revision of Article 27 in Mexico's 1917 revolutionary constitution, which protected Mexico communal *ejido* lands from privatization. Indigenous farmers in Chiapas feared that they would lose their communal lands. Control of lands, water supply, and other communal resources is a typical source of struggle for Indigenous peoples throughout the Americas, and the Zapatista revolt resulted from these ever-present grievances. Although the uprising did not last long, it made the world aware of the flagrant abuse of Indigenous peoples' rights in the Americas (Mentinis, 2006).

As part of this increased awareness, the World Bank produced a study that provided valuable detail on the possible reasons for

Indigenous peoples' severe economic and social disadvantages. The study analyzed them in four countries with large Indigenous populations: Bolivia (urban), Guatemala, Mexico, and Peru (Psacharopoulos and Patrinos, 1994). The study's description of the economic and social marginalization of Indigenous peoples and the main reasons for that marginalization are devastatingly simple: less access to education, less access to other social services, and probable economic discrimination even at the same level of education. These are all either the result of conscious public sector policies (lack of education, health, water, and other infrastructure) or of the absence of policies that guarantee rights of equal treatment regardless of race and ethnicity written into all these countries' constitutions.

Thus, on the one hand, Indigenous peoples are poor because they have low levels of education and health:

The indigenous people in Guatemala are the poorest of the poor. They have the lowest education levels, the least access to health services, the least access to basic services such as water and sanitation, and income levels half that of non-indigenous people. . . . Increasing the human capital attainment of Guatemalan indigenous males would lead to a substantial reduction in the gap in earnings between ethnic groups. Equalizing income-generating characteristics between ethnic groups, especially policy-relevant variables such as education, would reduce the wage gap by about 50 percent (Psacharopoulos and Patrinos, 1994: 125–126). . . . [In urban Bolivia] detailed decomposition analysis of earnings differentials shows that for the male sample, endowments of assessed characteristics account for 72 percent of the disparity between indigenous and non-indigenous earnings. Non-indigenous males in the labor force average almost three more years of schooling than their indigenous counterparts, while the disparity between indigenous and non-indigenous females is almost four years (94–95). [In Mexico] detailed decomposition of the earnings differentials shows that for the male sample, endowments of assessed characteristics account for 52 percent of the disparity between indigenous and non-indigenous workers' earnings. . . . Large educational differences exist between indigenous and non-indigenous *municipios* (145–146). In Peru, . . . if indigenous workers were endowed with the same productive characteristics as non-indigenous workers, the earnings differential between them would narrow by 50 percent. (202–203)

On the other hand, even with the same productive characteristics, Indigenous workers are paid less. In Bolivia, the "unexplained" gap in Indigenous earnings is the lowest, at 28 percent—that is, controlling for education, age, and other individual characteristics associated with higher productivity, Indigenous workers earn 28 percent less than a non-Indigenous worker. This might not be due entirely to discrimination, yet discrimination is likely to be an important factor in such unexplained differences. In the other three countries, the "unexplained" gap is much larger, at about one-half the lower earnings of the Indigenous. This means that even when we account for differences in education, age, and so forth, Indigenous peoples earn 50 percent lower wages.

> [In Mexico] the empirical results . . . show a clear socioeconomic disadvantage among those living in *municipios* with high percentages of indigenous people to those living in *municipios* with low percentages of indigenous people. . . . "Unexplained" factors such as variations in ability, quality of education, labor force participation, culture and labor market discrimination are responsible for . . . 48 percent of the earnings gap. . . . Indigenous people [in Peru] receive negligible and non-significant returns to their investments in education, except at the university level. . . . [W]age discrimination against the indigenous population may account for as much as 50 percent of the overall earnings differential. (Psachropoulos and Patrinos, 1994: 145–146, 202–203)

So it is not surprising that Indigenous peoples are frustrated by their situation and that in Mexico, an armed rebellion occurred in an area with a high concentration of Indigenous peoples. It had the positive effect of drawing attention to the powerlessness of Indigenous peoples. One political reaction to the Zapatista revolt was the United Nations proclamation of the International Decade of the World's Indigenous Peoples in December 1994. Did that proclamation have an effect on the conditions of life for Indigenous peoples in Latin America during the following decade?

The World Bank followed up its 1994 analysis cited above with a second study that assessed the gains made by Indigenous peoples during 1994–2004 (Hall and Patrinos, 2005). That second study concluded that although Indigenous peoples made important political gains during the decade, as measured by "indigenous political parties, indigenous elected representatives, constitutional provisions for indigenous people or indigenous-tailored health and education policies" (Hall and Patrinos, 2005: 2), few gains were made in reducing poverty among Indigenous peoples during the decade and little action took place to address the high proportion of the earnings gap attributable to pay discrimination (3).

> In four of the five countries studied, virtually no reduction occurred in the share of indigenous people in poverty, from the earliest to latest year for which data are available. . . . In two of these countries, poverty rates did fall for non-indigenous people (Mexico and Bolivia). This pattern suggests that where gains in poverty reduction are being made, indigenous people are benefiting less, and is repeated in the case of Guatemala (1989–2000), where indigenous poverty rates fell, but at a slower pace than for non-indigenous people. In two cases (Ecuador and Peru), national poverty rates rose over the period, yet indigenous peoples were less affected by that increase. (Hall and Patrinos, 2005: 3)

There are other interesting aspects of this World Bank report concerning bilingual education, which we will discuss later, but the main takeaway is that the UN's Indigenous Peoples decade, combined with important advances in democratic institutions in the region, helped Indigenous peoples to make some political gains, but did little to close the education gap between them and the non-Indigenous population, and did nothing to overcome the relatively lower earnings return that they realize from the education they do get—in other words, little or no progress in reducing the discrimination that Indigenous peoples face in Latin American societies.

A closer look at the political gains made by Indigenous peoples suggests that although there have been gains in recognizing Indigenous legal rights to self-determination and prior consultation, and political representation did increase, the recognition of legal rights has had little impact on the daily lives of Indigenous peoples. In addition, representation is still far short of proportional to the Indigenous share of population in all but two countries, Ecuador and Venezuela. Venezuela has only a small Indigenous population but has reserved parliamentary seats for Indigenous representatives (Hoffay and Rivas, 2016). For example, using an estimate of the Indigenous population of Bolivia as 41 percent of the total (other estimates of the Indigenous population are as high as 66 percent), that country had a "reasonable" representation of 26 percent of the seats in the Bolivian legislature and an Indigenous president, Evo Morales, but Guatemala, with a similar proportion of 41 percent Indigenous, had only 13 percent Indigenous representation in the legislature. My country, Peru, with 26 percent of the population estimated to be Indigenous, had only 7 percent of the seats in the Peruvian Congress in 2016 occupied by Indigenous representatives, and Mexico, with the largest absolute population of Indigenous peoples in the region (yet, only 15 percent of the total population) had only 3 percent of the representatives to the Mexico legislature who were Indigenous, despite a legislative policy that created Indigenous districts in high-density Indigenous areas (Hoffay and Rivas, 2016).

Thus, the picture is not as bad politically for Indigenous peoples as it was a generation ago, but these political gains have not translated into many legal victories for Indigenous peoples' control over their land and communal resources, nor have they resulted in reductions in the poverty gap or less economic discrimination. There has been increased discussion of what to do educationally, including bilingual education, and discussions about increasing public resources for Indigenous peoples, including improved targeted healthcare programs, yet, according to the World Bank study, not much progress has been made on that front either.

There is agreement that closing the education gap would help close *at least part* of the earnings and poverty gap. I want to emphasize that whatever we do in helping Indigenous peoples get more and higher quality education will not solve the problems of lower returns on that education for Indigenous peoples or pay discrimination in similar jobs. And without major policy changes, greater access to good education is not going to occur. This includes increased access to higher education for the children of Indigenous peoples, programs promoting functional literacy for Indigenous adults, especially in rural areas, and better quality of education in schools with high percentages of Indigenous children. In the rest of this chapter I discuss policies and strategies for achieving these goals.

The Autonomy vs. Assimilation Debate in Indigenous Education

An important question inherent in democratic nation-state educational policies for "minority" groups is how the nation-state views itself culturally and linguistically. This question becomes even more complex in a global economy, where the nation-state's dominant language is not the dominant global language. I draw heavily on University of Pennsylvania president Amy Gutmann's work in unraveling this issue of democratic education in culturally diverse societies (Gutmann, 1999, 2004). The underlying framework is spelled out by Gutmann.

> Democratic education—publicly supported education that is defensible according to a democratic ideal—should educate children so that they are capable of assuming the rights and correlative responsibilities of equal citizenship, which includes respecting other people's rights. In short, democratic education should both express and develop the capacity of all children to become equal citizens. . . . [I]ndividuals should be treated and treat one another as equal citizens, regardless of their gender, race, ethnicity, or religion. (Gutmann, 2004: 71)

Starting with this framework, for Indigenous peoples in Latin American nation-states to advance economically, socially, and politically two things need to happen: first, all students, whether Indigenous or non-Indigenous should receive a civic education in public schools that teaches both tolerance and recognition of cultural differences. This means that children who are from the dominant European/mestizo/mulatto culture of most Latin American nations (Bolivia may be an exception) should not only be taught to "tolerate" Indigenous and African-origin minority cultures but also "recognize" them as having equal value and standing in their democratic, multicultural society. Tolerance and recognition of European/mestizo/mulatto cultures should also be part of any education that serves minority cultural groups, such as Indigenous-run bilingual schools. As Gutmann points out, "liberal democracies can defend a set of multicultural practices that exhibit both toleration and recognition of cultural differences, depending on their content and social context . . . [under the condition that these practices] aid, or at least do not impede, the education of children as civic equals" (Gutmann, 2004: 72).

Second, within this space of tolerance and recognition, we have to consider the degree to which the nation-state should permit various communities to decide on the form and curriculum of their children's education. More specifically, to what degree should dominant European culture communities control what their children are taught, and should Indigenous communities have autonomy over their children's education? Of course, in practical terms, the dominant group in any nation-state sets the terms of what is taught to children in public education, as well as how it is taught. Thus, dominant group (majority) children are taught a type of majority consensual notion of tolerance and recognition even when there is some form of multicultural education in the schools. The dominant group also sets the terms of (regulates) what is taught to minority children, even if the minority community "controls" (has autonomy over) its schools. Thus, for Indigenous communities in Latin America that would like to have more control over their children's education as well as broader rights to control the use of their communal lands and other resources (such as water), the practical issue is how much they will be able to emphasize their own cultural history and language. In any case, they should not be able to teach Indigenous children intolerance of European culture, nor, in a democratic society, should they teach such intolerance, even while "recognizing cultural diversity is good . . . within democratically defensible grounds" (Gutmann, 2004: 82). They should also be able to emphasize their rich cultural history and bring it into equality with the non-Indigenous version of national history.

Therefore, a main focus of education in Indigenous communities *and* non-Indigenous communities in our region should certainly be teaching mutual respect, tolerance, and equal treatment of the various cultures and histories that make up our diverse societies. It is probably as or more important for Indigenous peoples to what degree this emphasis on tolerance takes place in schools where students are predominantly non-Indigenous. Were most students in Peru or in Guatemala or Mexico taught about the value of Indigenous culture and taught to fight against the pervasive racism against the Indigenous peoples in our midst, discrimination might be reduced and education and wage gaps might begin to diminish.

Yet, at the same time, as an Indigenous person, I am concerned that education for Indigenous students should also focus on what would be best for them to be successful economically and socially in each of their countries. That issue is as controversial as what it means to have a multicultural democratic education that focuses on the reduction of intolerance. As argued earlier, part of the economic and social gap faced by Indigenous peoples can be overcome by increasing access to more years of schooling and to increase the quality of schooling. Previous chapters have discussed what it would take to improve the quality of schooling for disadvantaged students in our region. In the case of Indigenous students, such improvements are made more complex by cultural and language issues. One question is whether just improving the quality of teachers and physical facilities would be enough to make a major difference in the quality of education that Indigenous students receive, or whether that education needs to also include the recruitment and specialized training of Indigenous, bilingual teachers, special curricula that focus heavily on Indigenous history and cultural identity, and Indigenous autonomy—giving major control of this education to Indigenous communities.

There is persuasive evidence that a curriculum that helps develop positive cultural identity in students—hence greater self-efficacy—improves academic performance across a wide range of subjects, including mathematics and science (Dee and Penner, 2017). There is also evidence that bilingual education that emphasizes the value of high skill levels in both languages can improve the academic performance of students who are not native speakers of the dominant language (Hakuta, 1986). I go into much more detail below about the numerous studies showing that the effects on achievement and attainment of bilingual education for Indigenous language speakers are positive. Many years ago, Paulo Freire, made the case in *Pedagogy of the Oppressed* (2018) for the need to engage oppressed adults and children through a pedagogy embedded in political consciousness—through their political reality and their class and cultural position in society, including using their language. That may seem terribly revolutionary, but in a real sense, any effort to promote ethnic identity and more balanced history of Indigenous peoples in the Americas necessarily means engaging with a history of inequality and, yes, oppression of Indigenous rights.

The unfortunate part of all this is that bilingual schools for Indigenous students have been much less available and less successful in Latin America than they could have been. In large part, this is because they have lacked the necessary resources to be successful, including bilingual teachers with adequate levels of math and language content knowledge and, simultaneously, well trained to teach in both the Indigenous language and in Spanish (or Portuguese). In addition, except for Mexico, they have been limited in coverage, especially in my country, where in the early 2000s, only 10 percent of Indigenous primary school age children had access to bilingual, bicultural education. And often, even when bilingual education exists in a school, it is only present in the first two or three grades, not long enough to develop an adequate level of reading and writing skills in native (L1) and dominant (L2) languages.

Lessons from Bilingual, Bicultural Education in Latin America

Bilingual education and the official recognition of Indigenous languages and Indigenous cultures made major, if sporadic, advances during the twentieth century in the countries with large Indigenous populations. However, it is important to distinguish many of the "transitional bilingual" programs that were put in place during this period—programs that focused on teaching Spanish to Indigenous children and adults as a way to "assimilate" Indigenous peoples into the dominant mestizo culture of the nation-state—from "intercultural bilingual education" (IBE, or EIB in Spanish) whose purpose is to "create a level playing field for the teaching of two different cultures . . . to eliminate the hierarchy that had been imposed since colonial times and that treated Spanish as superior and the language of schooling. . . . As a learning pedagogy, EIB teaches students in the Indigenous language and in Spanish so that they develop literacy in both languages and are prepared to continue their education past elementary school. Most importantly, the goal is for children to learn to recognize the value of their own culture at the same time that they acquire knowledge about and respect for others" (Cortina, 2014: 3–4).

"[A]s a result of the increasing demands and active participation of Indigenous leaders, intellectuals, and teachers," a major ideological shift occurred in the 1970s and early 1980s from transitional bilingual education toward educational programs that emphasized the value of Indigenous languages and culture and using that culture as a political resource for greater participation in the definition of the nation-state (López, 2014: 27–28). However, this shift only took hold after transitional bilingual education failed to incorporate and assimilate Indigenous populations.

For example, Mexico, the site of the Zapatista revolt in the early 1990s, had been leading the way in terms of using Indigenous languages in bilingual approaches to "Spanishization." This included "'cultural missions', Spanishization campaigns, boarding schools for indigenous boys and girls, community radios, cultural and linguistic brokers, L1 literacy, indigenous-language-speaking youth and adults teaching appointments, and also bilingual education" (López, 2010: 14). Although there were gradual changes to bilingual, bicultural education in the 1970s and 1980s, it was not until after the revolt in Chiapas that the Mexican government made Mexico officially a multicultural nation and made bilingual, bicultural approaches to Indigenous education the preferred model for Indigenous students—this in the context of expanding Indigenous peoples' rights (López, 2010: 15).

My country, Peru, was also a leader in bilingual education for Indigenous peoples, especially during the Leftist military regime of Juan Velasco in the early 1970s. The education reform of 1972 instituted bilingual education for the Indigenous peoples of the Andes and the Amazon, and in 1975, the regime made Quechua an official language equal to Spanish (Salazar-Bondy, 1976). But this law was never enforced and ceased to be valid under the new constitution of 1979. Nevertheless, the democratically elected Peruvian governments that succeeded the Velasco regime continued—with the involvement of international agencies—to implement bilingual primary education in Indigenous areas, but on a limited scale. During my presidency, I reestablished the National Directorate of Intercultural Bilingual Education, which had been downgraded in the 1980s, and it continued to develop bilingual textbooks in various Indigenous languages, engage in pilot pre-service and in-service teacher training programs at universities in Indigenous areas, and generally tried to inject new life into bilingual, bicultural education. This was an important project for me, because of my Indigenous roots and because I felt that it would help Indigenous youth develop greater ethnic pride in their language and culture. I faced some opposition to the project from powerful mine owners—they suspected that the directorate would stimulate opposition to mining among Indigenous peoples whose drinking water was being polluted by runoff from the mines. But this opposition was short-lived—too many groups (including bilingual teachers and textbook manufacturers) supported the directorate. Unfortunately, these efforts to support bilingual, bicultural education stagnated after 2006 when I left office and Alan Garcia became president (López, 2010: 19).

Similar initiatives have also taken place in Guatemala, with the same kind of tentative results as in Peru, and starting from even more extreme gaps in literacy than in Mexico or Peru. However, one major difference from Mexico and Peru is that in Guatemala, most bilingual education efforts are financed by international loans and grants and on technical assistance from a range of international donors (López, 2014: 36).

> For the past two decades [1990–2010], but more strongly since the Peace Accords, the country has adopted neoliberal multiculturalism as a government policy. New institutions were created:

among others the National Academy of Mayan languages (1990), the Guatemalan Indigenous Development Fund (1994), and the Presidential Commission on Racism and Discrimination (2003). The national constitution of 1985 recognizes the right of indigenous learners to education in their own language, and the legal and official rhetoric is both sound and politically correct, but vast gaps exist between the apparent desire and implementation. (López, 2010: 21)

According to Patrinos and Velez (2009), "Decades of research show that bilingual education has met with success in Latin America. . . . The bilingual approach produces better results in tests of reading comprehension. That is, reading comprehension is greater for those students taught in bilingual schools where they first learn to read in their native language and then transfer their reading skill to the second language: Spanish" (Patrinos and Velez, 2009: 595). Patrinos and Velez also summarize a number of evaluations of a bilingual education program in Guatemala, Programa Nacional de Educación Bilingue Intercultural (PRONEBI), which show that Indigenous children in bilingual schools have lower repetition rates, higher attendance rates, lower dropout rates, and have as high or higher achievement than Indigenous children being taught only in Spanish. López (2010) cites other studies in Mexico, Peru, and Guatemala similarly showing that even the transitional bilingual education programs implemented in these three countries in the 1970s, 1980s, and 1990s had positive learning outcomes for Indigenous students compared to Spanish only schooling. Thus, as McEwan and Trowbridge (2007) conclude in their assessment of differences in achievement between Indigenous and non-Indigenous students in Guatemala, bilingual education could be important for bridging this gap.

Bilingual education in Bolivia and Ecuador has had a somewhat different history, and may provide additional lessons for Indigenous education in Latin America. Both of these countries had, in some ways, more ambitious efforts in IBE than in Peru and Guatemala, and different from Mexico's. According to López (2010, 2014), IBE developed in Ecuador and Bolivia from the "bottom up."

In many ways the Bolivian reform ideology, principles, and strategies followed a democratic direction, granting power to local communities, and for the first time education officially adopted interculturalism for all and gave privileged attention to the education of the most underprivileged: the indigenous children and youth. Millions of pedagogically innovative and richly illustrated educational materials that depicted the indigenous way of life reached public school classrooms both in indigenous and mainstream communities and neighborhoods. Half of all Bolivian teacher training colleges adopted an IIBE [Indigenous intercultural bilingual education] curriculum with the participation of indigenous leaders and after their staff went through specialized seminars on language, culture, and active pedagogy. Several cohorts of professional IIBE teachers were trained. Renewed indigenous self-esteem and initial nationwide positioning of indigenous knowledge, culture, and languages practically invaded the educational and social scenario of the country, promoting a form of local indigenous Renaissance, which indeed paved the way for the indigenous political impetus Bolivia is now undergoing. . . .

In Bolivia and Ecuador, indigenous leaders negotiated with government authorities and, unlike other bottom-up experiences that remained only as micro-level initiatives, they managed to have some bearing on educational policies as well as on national politics in general. Indigenous educational proposals became national policies influencing the regular education system, obtained official funding, and were extended significantly. Indigenous leaders took advantage of the official educational platform just conquered to push the indigenous political agenda even further. Indeed, IIBE has never been an isolated demand, but part of a bigger agenda which includes other civil and political rights. (López, 2010: 25)

Other analysts of the Bolivian experience with IBE don't completely agree with López that IBE was driven mainly by a "bottom-up" movement of Indigenous peoples. These analyses claim that IBE was rather a case of government "nonreformist reform," part of the Bolivian state's neoliberal restructuring in the 1980s and 1990s, or a negotiation between the state and Indigenous movements (Cortina, 2014: 16). Yet, without getting into the subtleties of how to interpret the Bolivian (and Ecuadorian) histories of IBE, the lessons from Bolivia and Ecuador are rather clear that successful bilingual, bicultural education for Indigenous children and youth must have Indigenous community political support and must have the support of wider groups of stakeholders, such as teachers' unions, intellectuals (universities), and political leaders (the state). Furthermore, the entire effort cannot be viewed as part of a "nonreformist reform" to co-opt Indigenous peoples into an economy and society that regards them as second class and gives second-class status to their language, culture, and community organizations.

Indeed, these are also the lessons of Mexico, Peru, and Guatemala. We now know that bilingual education is more effective in keeping Indigenous children in school and is more effective in developing reading and other academic skills, but for it to be meaningful for Indigenous peoples it must be part of a larger effort to make Indigenous culture legitimate and equal in Latin America's multicultural societies. It must both be "owned" by Indigenous communities and be seen as contributing to the overall welfare of the nation-state by its non-Indigenous communities. As Mexican sociologist Sylvia Schmelkes has noted, "Achieving more equity in education necessarily entails improving the quality of the education offered to the indigenous population and the great challenge still lies in preschool and primary education. But it is essential to offer intercultural education to all the populations so that the quality improvement of the education offered to the indigenous population reaches the expected impact in the short and long term. Interculturalism . . . must be a necessary ingredient of our national education" (Schmelkes, 2006: 4, quoted in López, 2010: 16).

Thus, a key lesson of IBE in all these countries is that it is intensely political. The gains of the past generation in preserving Indigenous culture and recognizing the plight of Indigenous peoples in the Americas were largely the result of political actions in Mexico, then in other Latin American countries, as well as the United States and Canada to make this an international issue. IBE is a pedagogical intervention that can improve the quality of education for Indigenous peoples in our region, but for it to be implemented on a large scale, it must be part of a political process that gives recognition to Indigenous rights and power to Indigenous communities to participate in that process.

The Critical Role of Higher Education

As part and parcel of this underlying politics of Indigenous education, in Mexico, Bolivia, and Ecuador, Indigenous movements have understood that Indigenous education has to extend beyond primary schools and basic bilingual reading and math skills into secondary school and universities. This means that societal expectations for Indigenous peoples have to be sharply increased even as reforms in the education available to Indigenous children improve their academic skills. One of the unfortunate realities in Indigenous regions is that well-meaning educators see their task as just bringing literacy and basic academic skills to Indigenous children to train them for somewhat better but still relatively low-skilled occupations. For example, in Chile's Temuco region, home of many of the Indigenous Mapuche, an Organization for Economic Cooperation and Development (OECD) mission in 2003 visited secondary vocational schools serving Mapuche young people and found the training oriented largely to domestic service and manual occupations, not for attending university or even postsecondary technical schools (OECD, 2003).

Without access to university education, Indigenous young people will necessarily be kept out of the professions, including teaching. As I show in Chapter 10, because of the rapid expansion of primary and secondary education, and the increasing demand for higher order skills, the highest returns to education in Latin America over the past thirty years have shifted to those who complete university education. Indigenous peoples are much less likely to get access to higher education. In Mexico, where, as I discussed earlier, major advances were made in transitional bilingual education in the 1970s and 1980s, by 1990, when 17.4 percent of Mexicans aged fifteen years or older had completed normal school or some years of university or more, only 2.8 percent of Indigenous Mexicans had attained these levels. In the poor states of Chiapas and Oaxaca, where most Indigenous peoples lived in 1990, the percentages were 5.8 percent for the non-Indigenous and 1.3 percent for Indigenous peoples in Chiapas, and 6.4 percent and 3.2 percent in Oaxaca (Carnoy, Santibanez, Maldonado, and Ordorika, 2002: Table 3). In the past thirty years, the development of intercultural universities and advances in Indigenous studies have improved higher education access for Indigenous students significantly, but large gaps remain in the proportion of Indigenous and non-Indigenous young people who get higher education.

Continuing to increase Indigenous access to universities and the transformation of universities themselves in countries with significant Indigenous populations is crucial for national progress. In the 2000s in Mexico, Schmelkes (2014) found that "a university education provides unexpected opportunities for social mobility for indigenous students; it also contributes to graduate strengthening and redefining their indigenous cultural identity and helps ensure that indigenous knowledge and languages will persist through the generations" (Cortina, 2014: 13). Further, since universities are one of the key producers and legitimizers of knowledge (Weiler, 2011), the creation of programs of study and research in universities that focus on the multicultural nature of most Latin American societies is important to the construction and legitimation of multiculturalism in our societies. This includes teaching programs, intercultural studies, legal studies, economics, sociology, medicine, and environmental studies. All these disciplines would be transformed by framing them in a multicultural perspective.

It is also important to recognize that unless our universities in the region become more dedicated to supporting multiculturalism, Indigenous students not only face obstacles to maintaining their cultural identity, but also are less likely to succeed academically—a strong sense of identity and confidence in the value of that identity are key to academic success.

> Considered as privileged places for negotiating knowledge and for the construction of a new type of citizenship, indigenous leaders expect universities to also become intercultural since many of the IIBE graduates and more indigenous students in general are now entering tertiary education. They want to overcome indigenous identity fragility, since a student of indigenous origin who starts a university career is subject to strong institutional and social pressure to give up his indigenous identity and affiliation. (López, 2010: 26)

The establishment of "intercultural universities," in some countries of Latin America serve as an example of both the positive and negative aspects of creating higher education institutions that are organized to serve Indigenous peoples in the region (Mato, 2008). Mexico, with eight intercultural universities, including the Universidad Intercultural de Chiapas (UNICH), the Universidad Autónoma Indígena de México (UAIM), and the Universidad Veracruzana Intercultural (UVI); Bolivia, with the Universidad Intercultural Indígena Originaria Kawsay (UIIOK) and other programs; Ecuador, with the Universidad Intercultural de las Nacionalidades y Pueblos Indígenas "Amawtay Wasi" (UIAW), Universidad de las Nacionalidades Indígenas de la Amazonía Ecuatoriana, and other programs; Colombia, with the Universidad Autónoma, Indígena e Intercultural (UAIIN) and other programs; Guatemala, with its Universidad Maya; and Venezuela, with its Universidad Indígena de Venezuela (UIV), are all examples of more than fifty intercultural universities and programs in the region that have been founded in the past forty years in response to movements focused on promoting multicultural societies in Latin America (Mato, 2009). These are in addition to efforts to include Indigenous students and students of other disadvantaged groups (such as Latin Americans of African origin, for example) in traditional universities as "individuals" (Mato, 2009: 26). I discuss such "affirmative action" efforts in Chapter 10.

These experiences have been the object of a number of studies (Mato, 2008, 2009; Schmelkes, 2006, 2013; Martinez Novo, 2014, among others). They show that first, intercultural universities serve a relatively small number of students, even when a high percentage of the students are Indigenous (Mato, 2008). The poor quality of primary and secondary education available to Indigenous students and the low academic expectations that pervade lower levels of schooling in Indigenous regions are still major barriers for these students to graduate secondary school and enter postsecondary education. Second, most Indigenous secondary graduates, at least a decade ago, entered teaching or health care or other public sector professions— this makes sense because, historically, there has been less wage discrimination in Latin America's public sector than in the private sector. Even so, these Indigenous graduates play an important leadership role in Indigenous communities. The fact that many higher education opportunities now exist for Indigenous peoples that were not available in an earlier generation, and that these opportunities are at least partly oriented toward preserving and developing Indigenous cultures, is a big step forward.

The studies also show that intercultural universities and the programs promoting individual access to universities through affirmative action are in a permanently precarious situation. The intercultural universities are always under threat of losing funding, which comes mostly from federal or state ministries, and, depending on the politics of the moment, can face administrations that exploit ever-present anti-Indigenous views in the wider population. Further, as Martinez Novo points out in analyzing the intercultural universities in Ecuador, Indigenous secondary school graduates consider conventional universities as much higher quality and providing more opportunities for good professional jobs (Martinez Novo, 2014). In analyzing interviews with graduates from intercultural universities in Ecuador, Martinez Novo found that

> most students would have liked to attend a mainstream university but chose an intercultural college instead because of its lower tuition and flexible schedule that allowed them to continue working. As in elementary schools, Indigenous languages are taught in these institutions as the content to particular

classes, not as a means of advanced academic communication. Moreover, Indigenous professors typically teach Indigenous culture using the writings of non-Indigenous authors. . . . Meanwhile, students in intercultural universities struggle to achieve mainstream competencies and secure a university diploma that will lead to a good job. (Cortina, 2014: 11)

Thus, even in the much improved current political and social context regarding Indigenous education, including the teaching of Indigenous languages and Indigenous culture, we have to face the fact that the low status of Indigenous culture in our mestizo societies, still struggling to emerge from "colonialist" ideologies of European cultural superiority, makes IBE and intercultural university education difficult to establish on equal footing with conventional schools and universities. Because of that structural inequality built into our social and, hence, educational systems, it will take a major political effort to equalize the underlying educational opportunities for Indigenous peoples even though we have developed the outlines and examples of how to get there.

Some Takeaways on Indigenous Education and Multiculturalism

I am convinced by the experience of the past thirty years that it is possible to improve Indigenous education so that Indigenous children can get a much better education and therefore eliminate part of the gap in achievement and attainment that currently keeps them in much greater poverty and much less likely to become professionals and leaders than non-Indigenous peoples in our region. Nevertheless, the experience of the past thirty years also tells me that it will take sustained political effort to make this happen. In addition, whatever we do to improve Indigenous education will have to occur in the broader context of protecting the rights of Indigenous peoples and implementing a powerful element of multicultural education in the schooling of the non-Indigenous population.

In effect, we have to commit ourselves to increasing tolerance in the non-Indigenous population and creating a social consciousness that our nation-states are all multicultural and that multiculturalism and modernity can go hand-in-hand; indeed, that multiculturalism in the twenty-first century information age is the *new modernity*—the only way that we can achieve the kinds of democratic, socially integrated societies that will allow us to develop into modern, high-income nation-states increasing economic output while sustaining our natural resources and protecting the environment.

Beyond improving education for Indigenous students, bilingual, intercultural education has become part of a much larger effort by Indigenous peoples for territorial rights, the right to use water and to protect water against degradation by mineral exploitation, and the right for Indigenous peoples to govern themselves locally by their own community organizations, and to maintain their cultures and worldviews within the context of each nation-state. The ultimate goal of all these movements is to create more democratic societies that recognize the legitimate voice of Indigenous peoples in "the social, political, cultural, and economic process, as well as the full recognition of their citizenship, and the elimination of the ethnic and racial exclusion they have traditionally suffered" (Cortina, 2014: 3).

It is impossible to conceive of this happening in a democratic society without the support of the non-Indigenous population. This means that improving Indigenous education and, in addition, reducing the discrimination faced by Indigenous peoples in labor markets and in political representation requires developing the "tolerance and recognition" of Indigenous culture and rights in the mestizo cultures that currently dominate our Latin American societies. This means legal and political work that eliminates discrimination at all levels of society. It also means, in turn, introducing in all our schools curricula and teaching practices that foster such tolerance and recognition. Indigenous education at all levels cannot be separated from educational curricula and practices and political ideologies regarding multiculturalism in society as a whole. And educational practices must be conducted in a political and social context that fights against discrimination and racism in every institution of society.

Again, I am convinced we can accomplish this over the next generation. Yet, as I stress in the last chapter, it will take extraordinary leadership in the region to do it—leadership that sacrifices short-run expediency for long-run structural change.

7

Teachers and Teaching

Like everyone I have ever talked with about education, I
had a teacher or two who made a tremendous difference to me in
school. In my case, those teachers changed my life. There was one in
my primary school who saw a spark in me and my desire to do well,
and she told me that I should plan to go on to high school. She kept
telling me that and made sure that I did. Then there was the high
school teacher who encouraged me to enter the essay contest that
landed me a scholarship to go to college in the United States. These
were life-transforming events for me, and caring teachers were the
driving force that made them happen.

If there is a single fundamental axiom in education, it is that good
teachers are the key to good education. Most people would argue that
a good teacher is one that knows the subject well and engages students
to learn. There is no doubt that those are very important attributes of a
good teacher. But from my experience, good teachers also need to care
deeply about their students—not only to engage them, but to feel
responsible for their learning and their futures.

There have been some excellent analyses of teachers and teaching in Latin America, including a study from the World Bank (Bruns
and Luque, 2014), a book from the Inter-American Development
Bank (IDB) (Elacqua et al., 2018), and a comparison of teaching in
Cuba, Brazil, and Chile (Carnoy, Gove, and Marshall, 2007). The
World Bank study is very comprehensive: it discusses the relatively
low test scores in Latin American countries of those who want to

become teachers at fifteen years old (data from the PISA test), those who enter higher education in pedagogy programs, and those in teacher education programs; it also considers teacher wages and teacher classroom practices, particularly time on task. The Inter-American Development Bank study repeats many of the arguments and data in the World Bank analysis, but also puts more emphasis on teacher pre-service education reforms in the region. The Cuba-Brazil-Chile comparison focuses on classroom practices and their possible link to teacher preparation, both in pre-service teacher training programs and the induction period in schools.

In this chapter, I discuss the issues raised in the World Bank and Inter-American Development Bank studies on the relatively low level of knowledge of subject matter among Latin America's teachers and the difficulty of recruiting high school students with high levels of content knowledge into university teacher pre-service preparation programs. These are real problems in Latin America, and, as I will argue, recruiting higher academic achievers into teaching needs to be a long-term goal of Latin American governments.

However, I focus in the chapter on teacher preparation to teach—on the kinds of professional development and pre-service training programs for teachers that can help our current and near future teaching force in Latin America be much better teachers, even those with relatively lower levels of content knowledge. I believe that simply raising the content knowledge of high school students being recruited into teaching and giving tests to teachers to assure that they have minimum levels of content knowledge is not enough to make good teachers, and it is certainly not enough to improve student performance in Latin American schools, especially because most students in our region's schools come from families where parents have low levels of education and income, and many live in poverty. In addition, we need to take steps—including raising teacher salaries and improving the conditions in schools—to raise the prestige of the teaching profession and to incentivize high school students with higher levels of math and science skills.

Yet, these are very high cost reforms and are not enough to produce good teachers who know how to include all students in the class in the learning process. Even student teachers with adequate content knowledge must be trained to know how to manage their classrooms, cover the required curriculum, engage their students with tried and true teaching techniques that unify theory and practice, and help all students learn much more than they do now. Of course, that also means paying more attention to subject matter content in pre-service courses and reforming professional development to teach teachers how to teach the subject matter in the required curriculum.

But beyond that, it seems strange that most pre-service teacher training in Latin America does not put priority on teaching student teachers to teach the required curriculum effectively at whatever level they are being trained to teach. Yet, that is unfortunately the case. A main reason is that those who teach teachers are themselves not trained how to prepare teachers in these skills: "For example, a recent study by [United Nations Educational, Scientific, and Cultural Organization] (UNESCO, 2013) criticizes the fragmentation and the inadequacy of the curriculum content as well as the lack of connection between theory and practice in the limited presence of classroom practice of teacher preservice education in the region. . . . Similarly, those [who are] teaching teachers appeared to be inadequately prepared" (Elacqua et al., 2018: 33–35).

Then we ask student teachers to learn all these things on their own, giving them access to deficient supervised student teaching (Elacqua et al., 2018) and scantily supervised induction into their first teaching job. The result is that they are ill prepared to teach, and even less prepared to teach the mass of children in Latin America who come to school disadvantaged economically and academically. Fundamentally, at no stage of their training and induction into teaching do we give them the teaching (pedagogical content knowledge) and classroom management skills to teach the children the things we want those children to learn.

In addition to all that, teachers need to be taught how to be engaged with their students in ways that raise student aspirations like my teachers raised mine. We can help the existing teaching force do all these things if we mobilize and effectively utilize resources for improved teacher professional development and support continuous improvement systems in schools. At the same time, we need to build for the future by greatly improving pre-service teacher education and new teacher induction into classroom practice.

There are examples in Latin America of teacher training that does all this—that have unified theories of teaching with the practice of teaching to help the current teaching force do significantly better. Many analysts have argued that teachers' unions, universities, schools, and teachers themselves are resistant to the introduction of such changes. There is some truth to these claims. But my experience suggests that one reason there is such resistance is because available (and usually required) professional development and pre-service programs are not relevant or effective. And teachers know that. I have talked to many teachers, and they have told me that the professional development they are required to take rarely addresses helping them be more effective in their classrooms. When teachers, schools, universities, and teachers' unions participate in programs that really help teachers become better at teaching—that visibly affect student engagement and learning—these changes are not only accepted, but are generally embraced. I will talk about such teacher professional development innovations in this chapter.

The State of Teachers and Teaching

For many years, the World Bank, Inter-American Development Bank and many (probably most) national policymakers in Latin America have developed a valid but very incomplete argument about teachers and teaching in the region. They stress that teachers in Latin America are drawn from a pool of students entering higher education (including normal schools) who are of much lower ability—as measured by university entrance tests, and, more recently, by international tests given to fifteen-year-olds—than the average higher education student.

World Bank and IDB analysts recognize that there may be many reasons for this. Teaching is a relatively low-paying profession, and it is highly feminized. It is therefore lower prestige on both these criteria. As more and more students from lower social class families graduate from high school in Latin America and aspire to attend higher education, the number of teacher education programs—especially private institutions—have increased and absorbed these lower socioeconomic status students, greatly increasing the supply of teachers. This, too, puts downward pressure on teacher salaries, particularly as the fertility rate declines in Latin America and enrollment in primary and middle schools tails off and even decreases. Bruns and Luque suggest that most Latin American countries face a surplus of teachers overall:

> Virtually all countries in the region report difficulty finding sufficient teachers for specialty subjects such as secondary school math and science, or for bilingual schools in rural areas. But the broader picture across the region today is substantial excess production of teacher graduates of generally low aca-

demic quality. Recent data for Peru, Chile, Costa Rica, Panama and Uruguay suggests that 40–50 percent of graduates from teacher training schools will not find work as teachers. (Bruns and Luque, 2014: 11)

Thus, the main challenge facing Latin American education, according to this and the IDB analysis, is the low level of subject matter knowledge of teachers, and this results from the low academic quality of individuals being attracted into teaching, which is the result of low teacher salaries and the oversupply of low-quality teacher candidates.

Two decade-old international studies (Mathematics Teaching in the 21st Century [MT21] and Teacher Education and Development Study in Mathematics [TEDS-M]) of mathematics teacher pre-service training, conducted by the International Education Association (IEA) and Michigan State University (Schmidt et al., 2007; Tatto et al., 2008), showed that final-year student teachers in Mexico and Chile had lower mathematics scores on a content knowledge test than teachers in almost every other country in the study. According to the MT21 study (Schmidt et al., 2007), which did not include Chile, Mexican middle school teachers did reasonably well on algebra content knowledge, but poorly on geometry, functions, numbers, and statistics content. The TEDS-M study (which did not include Mexico) showed that the gap was especially large at the secondary school level, as shown for Chile in Figure 7.1. Even Chilean primary school teachers scored lower than their counterparts in the Philippines and Botswana. "All of the available evidence suggests that Latin America is not attracting the high caliber individuals it needs to build world-class education systems. Virtually all countries in the region appear trapped in a low-level equilibrium of low standards for entry into teaching, low quality candidates, relatively low and undifferentiated salaries, low professionalism in the classroom and poor education results" (Bruns and Luque, 2014: 11).

There is considerable truth in this analysis. But it places too much emphasis on the test scores of students enrolled in pedagogy programs compared to, say, engineering, computer science, medicine, or economics. First, many, if not most, secondary math and science teachers in Latin America are formed in math and science (for example, math and biology) departments, not in education schools. Second, those students who *complete* university-level programs in Latin America, even in pedagogy, in most countries are in the top 25 percent of academic

Figure 7.1   Mathematics Content Knowledge of Teachers Across Countries

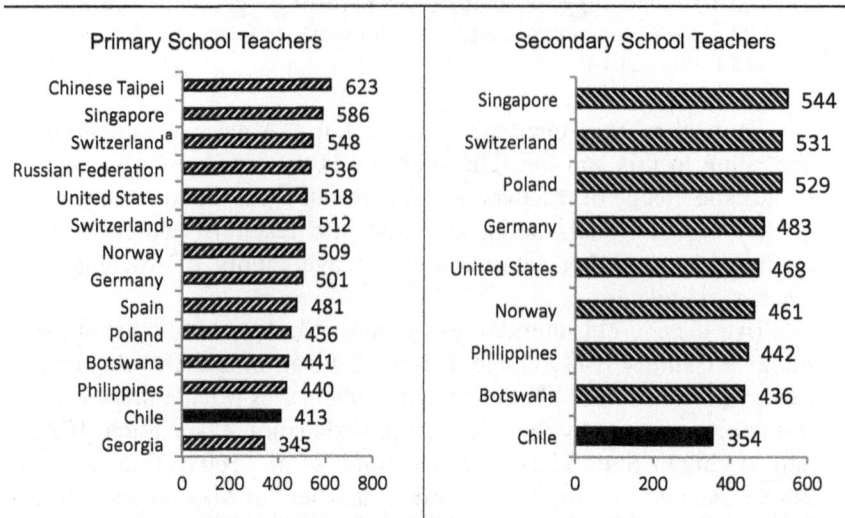

Primary School Teachers	
Chinese Taipei	623
Singapore	586
Switzerland[a]	548
Russian Federation	536
United States	518
Switzerland[b]	512
Norway	509
Germany	501
Spain	481
Poland	456
Botswana	441
Philippines	440
Chile	413
Georgia	345

0   200   400   600   800

Secondary School Teachers	
Singapore	544
Switzerland	531
Poland	529
Germany	483
United States	468
Norway	461
Philippines	442
Botswana	436
Chile	354

0   200   400   600

Source: Tatto et al., 2008.
Notes: a. Upper-primary grades in Switzerland. b. Lower-primary grades in Switzerland.

performers overall. Of course, Latin American students score low on international tests compared to their counterparts in Europe, but most individuals who end up in teaching are at least in the top quartile of test scores among Latin Americans in their age cohort.

This may not be adequate to produce the kind of school academic results we find in developed countries. I therefore agree that we should implement policies that would attract more high-scoring high school students into teaching. For example, in Chile, where all students pay tuition to attend universities, the government has provided sizable scholarships to lure students with high college entrance test scores to enter university teacher education programs. When I was president of Peru, I doubled teacher salaries during my five-year term, raising them from abysmally low levels. This was not easy politically because it was expensive, and I don't know whether this made teaching a more attractive profession, since salaries were still low, but it did raise morale among the teachers, and our students' PISA scores began to rise quite rapidly. These are useful steps toward raising the economic payoff to entering teaching, making it more prestigious, and therefore increasing the likelihood that academically better prepared high school graduates would enter teaching. Yet, as I will argue below, much more has to be done if we want to improve the quality of our teacher labor force.

Second, World Bank analysts (and many national educational policymakers) have recently also put a lot of emphasis on a second serious problem regarding the low-quality classroom teaching in the regions. A major multicountry Bank research project sent observers into classrooms to measure the time teachers spend engaging student in actual learning activities rather than classroom management and just plain "down time"—for example, writing text on the board for students to copy. To measure these activities, they used a rubric developed by Jane Stallings (Stallings, 1977). The results of their observations show that in samples of classrooms in six countries, the average proportion of time spent on academic activities is much lower than the Stallings benchmark of good practices, which she set at 85 percent.

Figure 7.2 shows that a typical Latin American teacher spends about 62–64 percent of her time on academic activities and about 10–12 percent of her time off-task. The Bank study shows further that almost none of the 10–12 percent is the teacher interacting with students—rather part of it is the teacher interacting with other school adults or out of the classroom entirely (Bruns and Luque, 2014: 83, see Figure 2.3). Not surprisingly, teachers in schools with higher performing students devote more time to academic activities than teachers in schools with lower performing (read lower social class) students. The example Bruns and Luque use is Rio de Janeiro schools. In schools performing in the top 10 percent on the Brazilian national test, teachers spend 70 percent of their time on academic activities—still below Stallings's benchmark—whereas in schools performing in the bottom 10 percent, they only spend 54 percent on academic activities. In both cases, almost all the rest of the teacher's time is spent on classroom organization (84, see Table 2.3). It should not be surprising that in these six countries, during about one-fourth of class time in the large number of classrooms observed, many students are not engaged in the class activities.

> In no country in the sample do teachers on average keep the entire class engaged in learning more than 25 percent of class time (Peru) and in Colombia and Honduras teachers achieve this less than 20 percent of time. This could reflect the conscious choice of teaching strategies that divide the class into groups working on parallel activities. But this was reported rarely by observer teams. More consistent with the classrooms observed in this study is that teachers arrive at school without

Figure 7.2   Proportion of Classroom Time on Academic Activities (percent)

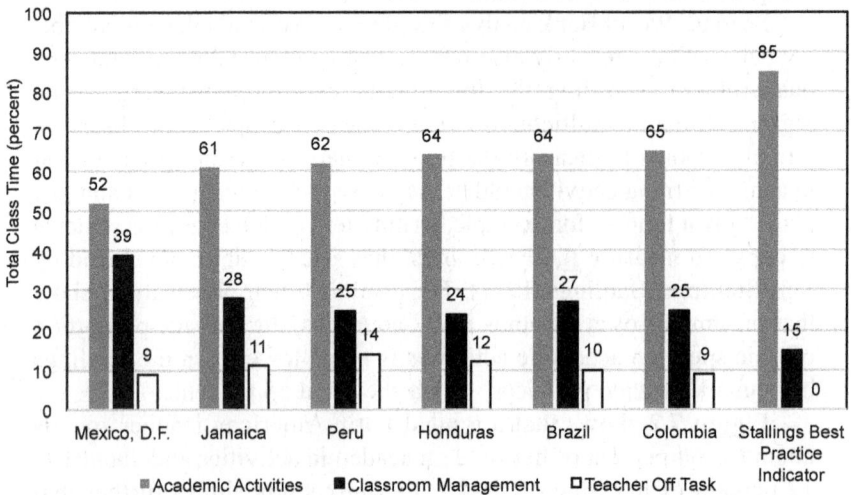

Source: Bruns and Luque, 2014: 83.

the detailed class preparation required to manage multiple activities simultaneously. In these contexts, a single teacher-led activity "pitched to the middle" of the learning distribution appears to leave some students bored and others falling behind. Both sets typically react by disengaging. (Bruns and Luque, 2014: 93)

It should also not be surprising that these researchers found large variation across schools in how much time teachers spend on academic activities and in student engagement. Perhaps it is more surprising that there is considerable variation even *within* schools—that is, that within a neighborhood school, there are some teachers spending significantly less time on academic activities.

But whatever the variation, the findings are disturbing and certainly help explain why students in Latin America's classrooms—especially in schools with low-income, lower-performing students—do not learn to read well or to attain adequate levels of mathematics skills. One of the countries that participated in the study was my home country, Peru, and the results there were often no better than in Honduras, a country much poorer than Peru. Thus, it is no accident that Peruvian students don't do well on international tests.

Bank researchers suggest many solutions to this problem of time on academic task, starting with observing classrooms regularly and making classroom observation part of teacher evaluation, as Peru and Chile have now implemented as an educational reform. They also suggest better in-service training, improving pre-service training by higher accreditation standards for teacher education programs, and improving beginning teacher induction into classrooms, as well as testing teachers before they can qualify to be teachers—some countries are already implementing such reforms.

The Bottom Line: Teachers Need to Be Better Trained to Teach

Even if we attract academically better students into undergraduate teaching programs, in today's Latin America they would receive such poor training and induction into teaching (Elacqua et al., 2018), it is unlikely that they would end up being good teachers, even if they knew the subject matter somewhat better. And testing them on subject knowledge before they become teachers (evaluating them), as recommended by the IDB study, would be useful at one level, but would not show whether they were effective classroom managers and knew how to engage students in learning activities.

The other side of this coin is that if the current "low-quality" students who enter teacher education or math or science programs in universities were to receive much more coherent and focused pre-service training plus carefully supervised student-teacher mentoring in schools that were partnered with these coherent and focused programs, it is much more likely that they would be effective teachers even if their subject matter knowledge were not as high as we would like.

In my view, we should put most of our chips on improving teacher education and professional development. One real problem, I believe, is that in many countries of the world, including most in Latin America, there is a sense that becoming a teacher does not require rigorous training—that good teachers are born, not trained. This contrasts with our view of engineers and doctors and even university professors, who most people believe should have years of high level education and training to practice their profession (although university professors are rarely taught how to be good teachers).

We just cannot avoid an important reality: like other professions, teachers need rigorous training. Indeed, because the nature of teaching requires many different skills—content knowledge, pedagogical content knowledge (knowing how to communicate the content knowledge to multiple types of learners), classroom management, relating to student's families, evaluative skills, psychological skills, and so forth—teachers need to be trained in all these and then given the opportunity to practice these skills in real-world classroom situations under the tutelage and feedback of well-trained supervisors.

I doubt many education policymakers and educational experts in Latin America would disagree with this view (see, for example, Cuenca, 2018; Schmelkes, 2016). Yet, the current situation in the region regarding teacher preparation for the multitasking of classroom instruction is so far from what it needs to be that all the incentives to attract "better" high school students into teaching, testing them for content knowledge, and even observing them in classrooms and making them realize how poorly they are engaging their students would not go very far in transforming Latin American classrooms into places where student learning significantly improves.

The main problem is that the capacity to improve professional development pre-service teacher training—to show current teachers how to effectively manage their classrooms, plan their lessons, and implement good teaching practices—is lacking in Latin America. The trainers of teachers in our region's universities and pedagogical institutes are themselves not well trained to provide a rigorous training that unites theory and practice. There are attempts to correct this problem, but it is not easy. For one thing, it is not cheap. For another, it requires training people in universities to be great trainers—to have the high-level skills to train teachers to teach complex instruction, to manage classrooms effectively, and to engage students to learn. It also requires universities to partner with school districts—whether they are municipalities or states or other relevant administrative units. These partnerships are needed so that the relevant educational management apparatus collaborates closely with the training apparatus (the universities and pedagogical institutions) to bring together the theoretical foundations of good teaching with carefully orchestrated supervision and feedback of classroom practice. That is what effective teacher education training requires, and that is what is lacking almost everywhere in Latin America. I am convinced that without world-class teacher professional development programs and pre-service teacher education programs that work hand-in-hand with schools and school districts, all the other efforts to improve teaching (and learning) will fall far short of excellence.

The Cuba Example

Although I am no fan of Cuba's authoritarian regime (or any non-democratic political system), there is little doubt that Cuba's basic education system is the best in Latin America. There are many reasons for this, as my former professor Martin Carnoy shows in his book, *Cuba's Academic Advantage* (Carnoy, Gove, and Marshall, 2007). He and his students systematically compared Cuban classrooms and the administration of the educational enterprise in Cuba with those in Brazil and Chile.

Reason one is that the Cuban government (and the Cuban people) considers the nation's education system as one of its most important assets—as contributing greatly to its political legitimacy. It also considers teachers as the centerpiece of the system, and, incidentally, along with doctors, one of Cuba's main exports. Thousands of Cuban teachers are sent every year to teach in other Latin American and some African countries. Reason two is that Cuba has been able to reduce child poverty, children's chronic illnesses, children's hunger, child labor, community violence, and school violence—all social factors that negatively impact children's and youths' capacity to learn—practically to zero. In contrast to other Latin American countries, where all these harmful influences on student achievement are part and parcel of the environment that teachers confront in their classrooms daily, Cuba has created a secure, healthful environment for young people. The contrast between Cuba and the rest of Latin America in these social environmental factors is especially great for children from lower income families. School children across social class and race in Cuba are uniformly well fed, healthy, and accustomed to attending school in a violence-free context.

Reason three is that teacher education is much more focused on unifying theory and practice in Cuba than in other Latin American countries. Cuban teachers are trained in pedagogical universities that put primary emphasis on teaching—this includes how to teach Cuba's centralized curriculum, which in math and science is an adaptation of the well-considered Russian curriculum. Furthermore, in the last year of their pedagogical training these teachers-to-be receive tight supervision from well-trained mentor teachers when they student teach. Finally, once assigned to a school, the new teachers are inducted for a probation period of three years under the close supervision of principals and vice principals, who regularly observe the young teachers' teaching in the classroom and provide regular feedback.

It is true that Cuba has a major advantage in the government's ability to recruit good high school students to become teachers because almost all Cuban professionals are equally badly paid and live largely on the same food subsidies in the same government housing. However, it would be a mistake to focus on this aspect and disregard the high quality of Cuban teacher training. The training is as good as it is partly because a centralized government is in direct charge of the pedagogical universities (the universities do not have autonomy) and in direct charge of the schools. Thus, primary and secondary schools must cooperate with the pedagogical universities, and both universities and schools have clear responsibilities and well-defined systems to ensure that teachers learn their craft both before working in the schools and in the probation induction period.

Finally, there is also a well-defined structure of accountability for the quality of student learning. That structure is governed by the state through its Communist party organization, which oversees the schools through the municipal governments and the party secretaries assigned to each school. School principals and vice principals answer to the party and are responsible for ensuring that school instruction is of high quality (that teachers are teaching what they are supposed to teach and how they are supposed to teach), that students are learning what they are supposed to learn (that they have good grades), and that families are taking responsibility for their students' attendance and high levels of effort. Teachers and families are held responsible for their students' good performance in school. In primary schools, students stay with the same teacher for four to six grades and rarely move from one school to another because housing is so tight. Thus, a student's primary school teacher becomes a quasi-parent, as in the Montessori method.

Ironically, from what Carnoy and others have seen, classrooms are very child-centered, caring places, and teaching methods are constructivist, in seeming contradiction with the top-down, centralized accountability system. The accountability system ensures, above all, that standards are adhered to and that children are not allowed to fall between the cracks of poorly managed classroom and schools. Thus, the system works to produce a well-educated population.

When we observe the Cuban education system, we can easily argue that an authoritarian Communist party–run government has a lot of advantages in forcibly reducing inequality and eliminating poverty, even as it eliminates fundamental political freedoms. Many would claim with good reason that it has accomplished this at the cost of reducing productivity and economic growth. But all that aside, a major question that comes to mind is why other countries in Latin America cannot train their teachers to be as good as Cuban teachers. This does not require an authoritarian government or a socialist philosophy. Cuban teacher education is modeled on good practices in developed countries and in the former Soviet Union. The rest of Latin America should be able to create partnerships between school districts and universities and to make universities adopt cutting-edge teacher education and professional development methodologies that unify theory and practice.

Elements of World-Class Teacher Education and Professional Development

The fundamental element in training teachers is to unite theories of effective teaching and learning with the practice of teaching. Many would argue that theories of teaching also must be rooted in practice. I noted above that good teacher preparation needs to include supervised practice in a classroom, first as a student teacher, then during a period of induction. It needs the support of schools and well-trained school administrators who work together with the initial preparers of teachers—usually universities and teacher education colleagues—on a well-defined, theoretically based conception of what good teaching requires. As Paula Louzano and Gabriela Miranda Moriconi argue, these are the characteristics of high-quality teacher preparation systems, such as Finland's and Singapore's, and, not coincidentally, they result in highly effective classroom practices (Louzano and Moriconi, 2015).

Beyond the unification of theory in universities and practice in the schools, if the theory of good teaching should be based on classroom practice, then the logic of teacher education in universities and teacher training colleges would be that these programs should themselves be directly linked to classroom practice—"to provide opportunities to enact teaching practices (e.g., organizing groupwork, orchestrating whole class discussion, giving feedback on pupils' work) and to ground learning in the real materials of teaching (e.g., texts, resources, pupils' work, real world examples of teaching using national or local curriculum)" (Klette et al., 2017: 5). This is a powerful conception of education that is just as relevant for training doctors and engineers and lawyers and corporate managers as it is teachers, and, indeed, good medical schools, engineering departments, law schools, and business schools all adhere to it, not just in the highly developed countries.

In developing a rubric for defining excellent teacher education programs, Klette, Hammerness, and Jenset (2017) came up with a detailed framework that I think can be used to distinguish the quality of programs in Latin America. In fact, their five-country study does include Cuba and Chile in the top-tier teacher education programs it evaluates in each country. Their framework is shown in Table 7.1.

The study analyzes eight top teacher education programs in five countries—these are Cuba, Chile, Finland, Norway, and the United States (see also Louzano and Mariconi, 2015, for Finland, the United States, and Singapore). All these programs were noted for their linking teacher preparation to classroom practice, and the study not only surveyed teacher candidates in each program but also observed teacher candidates teaching in classrooms. I found it very interesting that the program at the Varona Pedagogical University in Havana and the program at the Catholic University of Chile do very well on a number of these criteria (Table 7.1) compared to the teacher education program in Finland, although not as well as Stanford's teacher education program. This suggests that there are examples of excellence in teacher education in Latin America, even though few and far between.

All well and good. But in Latin America, even if we were to take seriously trying to implement these eight criteria in teacher education programs as well as implementing supervised student teaching and supervised induction in schools for two or three years, we have a serious lack of well-trained teacher educators and supervisors—either teachers or school directors—who themselves are well-steeped in the theory and practice of excellent teaching. This is the greatest barrier to passing these experiences and skills down to the next generation of teachers.

Despite these barriers, there are a few forays to start teacher education programs in Latin American universities that include all the components listed in Table 7.1. In the last section of this chapter I describe one such major effort in Brazil. Here I discuss teacher professional development—the massive amount that Latin America invests in in-service teacher training every year.

Teacher Professional Development in Latin America

About 80 million young people attend school in Latin America, and they are taught by about 3 million teachers. Most of these teachers attend teacher professional development courses, if not every year, every two years or so. Latin American governments spend hundreds

Table 7.1   Framework for Defining Excellent Teacher Education

Opportunities	Description of Dimension
Plan for teaching and teacher role(s)	The extent to which candidates have opportunities to plan lessons or units, or to develop instructional materials.
Practice and rehearse teacher role(s)	The extent to which candidates have opportunities to practice, rehearse, or approximate elements of practice. This includes practice leading a whole class or small group discussion, role-playing a discussion with the pupil, rehearsing a lesson introduction, or participating in the fishbowl discussion taking the part of the pupil or a teacher.
Analyze pupils' learning	The extent to which candidates have opportunities to practice analyzing pupil learning; to examine or analyze pupils' work; to work with pupils and analyze their skills, abilities, or needs; or to look at classroom transcripts or videos and analyze pupil learning.
Include teaching materials, artifacts, and resources	The extent to which candidates have opportunities to use, discuss, or analyze artifacts or resources from real classrooms and teaching, including videos of teachers, cases about teaching and teachers, samples of real pupils' work, and transcripts of classroom talk.
Talk about field placement	The extent to which candidates have opportunities to discuss what they are doing in class in relation to their own fieldwork or student teaching (e.g., bring in their own pupils' work).
Take pupils' perspective	The extent to which candidates have opportunities to do work that their own pupils will or might do (e.g., read texts or solve problems) or to take the pupils' perspective in terms of learning styles, adolescent perspectives and concerns, or pupils' needs and strengths.
See models of teaching	The extent to which candidates have opportunities to see teacher educators modeling the practices discussed in class (e.g., a good lecture for K–12 pupils, group work, or giving good feedback).
See connection to the national or state curriculum	The extent to which candidates have opportunities to read, review, or analyze materials specific to the national, state, or local context (e.g., read or analyze national, state, or local curriculum or local regulations for teacher evaluation or standards).

Source: Klette et al., 2017: 6, Table 1.

of millions of dollars on this professional development (PD). Its overall effect on the improvement of teaching and student learning seems to be minimal, and the reason for that is simple—PD in the region is almost universally *not* based on the unification of theory and practice features outlined by Klette and her colleagues.

Rather than harping on about all the things wrong with teacher professional development in Latin America (and just about everywhere else), however, I prefer to talk about the characteristics of PD that might produce positive results in the classroom, especially for students. A recent study of thirty-three professional development programs that had been impact evaluated (with student learning gains as the outcome measure) in low- and middle-income countries used a standard set of seventy indicators—the In-Service Teacher Training Survey Instrument (ITTSI)—to identify the characteristics that show higher student learning gains. The study shows that programs "[linking] participation to career incentives, have a specific subject focus, incorporate lesson enactment in the training, and include initial face-to-face training tend to show higher [student] gains" (Popova et al., 2018: 1).

To be clear, these are only "minimalist" criteria for assessing better PD programs, since they are necessarily based on what existing PD programs do in low- and middle-income countries. Yet, even such minimal criteria suggest that for these programs to impact student learning gains, they need to have a classroom reality focus and that the program needs to be face to face, focusing on subject matter and what teachers experience daily in their classrooms. When Popova and colleagues compared a much larger group of at-scale professional development programs in fourteen countries against the top performers in their smaller sample, they found many differences that suggested that most of the programs would not be likely to result in student learning gains.

If we were to apply the criteria that Klette and colleagues used to these at-scale PD programs, very few, if any, of them could claim high-quality status. As far as I am concerned, I think we should at least try to implement the highest quality PD programs possible, and that means also referring to the appropriate characteristics to evaluate them. This is important because the current teacher labor force is in classrooms right now, not in the future, and training them to be better teachers in a school environment that partners closely with PD programs could have a large effect on student learning in the near term.

The PED Program in Brazil

This is precisely what the Programa de Educação Docente (PED) in Brazil does. PED works with private and public universities to train teacher educators to deliver an eighteen-month *especialização* degree for working teachers in mathematics and sciences. The eighteen-month program uses a ten-module syllabus developed by Rachel Lotan, when she was director of the Stanford University Teacher Education Program and adapted for Brazil by her and the Instituto Canoa (São Paulo)—a syllabus rooted in years of studies on best teaching practices that covers classroom management and equal treatment of students, as well as how to teach mathematics and science in ways that optimize student learning in those subjects. The training of university faculty in the participating universities is conducted by a team from Stanford University in three to four weeklong training sessions in Brazil. Fundamental to the training of the Brazilian university faculty is that the weeklong seminars cover the modules in the syllabus and model the teaching of the modules in a university classroom setting. This modeling is then the basis for teaching the teachers who come to universities to participate in the eighteen-month-long professional development course in mathematics and science. Teachers who are trained in the PED program in participating universities are expected to teach their students in schools in the way that they were taught by PED-trained university educators.

The ten modules of the PED syllabus focus on managing the classroom, learning and teaching in student-centered ways, building equitable classrooms, developing pedagogical content knowledge in the subject to be taught, as well as planning and assessing student work. The participating teachers' work culminates in preparing a portfolio that includes a teaching performance assessment, an important component of teacher professional learning, and a consequential topic currently raised and discussed in Brazil. Importantly, the PED curriculum includes a significant clinical curriculum. Teachers who are trained in the PED program in participating universities are expected to teach their students in schools in the way that they were taught by PED-trained university educators. This means that PED mentors at the universities are in constant communication with the participating teachers (remotely or in person if possible) to address context-specific issues that might arise in the participating teachers' classrooms and schools. Many of the conversations among the mentors and the teachers are based on video recordings of the teachers' practices in their classrooms. Such conversations and feedback to the teachers are significant predictors of the implementation of PED strategies by the teachers. Core fundamentals of the syllabus combined with the mentoring program are shown in Figure 7.3.

The elements of the underlying theory that drives the PED program is shown in Figure 7.4. Element 1 is the connection between

Figure 7.3   The PED Curriculum Model

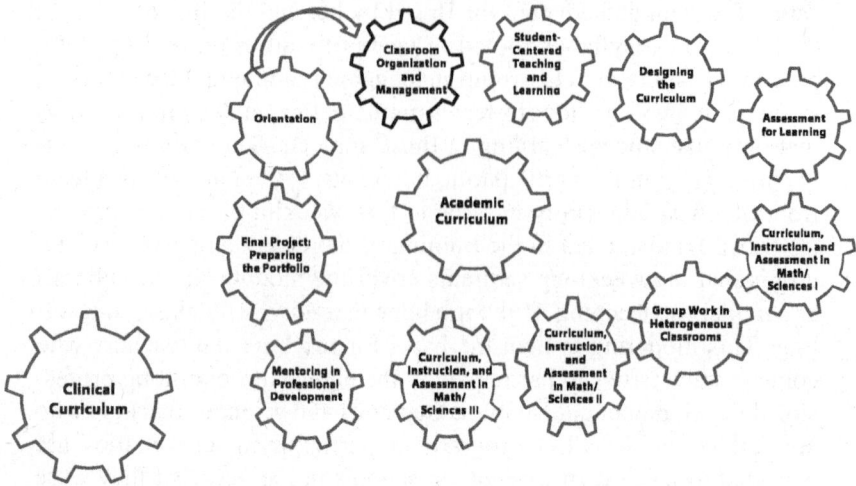

theory and practice—in other words, everything taught in the syllabus has to be connected with classroom practice. Concepts such as treating students equitably, for example, are not presented as an abstraction, but rather related to what actually happens in classrooms when students interact with each other and with the teacher. Thus, there has to be constant feedback between mentors, teachers in development, and university professors through connecting what is taught in the university classroom and what the teacher experiences in the school classroom. Element 2 is the need for universities to partner with schools in order to achieve the symbiosis between theory and practice and the transformation of teaching in the school. Element 3 is the overarching core themes of the program—namely, excellence and equity. The key is that all three of these elements must be "in coherence." Everything done in the program must be intimately entwined with all three elements.

In 2018 and again in 2019, the Stanford-Canoa team, organized through the Lemann Center for Educational Entrepreneurship and Innovation in Brazil and Brazil's Instituto Canoa, held the second and third years of weeklong seminars in São Paulo, Rio, and Curitiba for about eighty to ninety university faculty from twelve institutions in mathematics and science education. In addition, ten faculty each

Figure 7.4   The PED Theory of Action: Building Coherence

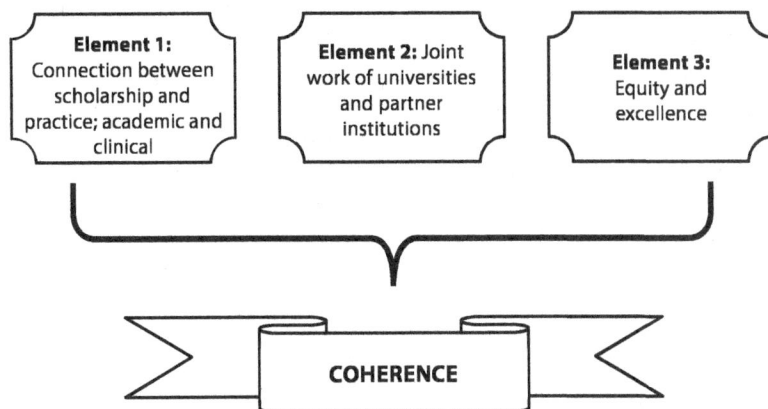

Source: Rachel Lotan, Stanford University Graduate School of Education.

year who had participated in the 2017 (or the 2018) seminars were trained as future trainers of university faculty.

The PED team from Stanford's Lemann Center and Instituto Canoa support teacher educators in participating universities throughout the eighteen-month courses, and, in turn, the university education teams include mentors who meet with groups of teachers being trained monthly to discuss classroom issues in applying the PED methodology to teaching math and science. Teachers in the *especialização* programs also make videos of themselves teaching every three months to use in their discussions of successes and difficulties of implementing the various modules of the syllabus.

Thus, in this high-end professional development program, teachers being trained in the universities come twice per week for eighteen months to engage in a detailed, classroom-modeled training that covers a wide range of skills, from classroom management to effective math and science pedagogical content. The university educators model the teaching that they expect their trainees to implement in the classroom with students, and the teacher trainees are supported by mentors who meet with them on a regular basis to discuss issues of implementation. The trainees are also assisted in assessing each other's progress with the mentors using videotapes of their classroom teaching.

Some of the teachers trained in PED university programs teach in private schools, and it is important that those schools (in some cases, systems of multiple private schools under the same ownership) are committed to training many, even most, of their teachers to the PED standard. Many of the teachers, however, are public school teachers. Thus, another important element of the PED program as it is gradually put in place is partnerships between municipalities and the universities where these teachers are trained by PED teacher educators. This is crucial because the teachers participating in the PED *especialização* programs need to be supported by their school administrations. The PED program is most likely to occur when municipal and state administrations buy into the PED project.

It would be misleading to claim that this is an easy program to scale up. However, as mentioned, PED is now training future trainers of university teacher educators to expand the number of seminars that can be offered every year. In addition, despite the pandemic, one large municipality, São Paulo, has committed to send up to 1,200 math and science teachers to *especialização* courses in universities in São Paulo from 2020 to 2025 where PED teacher education teams have already been trained in PED training courses. Thus, PED is poised to scale up on two fronts—both in training many more teachers in partnership with municipalities and in expanding the number of faculty in Brazilian universities who will be prepared to train teachers in the PED model.

The PED model offers the single best way of setting much higher standards in Latin America for teacher education. Although PED is a professional development program, it could, with some modifications, be adapted to pre-service teacher education, especially in those universities and municipalities already well advanced in the PED program. The modifications would include adding classroom mentoring (by PED-trained teachers) for undergraduate student teachers, and adding a well-structured induction program for new PED-trained teacher graduates entering their first teaching jobs.

Some Conclusions

The World Bank, IDB, and others have identified improved teaching as the key to raising the levels of student learning in Latin America, and improving the quality of teaching is especially crucial for the children of low-income families, who are most likely to face poorly prepared teachers in their classrooms. The Bank and others have put a lot of emphasis on recruiting young people into teaching who are better versed in subject matter knowledge and in developing accountability systems and incentives that could produce greater effort (time on task) by teachers in classrooms.

I don't disagree that programs that improve the academic quality of young people going into teaching, such as full scholarships for students willing to enter the teaching profession, and accountability and incentive systems to increase teacher effort could produce incrementally better learning experiences for students in Latin American schools, especially in low-income schools. However, my argument in this chapter is that the main reason that classroom teaching is generally at such a low level in Latin America, even in relatively high-income schools, is that teacher education in the region is not adequately preparing teachers to teach. Even if we recruit better academically prepared high school students into university teaching programs and develop accountability systems to incentivize greater effort, if classroom teachers don't understand the fundamentals of exercising their profession, they will not be able to function as high-quality teachers even if they were highly motivated to do so.

I have given the examples of the Cuban teacher education model, and of a major teacher professional development initiative in Brazil called PED. It will take many years for any country in Latin America (aside from Cuba, which has already done so) to transform its teacher labor force with a PED-type program, but my message to policymakers is that such transformation is the sine qua non for producing high-quality education. High-quality education for students and high-quality teacher education, which includes the elements of such teacher education I have discussed in this chapter, are simply inseparable.

Many have dreamed of some sort of technology, from educational television to computers to handheld devices acting as a substitute for a well-trained, effective teacher labor force, but this has turned out to be a pipe dream. To the contrary, technology—it turns out—is most effective as an aid to student learning when well-trained teachers are even better trained to add technology to their already high level of teaching skills. That is, effective computer-assisted instruction or computers as research tools in classrooms depend on highly trained teachers who, in addition, are skilled at working with students to incorporate information technology to improve student learning. I will discuss this in detail in a later chapter when I address the digital divide.

8

The Challenges of
Crime and Violence

As a child in Chimbote, Peru, living in poverty meant living with crime and violence, and things have gotten a lot worse since those days. A main feature of the poverty experience in Latin America—especially urban Latin America—was and is crime and violence. Although schools are marked by less violence than the neighborhoods around them, children in violent communities attend schools where assaults against and bullying of pupils and teachers are much more common than in communities that are relatively free of violence.

Since the time I was in school in Peru in the 1960s, poverty levels have declined substantially, but crime and violence have increased. In the 1980s and early 1990s, this was fueled by the Sendero Luminoso and other extremist armed groups, but since 2000, crime and violence in Peru, as in the rest of Latin America, has grown mainly because of increased urbanization, the rise of the drug trade, and the proliferation of urban gangs.

Data on crime are not very complete in Latin America. The best data are on homicide rates, and these are likely to be underestimated and may or may not be a good proxy for the more general crime rate and level of violence in a given country (Ayres, 1998). Nevertheless, in the countries for which we do have some data, it appears that where homicide rates are high, so are rates of theft, robbery, extortion, and threat (UNODC, 2019). The homicide rate in Latin America rose significantly from the early 1980s to the end of the first decade of the 2000s then tended to decline in the second decade. Despite the recent decrease, it is still the highest of any region in the world. It also varies greatly from country to country (Table 8.1). There are many different categories of homicide, ranging from domestic violence homicide to gang-related killings. Much more than other areas of the world, a relatively high percentage of homicides in Latin America is gang related, and much of this is drug related (UNODC, 2019: 32–33).

It should not be surprising that in schools and communities where violence is an issue, student learning is more difficult. Indeed, many studies show that violence inside and outside schools has a significant negative effect on student achievement and attainment (for example, Bowen and Bowen, 2006; Brown and Velásquez, 2017; Jarillo et al., 2016; Caudillo and Torche, 2014). These suggest that, in part, learning is affected because the main focus of the school becomes controlling violence. Administrators and teachers are spending their time, energy, and school resources policing the school, trying to protect the students and themselves from potential violence. Of course, this negatively affects the time that teachers focus on academics and that, consequently, affects how much time students spend

Table 8.1   Homicide Rates (homicides per 100,000 population), Late 1970s–2018

Country	Late 1970s/ Early 1980s	Late 1980s/ Early 1990s	Early 2000s	2011–2012	2018
Honduras		35.0 (1996)	55.7	83.0	38.9
Guatemala		32.0	30.0	39.3	22.5
El Salvador		NA	37.5	55.6	52.2
Colombia	34.5	89.5	64.5	32.2	25.3
Brazil	11.5	19.7	n.a.	24.3	27.4
Mexico	18.2	17.8	9.7	22.3	19.9 (2016)
Venezuela	11.7	15.2	36.8	50.8	36.7
Peru	2.4	11.5	4.6	9.6	7.9
Panama	2.1	10.9	10.5	20.5	9.4
Ecuador	6.4	10.3	14.2	13.9	5.8
Argentina	3.9	4.8	8.0	5.5 (2010)	5.3
Costa Rica	5.7	4.1	6.6	10.7	11.3
Uruguay	2.6	4.4	6.4	6.9	8.3
Paraguay	5.1	4.0	22.4	9.9	7.1
Chile	2.6	3.0	3.2	3.4	3.4
United States	10.7	10.1	5.7	4.7	5.0
Philippines		8.1 (1998)	7.7	9.0	6.5
Indonesia		0.9	0.8	0.6	0.4
Spain		0.9	1.4	0.8	0.6
Portugal		1.1	1.2	0.8

Sources: UNODC, 2010, 2020.

on learning. It is important to note that violence creates fear and insecurity in young people both in schools and in their everyday lives. If students are afraid of some of their fellow students or afraid of walking from home to school and back, they will be focused on these fears rather than trying to learn math or science.

We should be very concerned about the impact that street crime and in-school violence have on students' educational outcomes. But beyond that, students' capacity to learn in Latin America is hampered by high levels of domestic violence, which is not necessarily related to street crime or drugs, and resides more in the violence that (mostly) men feel they can perpetrate on women and children. Children's learning can be impacted by the devastating psychological and physical effects of violence at home directed at them or their mothers—the typical targets of domestic violence. Child abuse and violence directed at women with children has a major impact on human capital formation, especially among the poor, and especially in lower-income Latin American countries that have fewer resources to deal with children's learning disabilities stemming from trauma related to such abuse.

There is also an indirect effect of crime and violence on education through their drag on economic growth. When crime and violence reach the levels they have in places such as Honduras, El Salvador, Guatemala, Colombia, Brazil, Mexico, Panama, and even in Ecuador, Peru, and, more recently, Costa Rica, it has a negative effect on economic development. Crime and violence are costly—they require more police and military, especially when a high fraction of crime and violence are gang and drug related, as in our region. They increase risk and therefore reduce investment. Lower economic growth means that societies not only have a more difficult time reducing the rate of poverty through increasing the size of the economic pie, but because the poor are more likely to be impacted by crime and violence, whatever national economic improvement occurs, the poor are less likely to get the full benefits of that improvement (Ayres, 1998).

> An analysis of Colombia concludes that growth capital formation is about 38% lower today [late 1990s] than it would be if homicide rates had remained at their 1970 level. A World Bank study of Peru concludes that the country's cumulative wealth loss from terrorism was about $25 billion. The stagnation of the tourist industry in some countries is often attributed to the lack of new investment in hotels and other tourist infrastructure caused by increasing crime and violence. . . . [C]rime and violence have devastating effects on social capital. The norms of trust and reciprocity are replaced by the "war of all against all."

Community-based organizations and other social networks, increasingly deemed as critical for growth and poverty reduction, suffer attrition. . . . [T]he increase in crime and violence makes it increasingly difficult for any sort of community organizations not based on fear and coercion to function. (Ayres, 1998: 7–8)

In Latin America, violence disproportionately affects the poor, eroding their assets and livelihoods. The abnormally high levels of crime and violence constituted a key obstacle to the development of the region. The cost associated with these levels of crime and violence is astounding: it is estimated at 14.2% of the regional GDP. In terms of human capital, 1.9% of GDP is lost annually, which is equivalent to the region's spending on primary education. Over the past 15 years, the net accumulation of human capital has been cut in half due to the increase in crime and violence. (Heinemann and Verner, 2006: 2)

When we add up all these negative influences of crime and violence on educational outcomes—and the disproportionate impact that the high levels of violence in the region have on the poor and their children's capacity and opportunity to learn—we cannot avoid facing up to this major threat to human capital development and equalization of opportunity in Latin America. Indeed, it is safe to say that unless we can overcome the obstacle of violence, which is so intertwined with poverty in the region, it will be difficult to produce quality education for Latin America's low-income children.

With all this in mind, I want to lay out some of elements of broader political problems with the current situation regarding crime and violence in the region, outline the evidence for the relation between violence and lower educational outcomes, and then discuss some of the broader approaches to reduce crime and violence that are being taken up in the region and some of the more specific approaches that may soften its impact on students in schools.

Violence and the State

According to the 2018 Latinobarómetro report, Latin Americans consider crime the single most important problem facing their countries. One-fifth of those surveyed listed crime as the top national issue, and one-quarter said it was the top problem in their municipality (Latinobarómetro, 2018: 6). In addition, Latin Americans perceive that the most harmful types of violence for society are on the rise. About 60 percent of those surveyed considered domestic violence against women, domestic violence against children, street violence, and violence by organized criminals to be the most negative in terms of national interest. They cited the most frequent violence where they live to be violence in the street (35 percent), domestic violence against women (25 percent), and gang violence (25 percent). The importance of bullying as harmful to society rose from 25 percent to almost 50 percent in 2016–2018. Fully 40 percent of Latin Americans said that they experienced fear of being the victim of a crime "almost all the time" in 2018, and this figure has remained fairly constant for the past five years. The expectation to be a victim is, not surprisingly, highest in Honduras, Guatemala, and Colombia, where, according to Table 8.1, murder rates are also very high (Latinobarómetro, 2018: 58).

Thus, although actual violence varies across countries, the perception of high insecurity is common among inhabitants of the region. From the statistics we have on crime and violence, this is hardly shocking—for many Latin Americans in all but a few countries, violence is part of their daily lives. For children living in this environment, it means trauma at home and in the streets, and an inordinately high probability that even in their schools, they will have to confront violent situations.

This is a problem in and of itself. High levels of crime and violence are costly and directly reduce economic growth in several ways, such as the loss of scarce resources that go into fighting drug trafficking and gang violence associated with drugs, or the lower productivity of women injured in serious domestic violence, or the low levels of learning of children—Latin America's future labor force—because they are traumatized by violence in their homes or at school. Further, governments that are unable to reduce drug, gang, and domestic violence are usually too weak or corrupt to do so, which leaves citizens with a sense of defenselessness against violation of their rights, person, and property. This leads to a lack of trust of all institutions, which not only contributes to lower economic growth but also makes it less possible to create and maintain any semblance of democracy. The tendency in the current historical conjuncture is for the population to turn to populist authoritarian regimes backed by the military and police, but if these institutions are corrupted by drug money, crime and violence are simply institutionalized.

Domestic Violence

In their review of crime and violence in the Latin American and the Caribbean region, Heinemann and Verner (2006) confirm the

Latinobarómetro survey results that although domestic violence is less visible than street violence and much less accurately measurable than homicides, it is among the most pervasive types of violence in Latin America. They cite surveys in the 1990s that "between 10% and 50% of women declared having been beaten or mistreated physically by their current or former partner" (Buvinic, Morrison, and Orlando, 2003: 317), and that domestic violence in almost half the cases is associated with psychological and sexual violence (Buvinic, Morrison, and Orlando, 2003).

> The probability of being a victim of domestic violence rises as much as 10% from the top to the bottom quintile of the income distribution in urban Colombia. Empirical evidence suggests that the main risk factor for domestic violence is the lack of education: each year of schooling reduces the probability of domestic violence by more than 1%. The costs of domestic violence go beyond the public health burden, as domestic violence affects the productivity and employability of women. Cost projections based on the estimated number of national victims, estimate the total cost to society from domestic violence at 1.6% of GDP for Nicaragua and at 2% of GDP for Chile. (Heinemann and Verner, 2006: 5)

Furthermore, we can trace much of the crime and violence we observe in Latin America, especially youth gang and street violence, to earlier victimization of these youths as children and their later propensity to commit crimes as teenagers.

> It is estimated that 6 million minors in the region are the object of severe maltreatment and that 80,000 die each year as a result of injuries caused by their parents, relatives, or others. A recent study found that over 2 million children and youth, and 23% of families experience abuse in urban Colombia, and that in Mexico City 1 million children and 13% of households do so. This study also finds that abuse has a significant negative effect on human capital: it affects children's educational attainment and adult labor wages. (Heinemann and Verner, 2006: 6)

The "Special Problem" of Narcotrafficking in Latin America

The main reason for very high rates of crime and violence in some countries of Latin America is drug trafficking. Drug trafficking in the region is largely based on the production and transportation of cocaine. This cocaine is produced in Colombia, Peru, and Bolivia, and it used to go almost entirely to meet demand in the United States, but since the 1980s, the pattern has changed somewhat as the demand in Europe increased rapidly. In any case, the market in the United States still remains very large. It is difficult to estimate the total value of cocaine sold in the United States, but some estimates in 2008 were as high as $38 billion. The number of cocaine users in Europe doubled from 2 million in 1998 to 4.1 million in 2008. In this period, the market value of cocaine going to Europe rose from US$14 billion to US$34 billion, thus increasing the total value of cocaine sold on the two continents to more than $70 billion in 2008.

Until the 1990s, the Medellin and Cali cartels controlled narco-trafficking in the region. But the Colombian government's crackdown on organized crime was able to reduce their size and power. This vacuum created strong market incentives for the emergence of Mexican drug cartels because they are physically closer to the US market. The shift to Mexico has led to a sharp escalation of violence in Central America, including now in traditionally peaceful Costa Rica. As far as the equally large European market, Colombia is the main supplier of cocaine, followed by Peru and Bolivia. Shipments usually depart from Venezuela and Bolivia to West Africa before reaching the ports of Spain, Portugal, the Netherlands, and Belgium.

Although the proportion of total revenues from cocaine sales that end up in growers' pockets and in the pockets' of intermediaries and the cartels in Colombia and Mexico are estimated to total only about 20 percent of total sales—let's say about $15 billion annually in 2008—it is still big money and apparently worth killing a lot of people to access it. It is also large enough to create major barriers to eradicating it, especially because so much of it can be used to involve bribes to police, military, judges, and other government officials, who then become part of the problem. It is also the case that the giant profits flowing to sellers in the United States and Europe from drug sales also may act as obstacles to shutting down the flow of illegal drugs and therefore acting against the cartels.

Narcotrafficking is therefore particularly insidious and, simultaneously in Latin America, makes the crime and violence it generates especially difficult to eliminate because it threatens state capacity to govern and destabilizes democracies. It infiltrates the state and reduces the population's confidence in state capacity and people's trust in democratic institutions. The increasing power of drug cartels foments growing violence and crime, leaving numerous governments simply unable to handle the problem. Today, although the magnitude of the problem and the ability of governments to deal with it vary from country to country, Latin America faces the simultaneous threat of weakened democracies and increased violence, with all its destructive ramifications. Here is what I wrote in my book, *The Shared Society* (2015):

> The indirect impact of organized crime is centered on its threat to state capacity, undermining the state's institutions and rule of law. In this regard, "traditional organized crime groups displace state authority, by filling the governance niches neglected by the official structures and by co-opting whatever vestigial state agents remain" (UNDOC, 2010). Due to the financial profits derived from narcotrafficking, drug cartels tend to be powerful organizations that override the state and remain unaccountable to society. . . .
>
> Drug wars in Central America have led to the highest rates of homicides in the world, surpassing the deaths caused by civil wars in the 1980s and 1990s. The arms and financial power of drug cartels have left governments in Mexico and Central America bewildered by their ability to buy public officials and silence the press. Whenever bribery and corruption fail to work, cartels increase their use of violence in order to threaten state capacity and nullify police enforcement of laws and regulations. Thus, Mexico's state capacity to crack down on drug cartels has been called into question. The growing waves of crime and violence decrease confidence in the state and affect the quality of democracy, as citizens are left defenseless in the face of organized crime. In South America, narcotrafficking also threatens state capacity in countries that produce and transport drugs. In addition, narcotrafficking threatens the real economy across the region due to active money laundering activities. For all these reasons I argue that narcotrafficking has become Latin America's Achilles heel. It weakens state capacity and threatens to undermine our democracies. (Toledo, 2015: 152–153)

Circling back to the point I made earlier about the role of violence and insecurity in the decline of confidence in democracy among average Latin Americans, the question for many becomes whether to choose increased authoritarianism or to continue to live with personal insecurity caused by the weakness and/or compliance of the state apparatus in dealing with that violence, especially drug- and gang-related violence.

The Personal Security/Authoritarian Government Conundrum

However, let's assume that an authoritarian regime is able to reduce street crime and gang violence substantially and is able to make people feel safer. Let's assume further that an authoritarian regime implements measures that protect women and children against domestic violence. If this were the case, is the price of giving up individual freedom and the right to change governments worth the greater personal security and improved physical and mental health for children, plus better conditions for learning in school?

This poses an interesting dilemma—a real one in today's Latin America, as evidenced by the 2018 presidential election in Brazil. A successful campaign promising greater personal security has led to the election of a president and congress that are transparently promising reduced personal freedom and more leeway given to the police and military to fight crime with increasingly tough actions and less respect for human rights. Whether this will improve conditions for the poor and lower middle class, who suffer the main brunt of violence in Brazil, is a big question, but the fact is that a majority of Brazilians are willing to put democratic institutions at risk in return for lowering violence and potentially increasing economic growth.

It is much more difficult to build quality institutions of any kind, including schools and universities, with a weak, ineffectual state, and there is little doubt that authoritarian regimes can create and maintain "quality" education systems, as evidenced by the relatively high scores on international tests in today's China, Vietnam, and Cuba (PISA, TERCE), and yesterday's high scoring students in Eastern Europe under communist rule (Medrich and Griffith, 1992). One of the ways they are able to produce quality education is by keeping street and domestic violence low.

But there is a price for lowering violence through political authoritarianism. In societies run by communist governments, there is some commitment to allocating considerable resources to the lower income population—the rural and urban poor. There is no such commitment from authoritarian capitalist regimes, which are well known in Latin America, from El Salvador down to Argentina, as late as the 1980s and 1990s, and which have not provided solutions to personal insecurity, nor have they solved the underlying problems of sustaining economic growth or reducing inequality nor providing adequate social services. And all authoritarian regimes, capitalist and communist, rule through fear and repression and severe limitations on human rights, due process, and the right to democratically elected government representation. The one communist regime in Latin America, Cuba, has not been successful in sustaining economic growth—productivity is very low, and income per capita is as well, although there is little poverty and very little violence. The main promise that capitalist authoritarian regimes makes is to increase economic growth, but such growth, when it does happen, is usually accompanied by increased inequality in income and wealth. And in these regimes, what recourse do the poor have to improve the quality of their children's education, health care, and nutrition? The answer has historically been: not much.

To my mind, the promises of authoritarianism to solve crime and violence are largely false, and they have such a large downside, in terms of giving up on building stronger democratic institutions, that I believe that we have to stick with democracy. We need to do our best to reduce crime and violence within a democratic framework. It won't be easy, but it can be done. Below, I suggest some ways that seem to work. Before doing that, however, let me focus on the topic at hand, namely, the evidence for how violence impacts children's and young people's learning.

Violence and the Quality of Education

There is a lot of evidence that violence impacts student performance in school. The evidence varies from correlational to causal. In addition, there is good analysis of *why* there is a connection between violence and school outcomes. I want to review all this briefly and then turn to the steps needed to address systematically the underlying regional crime and violence in ways that could help the mass of Latin America's lower income young people get a better shot at improving their lives.

Big Picture Evidence

More than ten years ago, Carnoy and Marshall (2005) argued that some countries were able to develop greater "collective social capital" that provided more favorable social contexts for children to learn and do well in school. If sustained over a longer period of time, this collective social capital was closely related to higher school attainment among parents and more attractive conditions for recruiting more capable people into teaching, as well as a state apparatus that could organize well-functioning schools. Thus, the "virtuous circle" of underlying organizational features that enable societies and their states to create greater collective social capital also has payoffs in families because of better-educated parents and in schools with better instruction.

> The collective meaning of SES [socioeconomic status] can be strongly influenced by the ways that individuals and families organize socially and politically—particularly in the collective commitment to reduce (through the state) the most pernicious effects of socioeconomic difference. Following Coleman [1988] and other theorists, we characterize this as "collective social capital." In many contexts, low family SES is associated with greater violence, less access to early childhood education, poorer nutrition, and poorer health care. In many contexts, students from low-SES families face pressure to work outside the home after school. They may attend schools in which lower-SES students have been concentrated, leading to negative youth attitudes toward academic success. . . .
>
> If nation-states themselves generate social capital, then we would expect to find benefits to lower-SES children who attend schools in those neighborhoods, regions, and even countries that have more socially integrated, safer, cooperative, and coherent social climates, as compared with lower-SES children who attend equally academically resourced schools in less favorable social contexts. Most of the social capital discussion focuses on individual or family behavior that creates the social structures producing favorable results or on cooperative institutions in democratic states where individuals voluntarily adhere to organizations that promote networks of democratic institutions that help create social capital. . . . However, states themselves, whether democratic or authoritarian, also help to create social capital. Authoritarian states face difficulties in doing so, but can be successful in some societies if they deliver improved material and social conditions [across the SES spectrum]. (Carnoy and Marshall, 2005: 231, 233)

Carnoy and Marshall use three proxies for collective social capital—preschool attendance, whether a child works, and reported fights at school—to estimate their effects on individual students' fourth grade academic achievement in mathematics and language when controlling for parental resources, school resources, and the average performance of students in the same school on a third grade test in the same subjects. They made these estimates for seven Latin American countries using a UNESCO survey conducted in 1997. Their findings show that in every one of these countries, the reported average frequency of fights in the classroom—a proxy for violence in schools—was significantly and highly negatively related with students' fourth grade achievement relative to average third grade performance in school in both mathematics and language. When they estimated this effect across countries, including a country "fixed effect," reducing reported fights per student by one standard deviation (about 0.2 fights per student, which was also approximately the difference between the low average in Cuba—0.07—and the average in Argentina or Brazil—0.3 fights) resulted in an increase of about 0.12 standard deviations in math achievement and about 0.10 SD increase in language score from the third to fourth grade test.

This is a correlational, not causal, estimated effect of one measure of violence in schools, and the study assumes that fights in school are a proxy for a more violent social context. But even so, the results suggest that a more violent environment in schools is associated with lower student performance, controlling for a whole host of individual, classroom (teacher), and school characteristics.

Local Studies of the Impact of Violence on Student Outcomes

A number of studies takes a more direct look at the relation between violence outside school in individual Latin American countries. Most of these are about the effects of crime and violence in Mexico. All of them show a significant negative relationship between violence and educational outcomes in that national context. For example, Jarillo and colleagues (2016) related exposure to criminal violence in Mexico to student achievement and estimated that such exposure reduced math test scores for students in elementary and lower secondary education. Caudillo and Torche (2014) estimated that when Mexican elementary school students were exposed to local violence, they suffered a significant increase in the probability of failing a grade. MacGregor used data on the occurrence of drug-related gang turf wars in urban locations in Mexico to estimate a causal effect between the timing of such gang violence and lower exam results for students exposed to it. "The results show that the students who were exposed to violence prior to the exam performed significantly worse than those exposed afterward. Moreover, the negative impact of violence on education was greater for the male population than for the female population" (MacGregor, 2017: 1).

Studies in other Latin American countries show similarly negative effects of drug-related and other types of systematic violence. Monteiro and Rocha's (2013) results suggest that students exposed to drug battles in Rio de Janeiro had lower test scores than their counterparts who were not exposed, and, in Colombia, Ortiz-Correa (2014) estimated that scores in mathematics and language tests were somewhat lower for students exposed to armed conflict in that country.

These studies and those analyzing the effects of violence on student academic outcomes outside of Latin America suggest that there are several main mechanisms that explain why violence is negatively related to educational achievement and attainment. I have already discussed the relation of different types of violence on economic growth at the macro level and the impact that crime, street violence, and domestic violence can have on the individual or family capacity to maintain jobs or be productive and earn higher wages. A violent environment forces individuals and families to make financial and behavioral choices that reduce their earning capacity, and negatively affects their schooling choices for their children (Justino et al., 2013; Valente, 2014). Further, a violent environment necessarily makes it more difficult for families to focus on supporting their children's educational activities. Attending to personal security takes time and effort and tends to take precedence over children's education.

The more direct explanations we can identify for the relationship between violence and achievement are at the individual child level and at the school level. Exposure to domestic violence causes psychological distress and often trauma, including posttraumatic stress disorder, and this can result in emotional and behavioral problems (Berman et al., 1996; Wolfe et al., 2003; Thompson and Massat, 2005). These negative emotional consequences adversely affect student learning. Exposure to violence affects students' academic outcomes because it threatens their emotional and physical safety (Bowen and Bowen, 1999). Similarly, exposure to community violence can produce or at least make students more vulnerable to these same psychological symptoms, which can also lead to poor academic achievement (Thompson and Massat, 2005; Borofsky et al., 2013).

Violence also impacts teachers' capacity to deliver curriculum in their classrooms and can affect school operations, as I have already noted. Schools that have to organize themselves to prevent fighting and extreme violence will be less likely to focus on instruction. Teachers focused on classroom disruptions, especially on violent ones, have less time for students to engage in learning activities. Jarillo and colleagues' (2016) study of student (and school) exposure to local urban turf-war violence in Mexico also showed higher teacher turnover and subsequent loss of instructional time. Monteiro and Rocha (2013) also found that gang violence in Rio de Janeiro increased teacher turnover and, further, caused temporary school closings— again, loss of instruction time.

Thus, violence is a major problem for improving the quality of schooling and for improving students' capacity to learn. The problem is especially great for students living in poverty, particularly in urban areas of Latin America, although domestic violence is not restricted to cities and large towns, nor to poor families. The problem of violence is further exacerbated by narcotrafficking and the great amount of street violence it generates in many communities in Latin America. Education can improve even in the context of crime and violence, but combating violence effectively in families and communities can have a significant positive effect on student achievement through the reduction of psychological distress in children, the increase in the capacity of families to focus greater energy on their children's academic performance and educational attainment, and through allowing schools to organize themselves around instruction instead of student and teacher safety.

Reducing Crime and Violence

Domestic Violence

> To understand violence against women in Latin America and attempts to reduce it, start with Colombia. Every four days, a Colombian woman is killed by her male partner, according to Martha Ordonez, Colombia's Presidential Advisor on Equality for Women. Over half of Colombian men admit to abusing their wives or girlfriends, according to a 2010 U.N. report. Abuse is rampant, but lower-level officials often lack the tools or the will to combat it. Over half of Colombian officials think that "what happens in privacy should be solved in privacy," while 32% "don't care" about stories of spouse abuse and 11% believe that women should forgive husbands who commit violence while drunk, according to a 2014 survey carried out by Ordonez. (Attanasio, 2015: 1)

Despite these difficult conditions for addressing domestic violence, Colombia and many other Latin American countries have passed legislation designed to increase protection for women, who are the main objects of such attacks. Sixteen countries including Argentina, Bolivia, Colombia, and others have passed "femicide" laws that aim at reducing the murder of women and other types of attacks, including acid attacks meant to disfigure them. Colombia passed a law in 2012 that attempts to increase prosecution rates for domestic violence and went further by passing a "hate crime" law in 2015 that adds additional punishment for gender-based violence.

Activists don't think that such laws are enough, and they have a point. If the laws are weakly enforced, they will discourage reporting of domestic violence as well as fail to send an adequately strong message to perpetrators. Advocates rightly demand reforms of the justice systems' prosecutor accountability, expedited restraining orders, and exceptions in abortion laws for victims of rape (Attanasio, 2015).

Most analysts and activists agree that laws to protect women need to exist to form the basis for legal action, as long as they are enforced. But strengthening enforcement requires more funding at the national, state, and municipal levels for combating domestic violence and aiding victims. Prosecutors also need to get tough on perpetrators from the very first infraction. A common practice is to give first-time offenders the choice of counseling to avoid charges. In the United States, this does work to prevent future violence in some cases, but only in about 20 percent after twelve to eighteen months of counseling. "But precisely because the success rate is relatively low, experts think it's important that penalties be tough and consistent" (Cohn, 2014: 3).

It is difficult to determine what works to reduce domestic violence because data are still incomplete even in countries such as the United States, but we do know that money for programs that provides transitional housing for families escaping abusers and other services that support domestically abused women and allow them and their children to separate themselves physically from abusive situations can and do help reduce the repetition of abuse and violence. Further, another key way to reduce violence is by increasing the opportunities for women to become economically independent from abusive men through fairer divorce settlements, and making the justice system generally more able to recognize abusive domestic situations in divorce and child custody cases and more protective of women and children in such cases. Strange as it may seem to say this in the twenty-first century, but justice systems in many countries, including those in Latin America, implicitly treat women and children as the property of men. Changing that view is difficult, but it is a crucial step in making the police and courts effective mechanisms for reducing violence against women and children.

Finally, many analysts think that the best way to reduce abusive behavior is education that stops people from ever becoming abusers. "Broad, cultural messages appear to make a difference—not just what young children see and hear, from their families and neighbors but also from their role models on television and in sports arenas, may have an impact. In addition, many researchers think it's possible to reach kids more directly, through schools or through their parents. According to these researchers, themes should include how men treat women—and how they express their own emotions" (Cohn, 2014: 3).

Fighting Drug Violence

As I discussed earlier, the problem of drug violence in Latin America is rooted in the huge amount of user demand in developed countries. Without reducing the demand, the economic returns to producing and selling drugs will continue to be high. Although drug enforcement agencies have been successful in breaking up some of the big cartels, this has resulted in spawning multiple smaller organizations, and may have contributed to even greater violence as these smaller organizations compete for turf (Dudley, 2014). In addition, the drug trade and violence build on the more traditional reasons for crime and violence —namely, urban poverty, high unemployment among youth, low levels of social capital in poor urban neighborhoods, and the reasons that I would put most emphasis on, the low capacity of governments, especially urban municipal governments, and ineffectual and often corrupt justice systems.

Twenty years ago, the World Bank produced a well-done report that argued for programs to combat urban poverty with a special focus on vulnerable groups such as at-risk youth and women, programs to build and strengthen social networks and community organizations in poor urban neighborhoods, and programs that would help municipal governments to build community-police cooperation based not just on punishing criminals but also on developing community projects (Ayres, 1998). The report suggested simple things, such as improving the infrastructure of poor urban neighborhoods, including better lighting and paved streets, and youth development projects that focus on helping young people stay in school, helping them get training to improve their chances of finding employment, and developing facilities for sports and other youth activities that keep them off the street and create a better community environment.

Ultimately, however, governments have to be able to organize themselves to focus on such projects and to have the trust of people that they are on the side of the urban poor, not on the side of the drug dealers and gangs. Similarly, people have to have faith and trust in the justice system to put away the really bad guys and not just the small fish. Furthermore, as I wrote previously,

> The fight against narcotrafficking requires not only strengthening state institutions and the rule of law, but also focusing on decreasing opportunities for corruption and low enforcement of laws and regulations. We must also strengthen transnational cooperation and collaboration. Isolated efforts might reduce violence and the power of cartels in a specific region, but it will not root out the problem. This became clear in the case of Colombia and Mexico. The crack down on Colombian cartels did not eradicate the production of cocaine, it simply led to the emergence of new drug cartels in Mexico. Violence and crime decreased in Colombia, while they got worse in Mexico and Central America. Thus, a holistic approach is necessary to target the underlying source of the problem, which is the high and profitable demand for cocaine in developed countries. We must also continue to dismantle the production and transport of cocaine in South and Central America. This will require better transnational mechanisms and institutions to join forces in sharing information and resources in the fight against narcotrafficking. (Toledo, 2015: 153)

Effectively Reducing Violence in Schools

I realize that my main focus in reducing the problem of violence in schools, and hence attacking the effect of violence in school on student outcomes, seems to be on changing the violent environment in which many Latin American urban young people attend school. That perception is correct. But I also believe that schools can do better in handling the violence when it enters the school and of improving instruction in schools even if violence outside and inside the schools has a significant negative effect on student performance.

First, schools can play an important role in teaching children and young people to be aware of domestic abuse, to report it, and in teaching them the values that may prevent them from becoming abusers themselves. Second, professional development for teachers and principals needs to focus more on effective management and deterrence of school violence and on how to recognize the effects on students exposed to violence outside the school. Programs that offer therapy for students to recover from the traumas generated by violence should be part of the school infrastructure in high violence localities (MacGregor, 2017). Third, as I spelled out in the chapter on teaching,

Latin American teachers need to have high-quality training that teaches them how to engage students in learning and to develop confidence in students that they can succeed academically. When students can do better academically and are able to complete upper secondary schooling, they are less likely to get involved in criminal activities as youth and adults. Although there is no causal evidence that higher educational achievement and attainment among individuals reduces crime and violence, it makes economic sense that the higher educated have more to lose by committing crimes and engaging in criminal violence. If our educational systems in Latin America would also focus on teaching students about alternatives to acting violently, and our governments would themselves act as effective examples of protecting victims against the perpetrators of violence, education would certainly play a more forceful role in reducing criminality in our region.

9

Bridging the Digital Divide

As if it weren't challenging enough to eliminate gaps in access to education, health care, and food security, the information age has created a new gap—the *digital divide*—which has made it even more difficult for the poor to participate fully in economic and social development. The information age has moved the goalposts for our efforts to make the game fairer for Latin America's marginalized populations. Now it is not sufficient for the poor in Latin America to have clean water, better health care and schools, and more secure food supplies. Those are still the most important investments we can make to reduce the vast inequalities in our region. But the new communication and technology systems, which provide greater access to information and to better jobs and social mobility, have now also become crucial to inclusivity and greater equality. The question is how do we Latin Americans overcome the divide between us and the developed countries, and within our own very unequal societies.

What exactly is the digital divide and why is it important? One way to define it is in the availability and use of certain kinds of technological hardware and software, such as computers and internet access, and to compare the amount of equipment and services between societies or between groups within the same society. Of course, defining digital differences in this way does not capture intensity of use or the sophistication of use, both of which are important in understanding differences in the capacity to use technology. This capacity to use digital technology may be even more important than access to the technology itself.

> The digital divide is deepening. The divide of so-called physical access might be closing in certain respects; however, other digital divides have begun to grow. The digital divide as a whole is deepening because the divides of digital skills and unequal daily use of the digital media are increasing. . . . One can even claim that as higher stages of universal access to the digital media are reached, differences in skills and usage increase. . . . [We argue that] digital skills are the key to the entire process of the appropriation of these new technologies. These skills are vital for living, working, studying, and entertaining oneself in an information society. (van Dijk and van Deursen, 2014: 1)

The importance of the digital divide derives from the transformation of economies and societies into what Castells (1996) called the "network society." Underlying the network society is a digital infrastructure that steadily transforms the economy into the e-economy and society into the information society. In turn, to participate in this e-economy and information society, individuals need to have new types of education and skills, mainly associated with adeptly using computers, smartphones, and the various applications and programming languages needed to access and process information and turn it into productive activities.

> The acquisition of the appropriate education and skills to enable people to engage in economic life is differentiated among class, cultural capital and status, gender, ethnicity, digital literacy, and opportunities across the life course at the local, regional, and national level. Furthermore, as digital technology is embedded in political communication, individuals need access and skills to engage in the democratic process. Access to social and cultural networks is highly differentiated along class, status, and ethnic lines in terms of cultural capital, which relates to any quality and participation. Age and gender cuts across all of these divisions and undermines older people and women's ability to engage and participate. (Wessels, 2013: 21)

Thus, we can expect that even in Latin America, with its large rural populations, the future will be dominated by information technology, the internet, artificial intelligence, and a society where the capacity to network, to access information, and to use information, will increasingly determine the relation of individuals to the economy and society.

> Castells argues that the digital divide goes beyond those who have access to the Internet and those who do not have access. He writes that differing levels of access to, and usage of, digital services "adds a fundamental cleavage to existing sources of inequality and social exclusion in a complex interaction" (Castells, 2001: 247). The dimensions of digital divide can be understood as the dynamic of inclusion and exclusion that articulates the levels of digital and other resources that people have available to them within the social divisions in society. This means that people have unequal levels of opportunity to develop digital skills, to participate in democratic processes, and to enter the labor market. The digital divide involves social, democratic and global divides and is multidimensional. (Wessels, 2013: 18)

In keeping with the overall theme of the book, this chapter also discusses the possible role of schooling in bridging the digital divide. In addition to discussing how schools can provide access to computers and the internet in low-income communities that cannot afford individual access, I assess the conditions under which schools can bridge van Dijk and van Deursen's broader conception of the gap—namely, in digital skills and usage—among those young people attending schools.

How Large Is the Digital Divide in Latin America?

As I mentioned, the digital divide is almost always measured by available data on household access to computers, internet, and mobile devices, as well as the broader measure of internet use. At one level, we can make these assessments across countries and Latin America compared with the rest of the world. At another level, we need to compare these indicators across social class within Latin American countries.

One thing is clear: those living in the developed countries and even the former Soviet Republics have much greater access to computers and the internet at home than those living in Latin America and Asia. And digital access in Africa is far below that in Latin America (Table 9.1). The data in Table 9.1 end in 2017, but in 2020, as I was writing, more than 80 percent of Europeans and US residents had computers at home and were connected to the internet at home, whereas in Latin America, the average is closer to 50 percent. Of course, the numbers vary among European countries, among US states, and among Latin American countries. Table 9.2 shows how great this variation is in Latin America. Argentines, Chileans, and Uruguayans, for example, have access to computers and the internet in their homes in a proportion that is only somewhat lower than in the United States and Europe. On the other hand, families in my own country, Peru, and in Paraguay, Ecuador, and the three poorest Central American countries have very low access to computers and the internet. The digital divide between most people living in these nations and the average resident of the developed world and even Latin America's Southern Cone countries is very great.

This makes sense, because these countries are poorer, and, as Martin Hilbert (2010) has shown, family income is the single most important variable explaining internet access in Latin America— much more important than other explanatory variables, such as education, household size, or age. This is not only the case for differences in access between countries, but also, as Hilbert argues and we shall discuss below, within a country. Computers and internet access at home are even more expensive than internet access the way Hilbert defines it, so we would expect income to play an even more important part in home access.

Mobile phone subscriptions are the one exception to Latin America's low digital access (Table 9.2). By 2017, more than 80 percent— and in a number of countries more than 90 percent—of individuals living in Latin America had mobile phone subscriptions. These phones had, at minimum, texting and messaging capacity in various forms. Even in Peru, which has a low fraction of the population with computers and internet access, almost 90 percent of Peruvians had cell phone service in 2015, and this probably surpassed 90 percent in 2017. Thus, at some level, people in Latin America are "connected" to social media and can network through their cell phones. This is important politically, and political campaigns in Latin America are getting very adept in using cell phone messaging, unfortunately much of it by spreading fake news, as in Jair Bolsonaro's 2018 campaign for the Brazilian presidency, which focused on WhatsApp messaging. Researchers are also experimenting with educational interventions that involve advising low-income parents about their children's attendance and performance at school (positive and negative) and with improving young people's "mindset" (Dweck, 2008) to reduce dropouts and improve students' academic achievement. All this is possible because of the ubiquity of cellular phones and cellular service.

Table 9.1   Household Access to Digital Technology, 2005–2017, by Region (in percent)

Country	Technology Access	2005	2010	2013	2015	2017
Africa	Computers at home	4	5	7	8	9
	Internet at home	1	4	9	14	19
Arab States	Computers at home	14	29	38	42	47
	Internet at home	11	23	35	43	50
Asia and Pacific	Computers at home	20	27	33	36	39
	Internet at home	12	20	34	43	49
Latin America	Computers at home	—	30	42	45	46 (2016)
	Internet at home	—	28 (2011)	36	43	46 (2016)
CIS[a]	Computers at home	20	47	62	66	68
	Internet at home	13	37	61	69	74
Europe	Computers at home	49	68	75	76	79
	Internet at home	39	64	73	78	81
United States	Computers at home	66	77	82	87	89[b]
	Internet at home	58	71	77	82	84

Sources: Africa, Arab States, Asia Pacific, CIS, Europe: ITU World Telecommunication/ICT Indicators database; United States: Statista website; Latin America: CEPAL Statistics data tool. *Notes:* a. Former Soviet Republics. b. Estimate.

The most popular measure of technology access is overall internet use, since this picks up the opportunities that young people have to use the internet in school and at internet cafes, and it also picks up the fact that increasingly, people everywhere use the internet on mobile devices, and do not necessarily subscribe to it at home, nor have a home computer. Table 9.3 shows the percentage of the population in Latin America by country, and the overall figures for the United States and Europe. There are anomalies, such as a higher percentage in 2017 of households with internet access in Chile than the percentage of internet users, but generally, the percentages in Table 9.3 are slightly higher than the percentage of households with internet at home, as we expect. The differences between the poorer Central American countries along with Peru and Bolivia, and the Southern Cone countries, especially Argentina and Chile, are very large. Not surprisingly, the countries with the lowest income per capita, large rural populations, and a high fraction of those who are Indigenous use the internet less. In facing up to the digital divide, these characteristics of the countries with the biggest divides are just one more social gap that needs to be closed if we hope to create an inclusive economic and social development for the region. I will argue that we do not only have to invest in more digital infrastructure to

Table 9.2 Household Access to Digital Technology, 2005–2017, by Country (in percent)

Country	Technology Access	2005	2010	2013	2015	2017
Argentina	Computer at home	32	47	59	66	69
	Internet at home	13	34	49	62	81
	Mobile phone	—	86 (2011)	—	—	—
Bolivia	Computer at home	12	23	33	30	36
	Internet at home	4	6	13	24	32
	Mobile phone	39	82 (2011)	—	—	—
Brazil	Computer at home	19	35	49	50	46
	Internet at home	14	27	43	55	61
	Mobile phone	59	84	90	—	—
Chile	Computer at home	30	47	57	56	60
	Internet at home	17	35	50	60	88
	Mobile phone	84 (2006)	94 (2011)	—	—	—
Colombia	Computer at home	15	26	42	46	44
	Internet at home	6	19	36	42	50
	Mobile phone	65 (2006)	86	95	96	97
Costa Rica	Computer at home	27	44	53	53	51
	Internet at home	10	24	48	60	69
	Mobile phone	49	74	93	96	—
Dominican Rep.	Computer at home	9	16	26	29	34
	Internet at home	3	10	19	24	28
	Mobile phone	41	68	81	—	—
Ecuador	Computer at home	13	27	36	41	41
	Internet at home	4	12	28	33	37
	Mobile phone	64	76	86	—	—
El Salvador	Computer at home	7	13	22	20	22
	Internet at home	2	8	13	15	18
	Mobile phone	35	87	92	—	—

continues

close the gap, but also need to reach out to young people and adults with public spaces (schools, digital technology hubs, especially in rural areas) where these digitally marginalized populations have the opportunity to learn to use information technology.

The Distribution of Information Technology Within Latin American Countries

Of course, if a country's government can take steps to spread the use of information technology—such as making free internet service available in public places or, as I push for in my recommendation later in this chapter, bringing the internet and computers to all

Table 9.2   Continued

Country	Technology Access	2005	2010	2013	2015	2017
Guatemala	Computer at home	8	14	20	22	25
	Internet at home	1	5	12	17	24
	Mobile phone	55 (2006)	—	—	—	—
Honduras	Computer at home	6	13	20	20	17
	Internet at home	2	7	16	23	27
	Mobile phone	22	81	—	—	—
Mexico	Computer at home	19	30	36	45	45
	Internet at home	9	22	31	39	—
	Mobile phone	15	34	44	85	—
Nicaragua	Computer at home	4	8	11	13	14
	Internet at home	0	4	9	14	—
	Mobile phone	23	62 (2009)	—	—	—
Panama	Computer at home	15	28	38	40	47
	Internet at home	5	20	34	53	—
	Mobile phone	64 (2006)	—	—	71	—
Paraguay	Computer at home	9	19	32	29	26
	Internet at home	2	14	27	27	—
	Mobile phone	49	85	93	95	—
Peru	Computer at home	8	23	30	32	33
	Internet at home	4	13	22	23	—
	Mobile phone	20	70	82	87	—
Uruguay	Computer at home	22	53	66	68	71
	Internet at home	13	34	53	60	64
	Mobile phone	49 (2006)	85	90	—	—
Venezuela	Computer at home	10	19	41	44	46
	Internet at home	3	14	32	35	34
	Mobile phone	26	43	38	—	—

Source: CEPAL Statistics data tool.
Note: — = not available.

schools—this reduces the digital divide between the rich and the poor within a country. But even in developed countries with lots of technology, low-income families are less likely to have access to computers and the internet than better off families. The gap is larger in Latin American countries than in the United States or Europe, mainly because income and education inequality is greater and there is less information technology to go around.

Thus, in 2014, according to one estimate (Zechmeister et al., 2015), 76 percent of Latin Americans with postsecondary education regularly used the internet, 43 percent of those with secondary education regularly used it, but only 10 percent of those with primary education were regular internet users. If we divide Latin Americans by income levels, 69 percent of those in the highest 20 percent of

Table 9.3   **Proportion of Individuals Who Use the Internet, 2010–2017, by Country/Region (in percent)**

Country	2010	2011	2012	2013	2014	2015	2016	2017
Argentina	45	51	56	60	65	68	70	—
Bolivia	22	30	35	37	35	36	40	—
Brazil	41	46	49	51	55	58	60	—
Chile	45	52	55	58	61	64	66	82
Colombia	37	40	49	52	53	56	58	62
Costa Rica	37	39	48	46	53	60	66	72
Cuba	16	16	21	28	29	37	39	—
Dominican Republic	31	38	42	46	50	54	61	—
El Salvador	16	19	20	23	25	27	29	—
Guatemala	11	12	16	20	23	29	35	—
Honduras	11	16	18	18	19	28	30	—
Mexico	31	37	40	44	44	57	60	64
Nicaragua	10	11	14	16	18	20	25	—
Panama	40	43	40	44	45	51	54	—
Paraguay	20	25	29	37	43	48	51	61
Peru	35	36	38	39	40	41	46	49
Uruguay	46	51	55	58	62	65	66	—
Venezuela	37	40	49	55	57	62	60	—
Latin America & Caribbean	35	39	43	46	49	54	56	—
United States	72	70	79	84	87	88	89	90
Europe	70	73	76	79	81	83	85	87

Sources: Latin America: CEPAL statistics, data tool; United States: Internet Live Stats (www.internetLiveStats.com/internet-users/us/); Europe: Statista website.
Note: — = not available.

income were regular users, but only 14 percent of the lowest quintile regularly used the internet—this means that highest income Latin Americans were five times as likely to use the internet than the lowest income users.

We don't have very recent data estimating these social class breakdowns by internet use for each Latin American country, but the figures we have from 2009 (a long time ago when it comes to technology access) show very great inequalities in access between the highest and lowest income groups in each country (Table 9.4). In the past decade, we have seen very great increases in the proportion of young people with internet in the home and in the proportion of internet users. Yet, even in the countries with the highest percentage of internet in the home—Chile, Uruguay, and Brazil—the gaps are substantial, particularly in Brazil and Chile, two countries with very high levels of income inequality.

Table 9.4 Twelve- to Nineteen-Year-Olds with Internet in the Home,
by Country, 2009 (in percent)

Country	Total Internet in Home	Internet in Home, Highest Income Quintile	Internet in Home, Lowest Income Quintile
Bolivia (2007)	3	10	0
Brazil	28	50	5
Chile	35	50	15
Colombia	15	35	0
Costa Rica	18	40	5
Ecuador	7	15	0
El Salvador (2008)	6	20	0
Honduras (2007)	3	10	0
Panama (2007)	10	25	0
Paraguay	12	35	0
Peru	10	30	0
Uruguay	34	35	20
Venezuela (2008)	8	20	0

Source: Trucco, 2013: Figure 16.2.

Another source with somewhat later data shows similar gaps in internet and computers in high- and low-income households (Table 9.5). The percentages in some of the countries represent the difference in the highest and lowest deciles of income (Mexico and Uruguay), whereas others represent differences in highest and lowest quintiles (Argentina and Costa Rica). In Brazil and Ecuador, the lowest social class grouping (DE) is compared to the highest social class (A). The three main takeaways from Table 9.5 are that the gaps are generally large for computers and internet in the home between high- and low-income families; the gap is not large for the percentage of families with mobile phones; and, consistent with the data in Table 9.4, Uruguay has been able to achieve unusually equal access (for Latin America) to computers and, given that the difference shown for Uruguay is for the highest and lowest decile of family income, even much more equal access to the internet for the highest and lowest income families.

Estimates based on data in the early 2000s (up to 2007) show that the single most important family characteristic correlated with internet access in both Brazil and Uruguay, two countries with very different income distributions, was per capita household income, much more so than, for example, education of individuals in the family (Hilbert, 2010). This should be less true for fixed line or mobile telephone service, which is cheaper than internet service and

Table 9.5   Households with Access to Digital Technology, by Income Group and Country, 2013 (in percent)

Country	Technology Access	Lowest Income Group	Highest Income Group
Argentina (2011)[a]	Computer	22	85
	Internet	16	78
	Mobile phone	68	98
Brazil[b]	Computer	10	98
	Internet	8	98
Costa Rica[a]	Computer	20	80
	Internet	20	86
	Mobile phone	86	97
Mexico (2010)[c]	Computer	2	78
	Internet	1	67
	Mobile phone	22	92
Ecuador[b]	Internet	14	51
Uruguay[c]	Computer	76	89
	Internet	23	88

Source: Gallego and Gutiérrez, 2015.
Notes: a. Quintile; b. Social class DE (lowest) versus social class A (highest); c. Decile.

personal computers, although these differences vary from country to country (Hilbert, 2010).

Thus, the digital gap between countries could gradually equalize were the income per capita to increase steadily in Latin America overall and especially the lower income countries, such as Guatemala, Honduras, Nicaragua, El Salvador, Bolivia, Paraguay, and Peru—those facing the greatest digital divide. However, reducing the digital gap within countries is more challenging. Even if we grow economically, if we also sustain our actual high levels of income inequality, families at the bottom of the income distribution will continue to have far less access to information technology than the average family in their own country.

One way to reduce the digital divide within countries is to subsidize the use of computers and access to the internet for low-income families. Another way is turn schools into computer and internet centers, which would, first, increase computer skills among students and make internet available to them, and second, could increase computer and internet access to adults after school hours. In the next sections of this chapter, I discuss ways to reduce the digital divide more rapidly than would be possible by just waiting for economic growth to produce enough income for families to get access to current information technology privately.

Economic Approaches to Reducing the Digital Divide

In 2010, Martin Hilbert of the University of Southern California conducted an interesting exercise of estimating how much a low-income family in four Latin American countries would have to spend on information and communications technology (ICT) and what this implied for the price of ICT should these societies want to have everyone purchase computers and internet access individually and privately (Hilbert, 2010). Correspondingly, Hilbert also calculated the cost of subsidizing low-income families to buy ICT privately.

We can duplicate this exercise using more up-to-date information on the cost of computers and connectivity and the average income of the lowest 20 percent of the income distribution in Latin America. World Development Indicators show that in 2015, one-fourth of Latin America's population lived on $5.50 per day; 11 percent lived on $3.20 per day, and 4 percent, on $1.90 per day. Assuming that a poor family can spend 2.7 percent of its income on information and computer technology (ICT) (Hilbert, 2010), those in the bottom 11 percent would be able to spend $32 annually on all their ICT (computers, phones, and internet), and those in the bottom quarter, about $54 annually. Even buying a cheap computer every five years would mean that the bottom quarter of Latin Americans would only be able to pay $270 for the computer, and that would mean that they would have nothing left for internet service or mobile phone service. The figure for the bottom 11 percent would be $160 for the computer. Thus, in order to reduce the digital divide significantly, either the poor would have to spend more than 2.7 percent of their income on ICT or the price of ICT would have to fall considerably. We have seen hardware costs falling for computers, and many lower income users are substituting smaller hand-held devices for computers, but private mobile phone service and internet service prices have remained relatively high, especially as new types of uses are added (video streaming, for example).

One way to reduce the price of ICT to the poor would be to subsidize the purchase of hardware, software, internet service, and phone service for Latin American families that cannot afford them.

We can assume that the whole package of ICT hardware, internet, and phone services costs about $300–$400 annually (Hilbert, 2010: Table 2)—or if we don't include fixed-line telephone service about $230–$330 annually. Therefore, subsidizing private ICT for the bottom quarter of Latin America's population would require at least 0.3 percent of the region's gross domestic product in the form of subsidies to the poorest 25 percent of the population.

To convince Latin American governments to take even 0.3 percent of GDP to close the digital divide would be difficult. As Hilbert points out, such a large expenditure would also have to be justified in terms of the social benefits it would produce compared, for example, to spending the money on other important services for the bottom 25 percent of the population. These other services include improved access to health care, education, sanitation, and access to drinking water—all the investments we discussed in earlier chapters. Finally, since this strategy to close the digital divide is based on subsidizing the purchase of privately provided ICT hardware and services, the billions of dollars added to the demand for this ICT could raise its price, which would attenuate the total impact of the subsidies.

The high cost of government subsidies to promote the use of privately provided ICT among low-income Latin Americans and the unlikely reduction in the price of many of these services, particularly private internet and mobile phone access, mean that we have to find other ways to reduce the digital divide. One way is to create publicly run communications companies, such as Costa Rica's Grupo ICE, which provide cheaper mobile phone services than competing private companies. It would also be possible to create free Wi-Fi access in most urban areas, as is now the case in many US cities. Even though the speed of this free Wi-Fi is less than that of more expensive systems, for ordinary use, it could bring in tens of millions of Latin Americans now not connected. Combined with cheap smartphones, this combination of free Wi-Fi and handheld devices could incorporate a high fraction of currently excluded urban low-income users.

However, even with free Wi-Fi in cities, relatively low-cost smartphones, and lower priced mobile phone services provided by public companies such as Grupo ICE, the important fraction of poor Latin Americans in rural areas would still not be able to access ICT, mainly because internet access is not available to them. The question of solving the digital divide in rural communities has to be, in practical terms, mainly handled in terms of public access. Public access could also contribute to reducing the digital divide in urban centers, and, in many ways public access would be considerably cheaper and easier logistically for users in higher density populations areas.

The results of the analysis presented here show a reality in which it does not seem likely that the poor will gain sufficient purchasing power to obtain personalized access in the short term. The logical conclusion is to prepare for a long period in which public access is the only viable access solution to assure quality and up-to-date access for these income segments. An apparatus would be comparable to the institutional structure of today's public transportation system, which might of course consist of public and private components (similar to public transportation). Notwithstanding, any sustainable solution of such institution requires a reliable stream of resources. Currently, few financial mechanisms are in place to support such an institutional structure of public access to information. (Hilbert, 2010: 25)

One way to finance public (and private) access is through universal service funds (USFs). These funds exist in most Latin American countries and receive their revenues from an earmarked tax on telecom operators. Their purpose has always been to extend communications services to the poor, so they are ideal for closing the digital divide, but they have not always been used effectively:

Studies by the ITU (International Telecommunications Union, 2013) and the GMSA (Global Systems for Mobile Communications) show that across the world, more than half of the sums collected for USFs were never utilized and over a third of the funds were not able to distribute any of the levies collected. . . . [For example] in Brazil, where payments to the universal service fund have amounted to 1 percent of operator revenues since 2000, the fund is now $6bn and largely unused due to technology restrictions. (GSMA, 2016)

Nevertheless, there have been some USF success stories in Latin America reported by the ITU, and these suggest that USFs can be effectively used to greatly extend mobile phone and internet access to the poor and even into rural areas. Chile, Colombia, the Dominican Republic, Paraguay, and, I am proud to say, my own country, Peru, have achieved such expansion through the Telecommunications Investment Fund (FITEL) program, with the program's internet service component initiated during my presidency. By 2011, the program had reached almost 17,000 rural towns (ITU, 2013: 114).

In Latin America, FITEL [Fondo de Inversion de Telecomunica-
ciones] was the first successful example of a USF administration
adopting innovative approaches, now widely respected, to
achieve access in rural areas i.e., lowest-subsidy and technology
neutral auctions. FITEL's pioneering programmes resulted in a
number of social benefits and activities that have since been
expanded from public telephony to include broadband internet
access, and many of these concepts have been used as models in
other jurisdictions. . . . In 2001, FITEL initiated projects to provide internet services: the first, using VSAT to cover district
capitals at an average cost of USD 16,800 per town. Projects
became more ambitious regarding the number of locales and the
requirement that tele-centres must be installed to provide effective use of the internet access. The projects for expanding
internet access included an additional allocation of resources
(training subsidy) for teaching multimedia usage to local residents, creating local content and fostering the development of
micro enterprises responsible for the management and operation of the tele-centres. After 2004, all internet service projects
included broadband and a training subsidy. (ITU, 2013: 114)

Other Latin American countries that used USFs this way had
similarly successful results—reaching large numbers of unconnected
people with telephone and internet service. The Dominican Republic
used funds to create "tele-centers" to provide internet access to rural
towns, giving preferences to students, teachers, and professionals,
and to rural schools. Colombia also used USF money for tele-centers
and, in addition, for putting computers in schools and training people
to use computers and the internet. Chile used the funds to increase
broadband access to private households and to connect all schools to
the internet. Connecting schools—especially low-income, rural schools
to the internet—serves multiple functions, including, of course, preparing the least digitally served young people—the next generation—to
participate in the information society and to have schools also serve as
tele-centers for adults in rural communities. In the next section, I
explore these two possibilities.

Schools and the Digital Divide

Bridging the digital divide is not only important in terms of including low-income Latin Americans in their country's social and political life, and having access to information more generally, but it also

makes it possible for lower-income adults and particularly young people to learn skills important in the modern economy (such as using computers and the internet). This is where bringing technology into Latin American schools comes in.

Some IT advocates have argued for putting computers in schools as a new way of teaching mathematics and reading to children, and for older young people, as a new way to teach research skills using the internet. For many in the IT world, computer technology was touted as a way to improve educational outcomes, especially in countries with shortages of highly skilled teachers. An example of this argument is the One Laptop per Child (OLPC) movement initiated by Nicholas Negroponte of the MIT media lab (http://one.laptop.org /about/mission). Despite the appeal of this argument, more savvy analysts of the potential uses of computers in schools saw early on that for technology to be an effective tool to improve learning, it would require even more skilled teachers than the best teachers not using technology (Becker, 1984; Oppenheimer, 1997; Jara, 2018). The empirical evidence on the effectiveness of computers in schools in improving student achievement has always been mixed, with the best results taking place where considerable (and expensive) teacher training was added to the hardware and software costs (Levin and Meister, 1986; Becker, 1994).

So let's step away from the illusion that introducing computers and the internet into classrooms will—pretty much on their own—raise student achievement. Let's stop hoping that we can avoid making the large investments outlined in earlier chapters in social services other than schools and much greater and well-targeted investments in improving teacher education and training and improving the physical facilities of the schools themselves. Even if we abandon the IT illusion, we can still make a strong argument that computers in schools would help students improve their computer skills. This argument is especially cogent for young people who do not have computers and internet access at home. Unless a school has teachers very well trained to use computers and the internet as teaching enhancement tools, the main argument for putting computers in schools and connecting schools to the internet is to *bridge the digital divide*—to provide the opportunity for students without computers and internet at home to become adept at using information technology and therefore be much more ready for twenty-first-century jobs and participation in what Castells called the "network society" (Castells, 1996).

There have been several ambitious efforts in Latin America to computerize schools and connect them to the internet, some reaching down to rural schools in the hinterland. In late 2001, a few months after taking office as Peru's president, I initiated the Huascarán project, which over the next five years brought about 15,000 computers (to computer labs) and 1,700 internet connections to 3,000 schools. The project was ambitious, training 55,000 teachers how to use the software made available and to help the 2.5 million students reached by the program during those years to acquire digital skills and try to improve the quality of education in Peru. Each school appointed a teacher to be in charge of the computer lab, training his or her colleagues, and organizing a schedule for using ICT in different subjects. The program was never evaluated properly, so we don't know whether it did improve student performance, but for the first time in Peru, low-income urban and some rural schools had access to computers and had teachers trained to help students use them to learn subject matter.

Other projects followed in Peru—notably, the one laptop per child program that began in 2007 under Alan Garcia, my successor as president. That program focused on rural schools, almost all without internet access, supplying the laptops to Technology Resource Centers at each school rather than to individual pupils. One estimate had Peru buying 850,000 of these laptops in 2007–2011. The Inter-American Development Bank evaluated the project in 2012 and found that although it significantly increased access and use of IT in schools, and students acquired skills in using laptops, there were no gains in math and reading skills and some gains in abstract reasoning, verbal skills, and processing speed (Cristia et al., 2012).

Another very large educational IT project was implemented in Uruguay. As part of its El Ceibal program Uruguay also invested in OLPC and had already achieved fixed broadband connection by 2010 to 95 percent of primary schools and 100 percent of secondary schools (UNESCO, 2012: Figure 11), although this was possible in part because Uruguay has a relatively low proportion of rural schools. All secondary schools and 75 percent of primary schools were connected in Colombia, although almost none with fixed broadband in 2010. Colombia also had one of the lowest learner to computer ratios in 2010— about twelve students per computer (UNESCO, 2012: Figure 5).

The ambitious Enlaces program in Chile installed internet in Chilean schools with the support of private enterprise, reaching mass coverage by the early 2000s, except for rural schools (Claro and Jara,

2020). It provided about 55 percent of schools with internet connectivity at the primary and secondary levels, almost all schools with computers, and most communities with tele-centers for training and access for families in the school neighborhood (Hepp et al., 2004; Claro and Jara, 2020). Almost 90 percent of Chilean students were involved in computer-assisted instruction programs, and the number of computers per student in Chilean schools by 2015 was about the same as the average in the OECD. Further, Enlaces trained Chilean teachers in the use of digital technologies in support of school subjects and "defined a set of competencies and standards to identify and define the types of ICT usage expected from teachers in the various areas of their profession" (Claro and Jara, 2020: 100). Even in huge Brazil, three-quarters of secondary schools were already connected with fixed broadband internet as early as ten years ago. However, the figure for basic education schools is considerably lower even today.

The prospects of reaching most students in Latin American schools—especially at the middle and secondary levels—with access to computers and internet connectivity in the next ten years is very high. This implies that at least this youngest generation of Latin Americans will be familiar with and maybe even adept at using IT. This is not to say that computers and the internet will be a vehicle for improving education—to get into that process seriously would require developing a new kind of teacher, not only skilled in using computers and the internet, but also knowing how to use IT to enhance classroom teaching and student learning. That is a far longer-term project. The Chilean experience is revealing in this regard. As described above, in addition to making computers and the internet widely available to students, Enlaces provided rather extensive teacher education and support services for developing skills and using digital technologies in Chilean classrooms. Despite this, as in other countries, there is little evidence that all this positively influenced student performance in subject matter learning. Further, thanks to the opportunities provided to Chilean teachers to use IT in their classrooms, the hope was that this would motivate them to change traditional teaching practices in innovative ways. It turns out that although IT was used more in the classroom, it was mainly to support traditional practices (Claro and Jara, 2020).

Nevertheless, an important advantage of bringing computers and the internet into schools is that, after hours, computer labs and internet access in schools in low-income urban and in rural areas can serve adult populations as IT centers. This is much cheaper than trying to subsidize family access in individual homes. Providing after-hours instruction at schools for lower income adults without computers and internet access at home could help older generations pick up computer skills that could help them deal more effectively with IT in their everyday lives—at work and in getting access to social and political information. As discussed earlier, USFs could finance such community programs in schools equipped with IT.

And although not much thought has been given to this issue, we should consider how information technology is underutilized in school systems, which could be used to help teachers follow students' progress and, more generally, make more informed decisions about resource allocation and improving student performance. Throughout Latin America, students are being tested more often, but the data from these tests are rarely used to help teachers improve their teaching, improve the curriculum, or identify which interventions work or don't work. At the school and even at higher administrative levels, the vast power of computers to process data and inform decisionmaking are simply not part of the day-to-day work of educational administrators, mainly because they are not trained to use information technology. As far as I am concerned, we have put too much emphasis on computers as a teaching tool in the classroom, in the vague hope that they can compensate for how poorly we train classroom teachers, and too little emphasis in using information technology as it is used in every other industry, to gather and process data to enhance productivity at every level. Some countries, such as Brazil and Chile, have vast amounts of data on student performance and teacher and administrative resources at the school level. But the data are seriously underutilized at the local level. This can and should be changed.

Some Final Thoughts

An important element in providing access to information technology for low-income Latin Americans is instruction. A simple way to provide that instruction is for secondary school students to be paid to work with adults after school in school computer labs. These types of social-community efforts in spaces such as schools or tele-centers are the most effective way to bridge the digital divide in the short and medium run. Eventually, incomes will get high enough and the technology cheap enough (and largely handheld) that all public efforts and subsidies can be focused on the bottom 10 percent of the population—

still an expensive proposition but within the capacity of Latin American governments to eliminate this last gap.

As mentioned, it is an entirely different proposition to develop quality instruction in the use of IT to train the next generation in programming and higher level engineering and IT skills, and to develop a more sophisticated understanding in how to interpret the information they receive through social media. That will take long-term investments in high-quality science teachers and widespread programs that help adults and young people understand the human-information interaction. As artificial intelligence becomes more ubiquitous, this will raise the stakes and make this understanding even more crucial to functioning in the digital age. Further, the educational system itself can be made more robust in the way information and communications technology is administered and organized. This would, first and foremost, require the training of administrators to use ICT effectively down to the school level.

The most difficult of the challenges is to convince governments to find ways to provide access to ICT for the lowest 25 percent and the lowest 10 percent of their nation's population. Of course, private providers would love to see major resources go into this effort, but subsidizing private use is very expensive and—given other important investments needed for education, health, and other services to reduce the very high levels of economic and social inequality in the region, not the best use of public resources. Rather more "collective" community access solutions are the best way to reduce the digital divide, especially since so many of Latin America's poor still live in rural areas, dispersed across small communities. Furthermore, the increasingly ubiquitous use of cellular phones portends the shape of things to come—for most Latin Americans, these phones are the computers of the future—their access to information and media technology. Also, their ubiquitous television sets will also serve as internet access, with fewer functions than full-fledged computers, but nevertheless providing connectivity and access to information. Investing heavily in low-income access through privately owned computers may not even make sense in terms of where ICT is headed in the next decade or two.

10

Higher Education as a Force for Greater Equality

In 2017, there were more than 27 million students enrolled in higher education institutions in Latin America and the Caribbean, 24 million of them in bachelor's and advanced degree programs. This compared to 29 million students enrolled in bachelor's and advanced degree programs in North America and Western Europe combined. The enrollment rate of young people in college and graduate school is lower in Latin America than in more developed countries, and the percentage of young workers in the labor force with higher education degrees is also lower. But in the next decade or two, we should see both gaps between Latin America and the developed countries continue to close.

As I argued for the case of K–12 education in the region, except for the poorer countries of Central America, governments in our region have figured out ways to increase the number of places in education institutions, and higher education is going to continue to expand as long as more students enter and graduate from secondary schools. Student higher education enrollment in the region has increased more than three-fold since 1995, when the great expansion began (see Figure 1.2). It is likely that many, if not most, Latin American countries will have gross enrollment rates in bachelor's degree programs above 50 percent of college age youth by 2030. Thus, it is fair to argue that enrollment expansion itself is not the main challenge we need to meet in higher education. Latin American countries are generally locked into a political commitment of providing their secondary

school graduates more access to colleges and universities, and I don't
see that changing over the next generation.

However, there is a huge challenge in delivering *reasonable
quality* higher education and avoiding a two-tier or three-tier quality
system of colleges and universities. I am not referring to how the
state of California, for example, has organized its *public* higher education system into the University of California, the state university
system, and the community college system, which somewhat corre-
sponds to postsecondary technical schools in Latin America. There are
many critiques of the California system (for example, Clark, 1960),
but the so-called second-tier state university system delivers high-
quality education at a low price for hundreds of thousands of students
annually. For example, engineers trained at San Jose State University
and Cal Poly in San Luis Obispo form a major part of Silicon Valley's
engineering labor force.

Rather, I'm concerned that in many Latin American countries,
expansion has relied too much on very low-quality *private* institutions,
many of them low-cost and for-profit while the public sector and the
Catholic Church maintain, at high cost, a few very selective universities
to continue training a relatively small group of professionals and political elites. And, just as in primary and secondary schooling, these private (and many public) universities and other types of higher education
institutions are delivering very uneven quality of curriculum content
and teaching with too little accountability to the public at large. There
is also a huge challenge in reducing the financial and informational barriers that even highly qualified students from lower socioeconomic
backgrounds face in access to universities in Latin America, especially
access to high-quality programs.

These problems are especially acute for creating a more equal
society in Latin America while promoting future economic growth.
This is true for three main reasons: (1) productivity in the new man-
ufacturing industries, high value-added agriculture, and advanced
services (including public services) needed to fuel growth in the
post–commodity export future increasingly depend on the quality of
the higher education system; (2) if the K–12 and higher education
systems are structured to make it difficult for bright, lower social
class or minority (Black and Indigenous) students to find their way
into higher education, it greatly reduces the talent pool of high-level
human resources, dampening the possibilities for economic growth;
and (3) the earnings payoff to a higher education degree is unusually
high in most Latin American countries (Carnoy, 2011), which means
that the allocation of those degrees among individuals from lower

and higher social classes has a major impact on social mobility in Latin American societies.

What our region's two- and three-tier higher education policy has failed to discover is the real secret to the success of developed countries' higher education systems. This secret lies in plain sight: second-tier institutions, such as the public state universities in most US states are generally of reasonably high quality and produce graduates who are productive in a range of professional jobs. Indeed, a recent study has shown that many of these public state universities provide the highest likelihood of upward mobility for low-income students among US higher education institutions (Chetty et al., 2017). That is, although state universities have had problems with access to core classes in recent years because of public funding and faculty cutbacks, they still provide good preparation for a range of higher paying jobs. In fact, I would say that the big advantage of the US higher education system is not necessarily the prestigious US "world class" institutions that form such a high percentage of the top global universities, but rather the strength of second-tier public institutions producing the mass of well-trained professionals for the US labor force and the greatest source of upward mobility for low-income students. This appears to contrast sharply with the situation in Latin America, where low-income students are much more likely to attend low-quality private institutions (McCowan and Bertolin, 2020).

In this chapter, I discuss how higher education in most of Latin America has expanded since the 1990s by relying heavily on the growth of second-tier private institutions, most of them of low quality, and how this has changed the nature and structure of higher education in Latin America in the past thirty years. Once a level of education that was largely organized around training elites for professional and leadership positions, higher education is now increasingly bifurcated. Part of it still trains high-level professionals, but most students attend "mass" institutions that absorb the increasing demand for university degrees but are riven by high dropout rates and provide relatively low-quality training to those who attend.

I also discuss how we can do much more to expand higher education access to lower class students, to make the higher education system more equitable in terms of how we subsidize students who attend, and to improve the quality of the new "mass" part of higher education. This includes a discussion of whether students from lower socioeconomic classes should be encouraged to attend some form of postsecondary vocational education, as done in Chile (Garcia de Fanelli, 2019), by expanding such alternatives to traditional universities and technical institutions, or whether we could focus on improving the quality of second-tier institutions. I present examples of how the higher education system can be more development oriented—how it can train for innovation in sectors that promise more diverse economic growth in the future. Finally, I suggest ways for the higher education system to motivate higher standards of training in occupations and sectors that play an important role in providing services such as education and health care to the 40 percent lowest income Latin Americans. After all, the key to high-quality, human capital–intensive services for those not getting them now is that the higher education system produce the professionals needed for delivering those services.

One of the biggest obstacles in improving higher education in Latin America is that the system is largely autonomous from direct government control. Autonomy of universities and other higher education institutions is important. Traditionally, autonomy is a buffer against authoritarian rule and protects the exchange of ideas from government control. At least for public universities autonomy can somewhat ensure that public funding will not be used to influence who is selected to teach in universities, what they are allowed to discuss in classes, and what they write. However, autonomy does have a downside. To a very great degree, autonomy means that the training of professionals in higher education institutions is self-regulated, either by professional associations (law, engineering, medicine, and nursing, for example) or the universities themselves. In some cases where the public sector is a major employer of professionals, such as teachers, course requirements are somewhat regulated by government. Governments may also test professionals before they are eligible to be hired, so the tests can be a form of curriculum regulation. But all this is rather indirect, and the result is that autonomy can mean great variation in the quality of the degree, and in some cases such as teaching, can result in low standards across most programs and great difficulty in changing those standards by any outside agency. I discuss this downside and what can be done to motivate universities to initiate improvements.

The Shape of Higher Education Expansion in Latin America

Before going on to discuss higher education policies that could improve its quality and equity, I want to establish just a few important points about what has happened to Latin American universities and other institutions granting bachelor's degrees in the past thirty years.

Considerable Regional Variation in Enrollment Growth

The first point is fairly obvious but worth restating: there has been rapid growth in the gross enrollment rate (GER, the percentage of eighteen- to twenty-four-year-olds attending higher education) since 1990, although enrollment growth has varied from country to country. For example, the GER in Chile increased from 20 to 90 percent of the age group; in Argentina, from 40 to 90 percent; and in Peru, from 30 to 70 percent (Table 10.1). On the other hand, Mexico's GER in higher education only increased from 15 to 38 percent, and several of the Central American countries also had increases that left their GERs under 30 percent (Table 10.1). It is important to note that the gross enrollment rate incudes repeaters who are older than twenty-four, and there are many students in Latin American higher education institutions who started late and are older than twenty-four years old. This would make the gross enrollment ratio higher than the true estimate of the proportion of eighteen- to twenty-four-year-olds enrolled in higher education. Further, in some Latin American countries, such as Chile, there are many postsecondary programs that grant three-year vocational degrees. True, this is tertiary enrollment, but it is not equivalent to what we usually think of as college degrees. All these factors bias the GER as a true measure of the proportion of eighteen- to twenty-four-year-olds attending a bachelor's degree–granting institution. Yet, there is no doubt that the proportion of eighteen- to twenty-four-year-olds attending higher education institutions at the end of the second decade of the twenty-first century is a lot higher than in 1990.

Increased Higher Education Privatization in Most Countries

The second point I want to make is that in a number of Latin American countries, the percentage of higher education students attending private, fee-charging institutions, many of them for-profit, is high and, in some, has increased even in the past twenty years (Table 10.2). There are three important exceptions to this trend: Argentina and Uruguay, which have relatively high gross enrollment rates in higher education, but have reached these levels mainly by expanding

Table 10.1   Gross Enrollment Rates, Higher Education, by Country, 1990–2017 (total student enrollment in tertiary education as a percentage of population aged eighteen to twenty-four years)

Country	1990	1995	2000	2005	2010	2015	2017
Argentina	38.2	37.0	53.2	63.8	73.9	86.0	90.0
Brazil	—	10.0	16.0	26.0	40.0	51.1	50.0
Chile	20.8	27.9	36.2	48.7	68.8	88.3	91.5
Colombia	13.9	16.1	23.2	29.2	39.4	55.7	60.4
Ecuador	19.5	18.2	26.0	34.0	38.0	45.5	—
Mexico	15.0	13.6	19.1	23.4	26.3	30.8	38.2
Paraguay	8.3	9.4	15.9	25.9	35.1	—	—
Peru	30.1	27.0	34.6	33.2	50.0	68.0	70.0
Uruguay	29.9	29.0	33.9	45.3	51.2	59.6	64.0
Venezuela	26.8	27.0	28.5	42.0	75.0	—	—
Costa Rica	26.7	27.0	27.0	27.0	43.0	53.6	55.6
El Salvador	16.1	22.0	21.5	23.1	26.2	28.1	28.7
Guatemala	7.0	8.2	9.0	14.5	16.0	21.8	—
Honduras	8.8	9.7	13.1	16.0	19.4	20.8	—
Panama	21.0	27.9	41.3	42.1	44.3	47.3	—
Cuba	21.1	13.8	22.2	62.5	95.3	35.9	40.3

Sources: UNESCO Statistical Institute, 2019. UNESCO STAT. See also World Bank (2021). *World Development Indicators.*

public universities; and Colombia, which has greatly expanded access to higher education since 1990 (Table 10.1) and has done so by significantly reducing the high proportion of students attending private institutions from 70 to 50 percent—that is, by increasing places in public universities (Table 10.2).

The default for most countries, however, has been to rely increasingly on private higher education for expanding places, or to keep the pace of expansion relatively low. A great example of the first default option is my own country, Peru, or our neighbors, Chile and Brazil. A good example of the second default option is Mexico, whose higher education system certainly expanded enrollment substantially, but in the twenty-five years up to 2015, had only increased the GER from 20 to 30 percent, the lowest level among the large countries in the region. Note that after 2015, the GER jumped in Mexico (Table 10.1), and so did the proportion of students attending private institutions (Table 10.2).

No doubt that we should support good private higher education as a valid and important way to help expand the preparation of the next generation of engineers, scientists, poets, lawyers, doctors,

Table 10.2   Enrollment in Private Higher Education Institutions, by Country, 2000–2018 (as percentage of total higher education enrollment)

Country	2000	2005	2010	2015	2018
Argentina	20	24	27	25	25
Brazil	65	72	73	74	73
Chile	72	75	82	85	84
Colombia	64	50	45	49	50
Mexico	30	33	32	30	35
Paraguay	58	57	70	70	—
Peru	47	51	62	71	72
Uruguay	11	14	16	17	17
Costa Rica	—	—	51	51	49
El Salvador	71	65	67	70	69
Guatemala	—	49 (2007)	37	43	—
Honduras	21	25	40	37	45
Panama	12 (2002)	21	36	34	—

Source: UNESCO Statistical Institute, 2021. UNESCO STAT.
Note: — = not available.

teachers, and public policymakers. Yet, the issue in Latin America is that we have private higher education that is even more bifurcated, quality wise, than public institutions, and despite the autonomy of public institutions, private higher education is usually much less regulated, or is subject to much lower standards. Thus, we have our tradition of excellent Catholic universities, often catering to the most privileged groups in our societies—including those families who want to send their children to a more "protected" educational environment than offered by the large public universities. We also have a spate of excellent new secular private universities that are both expensive and deliver a relatively high-quality preparation in economics, business, medicine, and law—fields that have high earnings returns for students who complete them.

At the same time, the vast majority of private institutions in places such as Brazil, Chile, and Peru are of low quality, and they are not necessarily attended by students from families with low income. In Brazil, for example, despite federal subsidies to private universities to admit low-income students partially or totally tuition free, the vast majority of students attending low-quality private institutions are from middle-class families in that country—these young people were just not able to get into the free public universities or into the higher quality private institutions (Carnoy et al., 2013). Faced with the problem of high proportions of students attending low-quality private institutions, the questions I would put out there are: (1) Is it a good long-run strategy to rely on the expansion of such low-quality private higher education institutions to satisfy increased demand? (2) Are there regulations that would improve the content and the quality of teaching in these types of private institutions? (3) Is it feasible to regulate higher education institutions?

It is important, I believe, to guarantee that all higher education institutions are delivering reasonable quality education—if nothing else, to protect families from spending money on services that cannot provide what they promise. Thus, answering the questions about low-quality private education as a key element of higher education expansion is crucial to any country's education strategy. I do understand that most governments don't want to get into this quality question. There would probably be significant political costs to raising the quality bar in private higher education. The payoff to completing a bachelor's degree is generally high in Latin America, so public perception that government is "restricting" access to higher education by raising the standards that institutions need to meet would not endear governments to the middle class. Although families have to pay a lot to send their children to even low-quality private universities, taking this option away from them could have political consequences. The alternative, of course, is to raise more public revenues and expand reasonable quality, public, higher education. Some countries (Argentina, Uruguay, and Mexico, for example) have done this. I further discuss all these alternatives below.

Decreased Public Spending per Student in Higher Education

If many Latin American governments are falling back on private investments to absorb the rapidly increasing demand for higher education, is this associated with decreased government investment in higher education? In *public* higher education as well? If a government, such as Brazil's, for example, devotes a very high fraction of its public spending to federal and state universities, which rely almost entirely on public monies for their financing, an increase in the percentage of students attending private institutions and paying for the operations of those institutions through tuition and fees, would reduce *public* spending per student in the system as a whole. This is precisely what allowing the expansion of private higher education financed directly by family-paid tuition fees is intended to do.

Table 10.3 shows how public spending for the total of students in the higher education system evolved in a number of countries in Latin America from 1998 to 2016. Spending here is measured by constant purchasing power parity dollars (PPP$), which means that all amounts shown reflect cost-of-living differences between countries and are equivalent to what goods cost in the United States. Measuring costs of education in terms of a basket of consumer goods is not very accurate, since how much higher educated labor—the biggest single item in a higher education budget—may vary in price from country to country in ways not perfectly tied to the cost of a basket of consumer goods. Nevertheless, the data in Table 10.3 suggest that, first, how much the governments of larger Latin American countries spent per student varied a lot, from about $1,000 in Peru to almost $7,000 in Mexico as measured by PPP. This way of estimating spending on higher education reflects government "effort" to fund students at this level of education—to some degree, a measure of how much each Latin American government considers higher education a "public good" and is therefore willing to devote more or fewer public funds to the totality of students attending. From that viewpoint, Mexico spends much more than Peru on higher education as a public good, but Mexico has expanded its higher education enrollment less than Peru (Table 10.1) and has not increased public spending per student whereas Peru has. Chile, Uruguay, and Costa Rica have also increased public spending per higher education student in the past twenty years. Brazil is an important example of a major decline in public spending per student.

Part of the difference in spending per student between Peru and Mexico is due to the much higher proportion of students attending private institutions in Peru, so we would get a different comparison by comparing public spending differences on public higher education students. This estimate assumes that none of the public money goes to private education. That is, we can divide total public spending per student by the percentage of higher education students who attend public institutions. This gives us an upper-bound estimate of public spending per public higher education student—upper bound because in most countries, part of public spending on higher education does go to students attending private institutions. In Chile, for example, a significant part of public spending goes to financing elite private universities through student grants and loans and research funding; and

Table 10.3   Public Spending per Student for the Total of Students Enrolled in Public and Private Higher Education Institutions, 1998–2016 (constant PPP$)

Country	1998	2000	2002	2004	2006	2008	2010	2012	2014	2016
Argentina	3,479	2,799	1,756	1,703	2,354	3,001	3,285	3,408	3,320	3,258
Brazil	9,510	6,737	5,547	4,226	4,440	4,042	4,362	4,575	4,809	5,075
Chile	2,936	2,753	2,652	2,483	2,052	2,251	3,228	3,350	4,108	4,837
Colombia	3,164	2,705	2,523	2,015	2,287	2,960	3,439	2,945	2,858	3,072
Mexico	6,009	6,373	6,659	6,120	6,107	6,566	6,733	6,330	6,932	5,929
Paraguay	—	3,308	1,503	1,378	1,518	1,570	1,514	—	—	—
Peru	—	750	818	976	978	1,058	1,138	1,218	1,298	1,382
Uruguay	—	2,541	2,027	2,474	2,685	3,875	5,546	—	—	5,381
Costa Rica	—	—	—	4,823	—	—	5,056	5,282	5,927	6,978
El Salvador	661	595	757	844	1,097	1,246	1,532	804	893	912
Guatemala	—	—	—	—	—	1,418	1,442	1,633	1,509	—
Honduras	—	—	—	—			2,160	2,495	2,485	—
Panama	—	4,582	4,639	4,093	—	—	4,663	4,834	—	—

Source: UNESCO Statistical Institute, 2021. UNESCO STAT.

in Brazil, the federal government has used public funds to subsidize private higher education institutions in the past ten years to underwrite the tuition of low-income students.

Table 10.4 shows the spending per student in constant PPP dollars for a group of the larger countries in Latin America under the assumption that all public spending goes to students in public higher education institutions. We have left Chile out of the graph because, for Chile, our assumption that no public spending goes to students in private institutions is clearly violated. Now we see that the $1,000 to $7,000 difference between Peru and Mexico has been somewhat reduced to a $4,500 to $9,300 in constant PPP dollars. Table 10.4 also shows that Brazil spends much more per student attending public institutions than do other countries. This is well documented in the literature (Carnoy et al., 2013). Chile may be on a par with Brazil in recent years, but we cannot state that definitively.

Table 10.4 also suggests the answer to a question I asked earlier—does increased reliance on private institutions to absorb the increasing demand for places in higher education reduce public spending on students in public institutions? The story is mixed— some countries' governments did reduce public spending per student as the percentage enrolled in private institutions increase; others absorbed much of the increasing demand through private institutions, but still increased public spending per student in public institutions.

In Peru, for example, government increased spending per public higher education student, with the caveat that, as I well know, Peru began this period among the countries in the region with the lowest cost public higher education institutions. Some increase in spending per student in Peru was called for no matter the enrollment expansion strategy. In Colombia, spending per public higher education student declined even as the percentage of students attending private institutions also declined. In Brazil, public spending on public higher education students declined for ten years, but most recently increased. Conversely, Argentina and Uruguay absorbed some of their increase in higher education enrollment through expansion of private higher education, but increased spending per public higher education pupil. Thus, we cannot make a clear argument that expanding enrollment through a greater reliance on an increase in private higher education reduces government spending per student in public higher education. What we can say is that some countries in the region are increasing public funding per student and others are not.

We can also argue that most governments in the region spend relatively little per student when measured in values "comparable" to spending per student in Europe, the United States, and Canada. I would argue that the low level of funding is a major reason for generally low-quality public higher education in Latin America. However, when we observe the level of PPP dollars spent on students in public institutions in Brazil or Mexico, they are similar to the levels in developed countries. There are some very high-quality public universities in

Table 10.4 Estimated Public Spending per Public Higher Education Student, 2000–2015 (constant PPP$)

Country	2000	2005	2010	2015
Argentina	3,499	2,593	4,505	4,788
Brazil	19,483	16,358	16,057	20,224
Colombia	7,511	3,901	6,210	5,565
Mexico	9,151	9,321	9,939	9,348
Paraguay	7,875	7,815	5,008	5,167
Peru	1,415	1,553	2,958	4,539
Uruguay	2,852	2,883	6,602	7,221

Source: UNESCO Statistical Institute, 2021. UNESCO STAT.
Note: Public spending per total (public + private) enrollment in higher education (Table 10.3) divided by percentage of students enrolled in public institutions (Table 10.1 minus percentage of students enrolled in private institutions from Table 10.2).

those countries, but, on average, public higher education institutions in Mexico and Brazil are far less equipped and have far poorer capacity for cutting-edge teaching and research than average institutions in developed countries. Thus, money is important, but not sufficient to achieve the quality we in the region should have to develop the highly skilled labor needed for our continued development.

Two-Tiered Higher Education

What I have been leading up to is that much more so than in developed countries, most Latin American higher education systems have expanded enrollment by creating highly bifurcated, two-tiered systems, where one tier is not only selective, but students in those institutions also have access to many more resources than students in the second tier. I realize that the selective versus less or nonselective higher education tiers exist in every country, and that the resources per student are generally greater in the higher than in the lower tier everywhere. However, in many Latin American countries, the differences are much larger. For example, in the United States, a typical difference in spending per student between selective and nonselective public universities is about two to one. About 60 percent of four-year university students in the United States attend these public institutions. In Brazil, on the other hand, the spending per student in the public higher education sector as a whole compared to spending per student in private higher education increased from about 1.3 to 1 in 2003 to more than 3 to 1 in 2010 (Carnoy et al., 2013: Figure 4.6). Remember, more than 70 percent of students in Brazil attended private institutions in Brazil in 2010. In the public higher education sector, federal universities, on average, spend more per student than state universities. An important caveat: two of the most elite (and high cost) higher education institutions in Brazil are state, not federal, universities—the University of São Paulo and the University of Campinas, also in the state of São Paulo.

If this greater spending gap we observe in Brazil among higher and lower tier institutions is similar in other Latin American countries, it could mean that most students in Latin America now receive a very different version of higher education than those 15 percent attending more elite institutions (Carnoy et al., 2013). We could jump to the conclusion that this also means that low-income students receive, on average much lower quality higher education than higher social class students. That is generally true, since most lower-income students attend less selective institutions. But what this large spending per student gap really means is that most *middle social class* and many higher social class students receive a low-quality education, since only a small percentage of low-income students have access to institutions awarding bachelor's degrees.

Just a reminder: income distribution in Latin America is very unequal, so although with economic growth the middle class has increased substantially and poverty has decreased in the past twenty years, a high fraction of Latin American families have relatively little education and have low incomes. For example, in Brazil in 2015, more than 50 percent of those in the labor force earned 0–1 minimum wages, and only 3.5 percent had 6 minimum wages or more. Yet, only about 10–11 percent of higher education students came from families with 0–1 minimum wages, and about 30 percent came from families with 6 minimum wages or more. This means that a person born into a family earning 0–1 minimum wages—the bottom 50 percent on the income distribution—has 2.4 percent of the chance to go to higher education as someone born into a family with 6 minimum wages or more. If I come from a low-income family, my chance of attending a top 20 percent selective institution in Brazil is less than 1 percent of the chance of a high income (6 minimum wages or more) attending such an institution. The point I want to make, though, is that the chances of a low-income young person attending even one of the bottom 20 percent selective higher education institutions in Brazil are much lower than the chances of young people from high-income families—it only climbs to about 5 percent of the chances of someone from a high-income family (Fonseca, 2019). And this is despite the affirmative action law passed by the Brazilian government in 2012 that awards a significant fraction of places in federal (and some state) universities to Black and Indigenous students who attend public secondary schools. Although affirmative action policies have improved the probability of lower-income students attending higher education and more elite higher education, the probability is still low (see also McCowan and Bertolin, 2020).

These are grim statistics, but they tell us that in highly unequal societies such as those in Latin America, access to any kind of higher education is limited for youth from families with low socioeconomic status (SES), and when there is access, it is likely to very low-quality institutions. I might add that access is also most likely in studying for relatively lower paying professions. Programs such as engineering, law, and medicine are much more elite than pedagogy and humanities, in large part because the former are more expensive when attending a private higher education institution and more selective to enter in a public institution.

Is Higher Education Financing in Latin America Rational?

The financing of higher education varies from country to country, but except for Chile—where, since 1973, all universities charge full tuition, including public institutions—public higher education is free for those who can qualify. At one extreme, anyone with a valid secondary school degree in Argentina has access to a public higher education institution, although more recently the more prestigious ones, such as the University of Buenos Aires, require students to successfully complete an extra year of preparation before gaining admission. Many countries, such as Brazil, Chile, Colombia, and Mexico, give students entrance exams at the end of secondary school, and the score on that exam determines whether they will gain entrance to a particular program at a particular university. Higher scoring students in these countries tend to enter prestigious free public universities. In Chile, because of high tuition in all universities, the choice is less between public or private but rather between more prestigious and less prestigious. Further, in Chile, government loans and scholarships are only available for high-scoring students admitted to the top group of fewer than thirty institutions.

The financing of higher education is a subject of passionate political debate, but it is also important in defining the role of government and the use of public revenues. The main argument for free public higher education is that, just like education at lower levels, it should be a right—a purely pubic good, not just available to those who can afford it. There is even an economic argument for providing large public subsidies for higher education because graduates not only contribute to their own higher earnings, but also contribute to spillover effects called "externalities" that raise the productivity of other workers and benefit society at large (Carnoy et al., 2013).

Yet, there is plenty of evidence that higher education in Latin America, for all the benefits that its graduates may spin off for the general public good, also provides very large earnings benefits for those who complete their degrees, and even some benefits for those who do not complete one (Fonseca, 2019). The expected private rate of return to a university degree in the late 1990s and early 2000s in Argentina, Brazil, Chile, Colombia, Mexico, and Peru was between 12 and 20 percent annually over work lifetime (Carnoy, 2011: Table 4). Although it is likely that rates to university degrees fell in Latin America as income distribution became more equal (Lustig et al., 2016), completing higher education still means a substantial increase in earnings throughout the region. This suggests that asking students and their families to share in the cost of higher education is not unreasonable. Indeed, in countries where a high fraction of students attend private institutions, students and their families do pay a high fraction of the cost of higher education.

The question, then, is whether those who enter *public* universities—now free of tuition almost everywhere in the region—should also share in the costs of their education. A case could be made for free or very low tuition in a public university if the majority of students attending public institutions were from lower social class families. However, that is not at all the current situation, as I argued earlier. Many of the best universities in Latin America are public universities, and in many countries they are among the best funded institutions, and their student bodies are disproportionately upper middle–income students, especially in the highest payoff programs, such as medicine, law, engineering, and economics. In Brazil, for example, even in 2011–2014, almost 45–50 percent of the students in the federal universities were from families in the top 4 percent of the Brazilian income distribution. Among students studying law, the percentage from the top 4 percent of families was even higher, over 65 percent (Fonseca, 2019). In effect, these relatively wealthy students, most of whom attended private secondary schools, are being given a free ride to earn high incomes in the future at public expense. At the same time, the percentage of students from lower-income families attending the most selective 10 percent or 20 percent of Brazilian institutions represented less than 15 percent of all students.

The figures in university are probably less unequal in Chile and Argentina because of the high rates of secondary school completion in Chile and the high rate of admission of secondary school graduates to universities in Argentina. Most low-income secondary school graduates who go on to postsecondary institutions in Chile attend tertiary nonuniversity professional education (Garcia de Fanelli, 2019)—a category that is essentially nonexistent in Brazil. Similarly, the proportion of students from low-income families attending universities is probably only somewhat less unequal in Colombia and Mexico than in Brazil.

One culprit, of course, is that low-income students attend less resourced primary and secondary schools, and they do much worse on university entrance exams at the end of secondary school. Another culprit is that they are less informed about how to gain access to good quality institutions, even if qualified. The Chilean largely privately financed higher education system aside (with its inequalities), does it make sense for students from high-income families, most of whom attended private secondary school, to get a free ride in university? I think not, especially if the money raised through charging some tuition to those who can pay could be used to expand high-quality, free, public higher education for lower-income students and to provide additional preparatory education for these students so that they are ready to succeed at such institutions.

When I was president of Peru, the then rector of the elite, highly selective, agricultural university in Lima, La Molina, which produces many brilliant agricultural engineers and entrepreneurs in our country, responsible in the past thirty years for the development of Peru's important export agriculture (asparagus, artichokes, fruit), decided to ask students' families to contribute to the university an annual fee equal to the tuition they had paid in secondary school. Almost all complied, and greatly increased the budget of the university so it could maintain its expensive laboratories and extension services. La Molina, by law, could not charge tuition, but it could ask for contributions. Any student who had attended a public secondary school did not have to contribute, of course, and chances were, that this would be a student from a lower-ncome family.

Let me return to the case of Brazil. In 2017, there were 1 million students in federal universities. Assuming that 45 percent of them were from families with 6 minimum wages or more, and that that group of students could pay, on average, $2,500 in tuition, this would raise about $1.1 billion in revenues. Assuming a cost per student for the 1.8 million students in all public institutions in 2017, of $5,000–$6,000 in current dollars, this means a total budget of about $9.9 billion. Thus, this modest tuition fee—the monthly fee for a course at an average private university, would raise about 11 percent of the total budget for public higher education.

I know that it is not a popular position to charge fees at public universities, but I like the La Molina concept of charging university students the amount of tuition they paid at secondary school, or, even better, the alternative idea that once graduates who attended free public institutions start earning income, they are charged an additional tax on that income—the more they earn, the more they pay back to the system. A third alternative is to charge tuition but, at the same time, provide all students the possibility to borrow through a relatively low-interest student loan program. One increasingly popular version of loan programs is the income contingent loan (ICL), where students borrow money to attend higher education and pay it back not as a fixed amount but based on their ability to pay when they graduate. So if a doctor was trained at public expense and makes a good income, she would pay more than a teacher who was trained at a public university. The balance on the loan would be forgiven after a certain number of years or the death of the loan recipient (see Nascimento, 2018).

A wrinkle on the ICL plan or any plan involving tuition payments is to forgive a student's tuition or forgive future loan repayments if the graduate spends five years working in the public service—for example, as a teacher in a public school, a doctor in a rural area, an engineer in a low-income community, a police officer, or a firefighter. For example, the Chilean government has a program to attract students with high grades and high university entrance test scores into studying to be teachers by offering them free tuition to enroll in teacher education programs. This inventive program does have a positive effect on drawing higher-scoring high school students into teaching, and they end up teaching largely in low-income public or private subsidized schools (Perez, 2020). The good part of any of these plans is that they favor low-income students or low-earning students and those working in jobs that have high social payoffs rather than high private payoffs. Just to be clear, none of these plans work unless there is a tuition fee in public higher education or students are effectively charged a fee by paying additional taxes once they leave or graduate from a public higher education institution. I also want to emphasize that all of these efforts to make the higher education system more "efficient" and "equitable" financially should be accompanied by well-funded scholarship programs and investment in information directed at very low-income high school students, who are now severely underrepresented in Latin American higher education.

Affirmative Action

Affirmative action programs are controversial. The essence of the controversy is whether "leveling the playing field" by favoring disadvantaged groups in access to university should displace more "meritorious" young people from the best higher education institutions. To what extent should "forced" equalization penalize students who are higher achievers but not members of a disadvantaged group? As an indication of how deeply rooted in our societies is the notion of so-called merit, instituting affirmative action policies has involved the nation's high courts in considering such programs' constitutional legality.

Besides the displacement argument, there are other critiques made of these equalization programs. One is that despite their intention to bring more talented disadvantaged individuals into the mainstream of society, they mainly benefit only the already very advantaged of the disadvantaged. Another critique is that the disadvantaged students admitted into universities under affirmative action are likely to do poorly in better institutions and are less likely to succeed than if they had just attended second-tier institutions where they would be more comfortable and confident.

Despite these arguments against using this mechanism to equalize access, some Latin American countries have legislated affirmative action programs to increase the number of lower social class and Black students attending first-tier universities. The most established of these programs is in Brazil, but Colombia, Ecuador, Honduras, and Uruguay have also made some moves in this direction (Hernandez, 2013). Brazil began implementing workplace affirmative action policies in federal workplaces in 2001 for *preto* (Black) and *pardo* (Brown) Brazilians. Some states have also implemented similar programs for public jobs. In the early 2000s, a variety of public universities voluntarily began affirmative action admissions, and by 2010, more than 100 higher education institutions had adopted affirmative action programs that included race-based quotas as well as social class quotas that were based on whether students attended public high schools (Downie and Lloyd, 2010). Brazilian courts upheld the constitutionality of these programs, and in April 2012, the Federal Supreme Court ruled that the University of Brasilia's affirmative action policy was constitutionally valid.

After this ruling, in August 2012, the federal legislature passed the Law of Social Quotas, which "requires federal public universities to reserve half of all new admission spots for public high school graduates. Half of those reserve spots are set aside for students whose household family income falls below 1.5 times the minimum wage . . . per family member. The law also mandates that within that 50 percent set aside, spots be reserved for Afro-descendants and persons of indigenous ancestry, proportional to their relative populations within each state" (Hernandez, 2013, p. 6).

Not surprisingly, studies show that affirmative action in Brazil has had a significant impact on the enrollment of Black students and lower-income students in public universities (Carnoy et al., 2013: Chapter 8). Also not surprisingly, a higher fraction of affirmative action admissions enter humanities and social sciences rather than engineering and medicine (Dias Lopes, 2017), and when universities ran the programs before the government passed the affirmative action bill in 2012, in those institutions not using strict systems of checking the validity of affirmative action applications, there was considerable abuse of self-identification (Mulholland, 2005). However, contrary to expectations and to critics' claims, a number of studies of programs at individual universities suggest that Black and lower-income students admitted under affirmative action quotas perform no less well than the students admitted through normal channels (Childs and Stromquist, 2015; Hernandez, 2013).

How Can Higher Education Systems Contribute to Greater Equality?

In this chapter, I have tried to describe how Latin America's higher education systems are expanding to incorporate increasing numbers of students, but how, at the same time, the structures of that expansion are not oriented toward the welfare of those from the lower half of the region's income distribution. In theory, expanding higher education enrollment and the number of graduates entering the labor force with bachelor's degrees should drive down the payoff to higher education, and, all other things equal, should therefore help equalize income distribution. This may have happened in Brazil after 2000— the rate of return to investing in higher education did fall and income distribution did equalize somewhat (Ferreira et al., 2016).

However, the case I am making is that the contribution of such an expansion to greater income equality and social mobility could be considerably increased by lowering the financial and other barriers to higher education for profoundly underrepresented lower-income students, by substantially increasing the quality of the second-tier institutions that most of that group of students attends, and by increasing underrepresented students' access to first-tier institutions.

I have argued that most Latin American countries have chosen to move from elite to mass higher education by allowing for the rapid growth of largely low-quality tuition-charging private institutions. In some ways, this has an "equalizing" effect because most students attending such institutions are from middle- and higher-income families. So, at least, better off students unable to get into the tuition-free public universities have to pay the full cost of their higher education. On the other hand, going private has a dis-equalizing effect because the financial barriers to entry to private institutions for low-income students make attending them difficult. Students from low-income families who manage to finish secondary school are likely to average lower college entrance scores partly because they attend lower-resourced K–12 schools. It is therefore harder for them to gain access to (more selective) free public universities. Thus, we have the ironic situation that although a relatively low percentage of students who attend mass private higher education in Latin America are from poor families, for a relatively high percentage of students from poor families, these private, tuition-charging institutions are the only higher education option available.

The situation I am describing is clearest in the region's largest country, Brazil. The way Brazil's federal government has responded to increase access for students from low-income families is instructive, but, to my mind, not adequate. All Brazil's federal universities now have quotas for Black students and, in many cases, require that to qualify under the quota, students must have attended a public secondary school. In addition, the federal government provides subsidies to private universities to accept very low-income students who cannot pay tuition and provides loans for somewhat less low-income students to pay tuition. All these measures have increased the percentage of students from low-income families attending federal and private higher education institutions.

Why do I say that this is inadequate? For two reasons: first, many of the private higher education institutions attended by students from low-income families using federal scholarships and loans are of very low quality. Second, without a considerable expansion of better-resourced public institutions, the number of low-income students brought into higher education has still been very limited. It is also the case that a large expansion of students from lower-income families into higher education will require additional measures, such as those at the University of Buenos Aires requiring students to prepare for an extra year after secondary school to gain entrance at UBA.

A completely different argument also supports the expansion of higher quality second-tier public institutions. Besides the ability of governments to subsidize such institutions directly by keeping student tuition and fees below the actual costs of providing educational services, governments are also less likely to implement policies that drive quality down to increase profits. Indeed, this has been a major critique of public education—namely, that it is inefficient. Yet, the kinds of efficiencies implemented by private higher educational enterprises—

in an industry where it is difficult for the consumer to know whether the product is "good" or not—are often to save money by reducing quality. This tends to hurt students and their families, who have no way of comparing the education they are getting with the higher quality education at more expensive, higher-tier institutions.

For me, this is a major reason for the public sector to be the main provider of mass higher education. At the same time, the public sector has to come to the understanding that these second-tier institutions are the "heart and soul" of the mass higher education system. They are the providers responsible for producing a mass of reasonably high-quality, university-trained professionals for the private and public sectors— these are the large numbers of nurses, teachers, engineers, public administrators, and private managers who have learned the problem solving skills to be effective in twenty-first-century labor markets.

This brings me back to the subject of how we can create a higher education system that produces the high skilled labor needed to fill the service gaps faced by the lower-income half of our populations. In earlier chapters I argued for investing in better schools in rural and low-income urban areas, in public preschools, in improved health care and nutrition, in quality education for Indigenous peoples, and for better physical infrastructure in low-income areas. How can we achieve all this without the teachers, nurses, doctors, engineers, agricultural experts, and public administrators who can provide these services to our poor at a high level of quality? Ultimately, it is our higher education systems that have to form the human capital that can "deliver the goods." In much of Latin America, for example, we lack enough well-trained teachers to fill our rural and low-income urban classrooms and the doctors and nurses to staff clinics accessible to the rural poor. A very high percentage of teachers work in schools not far from where they went to secondary school. So we need high-quality, public higher education institutions throughout the country so that secondary school graduates can learn professional skills and use them locally. As long as the only way to get a good higher education is to come to large urban centers, we will always have a shortage of high-quality labor in our most human resource–poor regions. Simultaneously, local higher education institutions need to specialize in the training of professionals who can improve the quality of infrastructure and services for these poorer regions.

I have focused on this second-tier issue because I think it is the most misunderstood of what makes higher education systems successful in both promoting economic growth, helping to equalize opportunity for the mass of students who do not attend elite institutions, and producing the well-trained service sector professionals who then deliver higher quality education, health care, and other core services to the bottom 40 percent of Latin Americans who currently have very limited access to them.

However, that does not mean I don't care about what the elite higher education institutions are doing in Latin America. Their role is also key for promoting economic growth, innovation, and especially developing leadership with a social purpose. In terms of the first two of these objectives, there is a great example of such an institution in Peru. La Molina University has for years produced well-trained agriculture engineers and entrepreneurs. During the past half-century, the graduates of La Molina have transformed the agriculture sector in Peru into an export powerhouse of asparagus, grapes, avocados, mangos, and other nontraditional crops. These have required new technologies and sophisticated business strategies, and this is precisely what La Molina has taught its graduates to develop. There are other examples in Latin America of higher education institutions producing graduates with high-level technological and entrepreneurial skills—the National University of Mexico has one of the best medical schools in the world; the two leading universities in Chile, the University of Chile and La Universidad Católica have produced the technical and intellectual leaders of that country for more than a century; the two state universities in the state of São Paulo have done the same in Brazil, and the Federal University of Rio trained a generation of Brazilian software developers back in the 1980s, among other scientific research leaders.

The question is how to continue this mission, and, in my view, to do this we have to invest heavily in the public university as the promoter and producer of high-quality *public* leaders and business leaders who have a larger social vision than simply profits. This includes environmental responsibility and a broad conception of the social good, but it also must include an understanding that the public sector has an important role to play beyond simply fostering capital accumulation, high profits, and a good business climate. The distribution of income and wealth is a public concern and paying attention to these issues and the environment is crucial for the health of private business as well. It is good public sector leadership that sets the tone for the long-run concerns and investments in society, and the discussions of what that means should take place in public universities.

11

The Crucial Role of Sustained Public Leadership

In the first ten chapters of this book, I discussed what I consider to be the most important challenges we face in providing great education and more equal opportunity to every Latin American child. I also analyzed how best to meet these challenges, based on the extensive empirical research available. Evidence helps us understand both the essence of each of the issues we have covered and what appears to work in improving student learning and making education and society more equal. Evidence should also make us realists in our expectations of how much education can and cannot do in solving our social problems. But we should also be idealists in demanding much more from our educational systems than they have delivered until now.

I have laid out all this analysis to make clear what needs to be done. But this does not guarantee that appropriate action will be taken to significantly improve the educational system or make it fairer. In some version of such action, we might be able to rely on the private sector—businesses, nongovernmental agencies, and foundations—to get involved and actually make a difference on a number of fronts. There is a history of that in the United States, especially in private philanthropy for Black education in the eighteenth and early nineteenth century, in higher education for the past 150 years, and, more recently, in broader educational reforms. Similarly, in our Latin American region, Brazil is a good example of private foundations actively pushing educational improvement (Tarlau and Moeller, 2019).

However, government is the big player in education, and public leadership is crucial for making the big changes happen—the kind of changes we are talking about in this book. Most of these changes require simultaneously increasing and redistributing public funding for education, health services, housing, clean water, and other investments in human capital. They involve large sums of money, much more than the private sector is willing and able to come up with. In democratic regimes, they require intricate institutional cooperation between the executive and legislative branches (Scartascini et al., 2010), and, in education, between the government and educational institutional actors, such as teachers' unions—in most countries of Latin America, teachers' unions are powerful politically and have a lot to say about educational reforms. Most of the changes also require political mobilizations, either from the grassroots, which pushes the government to act (see, for example, Tarlau, 2019), or, as I focus on here, mobilizations around greater equity or better quality schools, driven by political leadership and broader civic coalitions around political leadership.

The underlying premise of my discussion in this chapter is the crucial point made by Scartascini and colleagues (2010) that long-term public policy reforms require a respect by political players for the rules of the democratic process—it is this adherence to the rules of the game that promote the cooperation needed for systematic change. I also agree with Juan Carlos Navarro (2007) that the major education reforms in Latin America have been institutional. The case I make in this chapter is that for such institutional reforms to have a significant effect on the educational lives of students—especially low-income students—the reforms have to be carried out over a long period of time. Therefore these changes must be conceived as part of a long-term vision of change and be supported by a continuity of leadership that transcends the usual term of office of a single person.

Having served in a national leadership position, I am fully conscious of how difficult it is to figure out what the best changes to make are and how to mobilize support for them. Nevertheless, there are examples of countries and states within federal countries that have made enormous progress in developing more effective and more equitable educational systems. These have been characterized by very impressive improvements in student performance, especially for low-income students. One common feature of these cases is that they had sustained leadership either from individual politicians or, more usually, from a coalition of political actors who provided consistent policy direction for a significant period of time—usually a minimum of two decades. In all these cases, educational improvement and greater equity were a constant focus of government leadership over a substantial period of time, considerably longer than one five-year presidential term.

There are five more features of these successful transformations of educational systems. The first is that educational reform and improvement was central to the government's economic and social development policy—it was a star player in the overall strategy of the government to implement broader social change. The second is that education curriculum standards were raised and assistance was provided to teachers to implement those standards. The third is that school accountability for improvement was built into the everyday operation of schools and the overall system. The fourth is that although driven in part by progressive ideals, the reforms were also evidence based. Finally, in each of these cases, leadership was able to mobilize increased resources for education and spend these resources strategically, usually raising the relative amount of resources going to more disadvantaged students.

In this chapter, I want to close my impassioned push for improving the lot of Latin America's marginalized poor and investing in Latin America's human resources by presenting a few of these relevant case studies of educational leadership and showing how, in each case, this leadership was able to accomplish its goal of transforming the educational system under its jurisdiction.

In all these cases the major expansions, improvements, and modest equalizations in education were associated with increased economic growth and, in some cases, were also associated with declining income inequality. That said, we need to be very cautious in leaping to any conclusions regarding the effects of educational expansion and quality improvements on either income growth or income inequality Although increasing human skills in the labor force through more and better education contributes to economic growth and can contribute to decreasing economic inequality (Lopez-Calva and Lustig, 2010), education alone cannot improve the economic growth rate; equalize income and wealth distribution; or eliminate poverty, wage discrimination, or racism in our societies. Good macroeconomic policy, political stability, and the rule of law go a long way toward improving economic growth even if educational quality remains unchanged, and without sustained economic growth, it is very difficult to alleviate poverty, even with drastic educational improvement. Further, progressive taxation and the kinds of policies recommended in this book— such as shifting spending to conditional cash transfers, improving nutrition and health care, providing clean water and decent housing, and reducing violence in poor communities, as well as shifting educational spending into these low-income communities—are more directly related to more equal income distribution than increasing the number of years children go to school or even increasing how much they learn in a given year of schooling.

These cases also provide evidence for an "opposite" relation between economic growth and improved schooling: it is much easier when the economy is growing to achieve sustained increases in needed resources for improving education and to provide more equal opportunity for the poor and marginalized in society. I stressed this in *The Shared Society*, and I emphatically stress it again here.

The cases of sustained educational leadership I discuss in this chapter had one more feature in common. They occurred in a democratic political context. Thus, the leaders or sets of leaders that implemented these policies were subject to accountability to the people they governed, not to the military or to the dictatorship of a military- or police-supported ruling party. There are many instances of communist countries that developed rather high performing and rather equal educational systems—the Soviet Union, the People's Republic of China, Cuba, and Vietnam, for example. It is interesting to discuss how this was accomplished in these countries (see Carnoy and Samoff, 1989, and Carnoy et al., 2007, for this discussion). However, because I believe that democratic ideals and living in a democracy are so important for human progress, these authoritarian examples are much less relevant to accomplishing our educational goals and a more equal society. To the contrary, the very process of building better and more equal educational systems in a democratic political context can help deepen democracy and make our Latin American societies much better and more equal places to live and work.

Cases Studies of Successful Educational Leadership

North Carolina, 1980–2000

It is not well known in international circles, but the state of North Carolina, in the bottom fourth of US states by per capita GDP in 1980, with a diverse student population (22 percent African American) and a history of racial segregation, implemented a series of high impact educational reforms beginning in the late 1970s. These reforms increased student mathematics achievement scores on the US National Assessment of Educational Progress (NAEP) more rapidly in eleven years, 1992–2003, than increases in any other state in the United States. The gain in eighth grade mathematics in that period, adjusted for changes in students' family academic resources over time, was 27 points, almost 0.8 standard deviations. The scores continued to increase at a slower pace until 2013. Even so, when mathematics scores are adjusted for students' family background and race, North Carolina's eighth grade achievement was the highest in the United States in 2003 and the second highest in 2013 (behind Massachusetts, which had its own major education reforms in the 1990s) (Carnoy et al., 2015a).

No single intervention explains this very large and sustained increase in student mathematics performance, but two factors definitely had a major influence on changing the educational system in the state: the first was leadership from the longest serving governor in the state's history, James Hunt Jr., who helped transform North Carolina in his two eight-year terms (1977–1985 and 1993–2001) through remarkable economic change, education reforms, and cultural growth, including progress toward racial integration. The second factor was that the reforms were sustained over more than two decades.

Hunt brought African Americans and women into high positions, enforced civil rights in the state, and developed a strong business climate to attract electronic, pharmaceutical, and biotechnology firms. In his first eight years as governor, he set up a primary reading program, reduced class size, created dropout prevention programs, and established the North Carolina School of Science and Mathematics. In his second term, he focused on expanding early childhood education (Smart Start) and improving teaching. Thus, from the mid-1970s until 2001, the state's leadership was dedicated to creating a good business climate, supporting inclusive policies for minorities and women, and transforming the educational system.

A 1998 analysis of North Carolina (and Texas) educational reforms undertaken for the National Education Goals Panel (James Hunt was one of eight governors on that panel) suggests that the great impact of the reforms was the result of

> establishing clear learning objectives by grade through state-wide learning standards; implementing new state-wide assessments closely linked to the learning standards; establishing a system of accountability with both sanctions and rewards linked to assessment results; establishing a computerized system of feedback on test score performance at the student, classroom, schools and district level that can be used for diagnostic purposes; emphasizing strongly that all students were expected to meet the standards; deregulating the teaching and school environment and giving teachers and administrators more local control and increased flexibility in determining how to meet the standards;

sustaining the system of assessment and accountability without significant changes over [many] years; explicit shifting of resources to schools with more disadvantaged students. (Grissmer and Flanagan, 1998: 19–20)

The business community played a crucial role at the strategic and legislative level in developing and funding key organizations to discuss the reforms and mobilize support for legislation. "A handful of businessmen . . . devoted considerable time and energy to learning the education issues, [formed] relationships with key stakeholders and remained involved over long time periods" (Grissmer and Flanagan, 1998: 25). A Commission on Education for Economic Growth prepared the first comprehensive reform agenda in 1984. The commission recommended pay increases and a pilot development program for teachers and increased funding for school facilities and for basic education. The next round of reform, organized through the North Carolina Public School Forum, composed of business leaders, educators, and state policymakers, which produced a strategic plan in late 1988.

The major principles of the strategic plan called for alignment of standards, curriculum and assessment tests, called for a strong system of accountability at the school building level with the deregulation of the education environment and shifting more control and flexibility to the local level. Accountability included publishing school report cards based on assessment performance and other measures and linking teacher career development and pay to student performance. The report also called for stronger training for principals and increased attention to early childhood programs. Provisions were passed for "taking over" schools or school systems based on sustained poor performance as well as mechanisms of intervention and support for such districts. . . . Partly as a response to this plan, North Carolina undertook the development of statewide learning standards by grade and new assessment testing linked to those standards. The standards and assessment tests were created based both on the NCTM [National Council of Mathematics Teachers] national standards as well as being aligned with the national NAEP tests. . . . Funding was also provided for extensive professional development for elementary school teachers based on the new curriculum and textbooks aligned to the standards. . . . While achieving a higher quality teaching force remains an important goal, the evidence to date indicates that the current teaching force is capable of producing achievement gains if given an appropriate organizational environment and working conditions. (Grissom and Flanagan, 1998: 31–33)

A final element of this educational transformation in North Carolina was that it took place during a period of relatively high economic growth—in part stimulated by the pro-growth policies initiated by the first Hunt administration—and a major increase in per pupil spending, certainly made easier by the increases in state tax revenues accruing from economic growth. In the years (1980–1990) preceding North Carolina's large test score gains in the 1990s, the state increased per pupil real spending (adjusted for inflation) by 46 percent compared to a national average of 20 percent (Texas increased per pupil spending in the 1980s by 43 percent). Although this was a major increase in spending, a number of other states (especially in the Northeast) increased spending more. And even with the increase, North Carolina per pupil spending remained considerably below the US average, and still does (NCES, 2000: Table 169; NCES, 2016: Table 236.75).

In sum, North Carolina drastically changed its educational system in the 1980s and 1990s, orienting it toward increasing student achievement. The state was able to do so through a concerted effort from political, business, and educational leaders to raise curriculum standards and to reorganize the system to assist teachers and schools to meet those new standards. The state also put in place a strong accountability system that provided a steady stream of information to schools and teachers about their progress toward raising student achievement. The effort was certainly successful, and it was just as successful for low-income students as for high-income students. Critics argue that it was a "business model," emphasizing teaching to standards-based tests, but it also included devolving most responsibility to schools and teachers for reaching ambitious goals, and it included major emphasis on improving the university system, increasing minority educational attainment, and supporting scientific research and high-end job growth, all of which benefited previously marginalized groups in the state.

The main lesson is that none of this would have been possible without a long-term, sustained effort to transform education, the economy, and society in the state, and without the combined leadership of the governor, business executives, and educators who believed in this process.

Chile, 1990–2018

The Chilean economy went through a period of severe restructuring during the early years of the military regime (1975–1982). Neoliberals claimed that the free-market privatization and anti-inflation reforms put in place by the Chicago Boys in the 1970s were responsible for the Chilean "miracle" of much higher growth in Chile during the 1980s than in Latin America as a whole. However, at least part of the improvement in the quality of life during this period was the paradoxical result of the right-wing military expanding public health and nutrition services. That is, by the early 1980s, the Chilean government had reverted to considerable public sector intervention in the economy (Drèze and Sen, 2002). Despite this and the higher levels of economic growth stimulated by many of the reforms of the 1970s, development in this period was marked by greatly increased inequality (Ruis-Tagle, 1998) and relatively high levels of poverty (almost 30 percent in 1987). With the formal end of the military dictatorship in 1990, a left of center democratically elected coalition came to power and remained in political control until 2010, when a right-wing politician, Sebastian Pinera, was elected. In 2014, with the reelection of Michelle Bachelet, a socialist, the coalition returned to power and continued its earlier political economic agenda.

This period of twenty years of coalition rule (1990–2010) drastically shifted economic policy toward a much greater emphasis on social equalization. Poverty rates were reduced by more than one-half in the 1990s, most due to relatively high rates of economic growth, but about 40 percent due to social policies (Wodon, 2000). Income inequality also began to fall substantially in the 2000s, but even so, Chile's income inequality remains very high, comparable to the most unequal Latin American countries.

In the context of this forty-year historical trajectory, Chile's educational system also went through radical changes, first in the 1970s and early 1980s, and then in a different direction in the 1990s and 2000s. Until 1973, higher education in Chile was free, but a relatively small percentage of the age cohort attended universities. The system was largely financed with the export tax on copper, Chile's main source of foreign trade revenue. When the military took power, they appropriated this copper tax for themselves and made higher education largely self-funded through student tuition. Also, in 1981, they implemented a voucher system, in which students could attend privately run primary and secondary schools at government expense. Primary and secondary school students received the same amount of funding whether they attended private or public schools. The fraction of students attending private schools subsidized by government funds increased steadily in the 1980s and continues today, with more than 50 percent now in such schools, with another 7–8 percent in elite private schools that do not accept vouchers. In the late 1980s, the government also implemented a national test given to fourth graders in even years and eighth graders in odd years. In the 1990s, a tenth grade test was added, and in the 2000s, the fourth grade test was applied every year.

The voucher reform was based on an idea that Milton Friedman had originated in the 1950s that the public education system was a monopoly and that school competition and choice would increase family satisfaction and reduce the price of schooling, increasing cost-efficiency (Friedman, 1962). Public subsidies for private schooling through vouchers, combined with a national test in which the results were given to schools and eventually made public on a school-by-school basis, were designed to give parents increased choice of schools along with "quality" information about schools as measured by test scores to inform that choice. Also consistent with Friedman's notion of making schools more "efficient," the teachers' unions were dismantled and teachers' special status as civil servants was eliminated. The military government fully expected that with vouchers and competition, students in private subsidized schools would achieve at higher levels than in public schools, and with the shift of students from public to private schools, "ineffective" public schools could be closed and student achievement in public schools would also rise.

By the end of the 1980s, parents had more school choice (over-subscribed schools also could choose students, however), but the measured effects on educational effectiveness and efficiency were dubious. At the end of the military regime (1988), the government began a national testing regime (called SIMCE) in the fourth and eighth grades of all Chilean schools, public and private, voucher and non-voucher. These test scores were used to "judge" school quality and, more important, were used by researchers to evaluate the impact of vouchers on student performance. A large new group of private schools organized to profit from vouchers had somewhat lower costs per student, mainly because they hired younger teachers and had larger class sizes, so were more "efficient." But they had lower student achievement than corresponding public schools (McEwan and Carnoy, 2000). Neither did public school test scores rise because of increased competition from private schools (Hsieh and Urquiola, 2006; Bellei, 2009). Vouchers and increased enrollment in private subsidized schools exacerbated already high social class segregation among schools (Mizala and Torche, 2012; Valenzuela et al., 2014).

With the return to democracy in 1990, the main concerns of the new coalition (Concertación) government was national reconciliation and reestablishing democratic public institutions. The Concertación made no attempt to eliminate school vouchers or tuition as the basis for financing university education (Bellei and Vanni, 2015). Indeed, in 1993, the Ministry of Education legalized existing under-the-table practices by private subsidized schools of accepting tuition payments from families and illegally using selection criteria such as interviewing families and reviewing students' previous grades to admit students. This resulted in the spread of these practices and even greater school system social class segregation than in the 1980s (Valenzuela et al., 2014).

Thus, the democratically elected governments of the 1990s did not roll back vouchers—the key radical reform of the 1970s and 1980s—and may have even exacerbated some of the reform's more perverse aspects. Nevertheless, teachers' unions were allowed to reconstitute themselves early on with the Statute for Teachers, and the Concertación governments did begin a series of investments and educational changes that had major impacts on the quantity and quality of education Chileans received. As in North Carolina, an initial curriculum reform was an important first step. Also as in North Carolina, an important feature of these changes was political continuity, a willingness to increase spending per student significantly to improve educational quality, and an emphasis on educational evaluation using large-scale testing programs, and, later, extensive teacher evaluation.

The first head of the quality and equity strategy in the Ministry of Education during the two decades of continuous Concertación coalition governments in Chile was Cristian Cox. He then became director of Curriculum and Evaluation in the Ministry of Education and was in that position managing policy for sixteen years. He and another long-standing leader in the ministry during this period, Juan Eduardo García-Huidobro, rapidly implemented the P-900 program, which increased resources going to low-income schools. It began in 1990 in Chile and extended to almost 2,500 schools by the end of the decade. It raised test scores of pupils significantly in low-scoring schools (Carnoy et al., 2004; McEwan and Carnoy, 2000). Ministry leadership institutionalized the SIMCE testing regime, and in the 2000s, expanded it to secondary school (tenth grade), and eventually to a national end-of-high-school/college entrance test.

Aided by relatively high economic growth in the 1980s and early 1990s, these same ministry reformers also implemented a major injection of spending on primary and secondary education through a series of teacher salary increases. In the decade of the 1990s, teacher salaries more than doubled in real terms. Teacher base monthly salaries in municipal (public) schools increased an average of 8.4

percent annually from 1990 to 2000, but slowed to 3.9 percent annually in 1996–2000 (Carnoy, 2007). These increases in teacher salaries resulted in academically better prepared high school students entering teaching programs in universities and the teaching profession. Part of the increase in salaries came through a salary premium scheme, SNED, begun in the mid-1990s, in which 25 percent of Chilean schools received teacher bonuses every two years based on a complex formula of increases in the schools' fourth and eighth grade SIMCE scores and student attainment progress (Mizala and Romaguera, 2002). Although SNED was intended to incentivize schools to increase test scores, evaluations of the program suggest that schools were able to increase fourth grade scores but not cohort gains between fourth and eighth grade (Carnoy et al., 2007).

Further, in the late 1990s, the ministry began to convert all Chilean primary and secondary schools to full-day, increasing the amount of time that students spent learning core subjects. This reform resulted in modest gains in test scores (Bellei, 2009). And in 2008, the Congress voted to increase the voucher for low-income students by 50 percent. This reform, called the Preferential School Subsidy (SEP), had a significant effect on the achievement of low-income primary school students (Carrasco, 2014; Murnane et al., 2017).

> The Preferential School Subsidy (SEP) law . . . recognized that it costs more to educate students well from low-income families, especially in schools serving large percentages of poor children. Under SEP, the vouchers provided to students from families in the bottom 40 percent of the income distribution were worth 50 percent more than those provided to wealthier students. Further, certain schools received additional bonuses based on the percentage of priority students in the school. . . . After SEP was introduced in 2008, student test scores in all types of schools improved, but the improvement was greatest among public and non-fee charging private schools. . . . In addition, the size of the income-based test score gap declined by at least one-third (from 20.8 to 13.3 points). (Vegas, 2018: 2–5)

This sustained effort to improve education by a series of Chilean governments eventually increased student achievement in Chilean schools, including sustained gains by low-income students, both on the national SIMCE test and international tests such as the PISA. However, it is important to note that the improvement in test scores did not come right away (Bellei and Vanni, 2015). Results on the SIMCE, Trends in International Mathematics and Science Study

(TIMMS), and PISA in the early 2000s—the first evaluations after five years of major reforms—were disappointing and prompted pushback, including pressure to make some changes in the primary school curriculum and increased emphasis on accountability, including more student testing and a national system of evaluating teacher performance. Yet, by 2006, Chilean PISA scores had risen substantially, and so did SIMCE scores after 2008. In both tests, disadvantaged students made larger gains than did advantaged students (Carnoy, Khavenson, Fonseca, Costa, and Marotta, 2015; Vegas, 2018).

The reforms were expensive and a significant part of the cost of education was borne by families paying tuition to private subsidized schools and especially for postsecondary education. More recently, a series of social movements have organized against structural inequalities in education and in Chilean society as a whole. A major problem not addressed in the twenty years after 1990 was the high tuition cost of even public universities, and this led to massive student demonstrations in 2011–2012. These movements suggest—as put forward in this book—that educational improvement has limits in solving larger problems of structural inequality in Latin America. Despite this important contradiction in these educational reforms, over two decades, Chilean leaders were able to mobilize much of the population behind educational improvements and were able to produce significant gains in student learning.

Ceará, Brazil, 2000–2018

Ceará is a relatively small and relatively poor state in northeast Brazil—twenty-third out of twenty-seven states in gross domestic product per capita. Yet, fifth and ninth graders in Ceará placed in seventh to eighth place among states in the national test (SAEB) in 2017, without any correction for the much lower socioeconomic background of Ceará students compared to students in the states that score higher. Further, the gains in average SAEB scores of Ceará's fifth and ninth graders in the period 2011–2017 are the highest or second highest depending on the subject and grade. The level of inequality in Ceará between the average in the top quintile scoring and lowest quintile scoring schools on the 2017 SAEB for fifth and ninth graders was also by far the lowest among all the Brazilian states (INEP, 2019).

Ceará students do not do as well on the SAEB test at the end of secondary school compared to students in other states, and, as I will explain, it is secondary schools that are most under the control of the state. However, the story behind raising primary (K–5) and middle school (6–9) achievement scores to such high levels in a relatively poor state—and, further, reducing achievement inequality so greatly among schools—is a unique one of educational leadership emerging at the local (municipal) level and, through example, shaping and eventually taking over state education policy to spread reform throughout the state's municipalities.

In Brazil, schools are administered by two largely separate systems—states and municipalities. Under the constitution of 1988, the two systems are autonomous but are supposed to cooperate in coordinating educational policies. This dictum is implemented to varying degrees across states. Secondary schools nationwide are operated almost universally by states, and primary schools, largely by municipalities. In most states, middle schools are operated by both states and municipalities, which means that in each municipality, there are both municipal and state middle schools. With the advent of municipalization policies coming from the federal government in the 1990s, middle schools have gradually shifted from state to municipal administrations, but again, this varies from state to state. The largest state in Brazil, São Paulo, still has a large fraction of its middle school students in state-run schools. Ceará is at the other end of the spectrum, with almost all middle schools run by municipalities.

The beginnings of the educational reforms that took place in Ceará can be situated in the mid-1990s to early 2000s during the second and third governments of Tasso Jereissati (1995–1998 and 1999–2002), and his successor from the same Brazilian Social Democracy Party (PSDB), Lúcio Alcântara (2003–2006). These governments of a very poor state established the fiscal and administrative conditions for the expansion and improvement of educational services in the state (Vieira et al., 2019). For example, the government implemented a reform in 1997 to select teachers based on merit, with the initial participation of 124 municipalities, which simultaneously promoted a process of collaboration between the state government and municipalities. Teacher hiring by meritocratic competition became a staple at the state (secondary schools) and local levels in the years that followed. This collaboration between state and municipalities, meant to implement a "better" form of government practice (hiring teachers by merit), had important implications for later and much broader collaboration on educational reforms in 2005–2007 (Vieira et al., 2019).

The expansion and improvement of education at the municipal level was also greatly aided, starting in 1998, by a federal financial equalization plan for education—the Fund for Maintenance and Development of the Basic Education and Valorization of Teaching

(FUNDEF), which redistributed funding for elementary education to poorer states and municipalities. In 2006, FUNDEF was replaced by the Fund for the Maintenance and Development of Basic Education and Valorization of Education Professionals (FUNDEB), and because this redistribution included middle and secondary education, it greatly increased funding per student at both the municipal and state level (Vieira et al., 2019: Graph 1).

Yet, there is a unique aspect of the educational improvement process in Ceará that distinguishes it from the other cases discussed here. Within the favorable reformist context at the state level in the 1990s and early 2000s, the main innovations that led to later statewide educational improvements began in one of the state's small rural municipalities. This municipality, Sobral, had local leaders who were determined to transform a low-performing, badly functioning school system in one of the poorer communities in the state. The innovative ideas emerging from Sobral affected state policy indirectly at first, but more directly after 2006, when the mayor of Sobral became governor of the state, and brought in Sobral's education reformers to run the state education secretariat.

In 1996, Cid Gomes was elected mayor of Sobral, and he, along with a group of local officials, including his younger brother, Ivo Gomes, as municipal secretary of education, initiated two decades of major educational improvements that transformed the municipality's educational system. They first took on the challenge of increasing the low levels of school attendance and high levels of dropouts in Sobral's schools. During the four years that followed, the municipal schools held their first public competition for teachers, guaranteed higher education for teachers chosen in the competition, constructed many new schools, refitted existing schools, and implemented programs that focused on reducing student repetition and dropouts. By 2000, enrollment in municipal schools had increased from 9,000 to 20,000 students, accompanied by a sharp reduction in dropouts, from 26 percent to 7 percent (Arruda, 2019). Thus, in this first phase of the reform, the main accomplishment was to increase student attainment through better management of the schools and recruiting teachers on the basis of merit rather than political connections.

The second stage of the reform focused on student literacy and lowering the entry age for primary school from seven to six years. At the end of the 2000 school year, again initiated by Gomes's leadership, second year primary students were given a simple literacy test and only about one-half were able to pass. The municipal administration responded by initiating a literacy program in the first three grades of primary school, teacher training for implementing the literacy program, and an accountability system that measured student literacy progress. This literacy program came to be known as the Programa Alfabetização na Idade Certa (PAIC) and was eventually adopted at the state level in Ceará with the creation of a commission in 2004 organized to combat illiteracy among school leavers. Also in 2001–2002, Sobral became one of the first municipalities in Brazil to introduce what eventually (2007) became the national "nine-year reform," lowering the entry age to primary school by a year and therefore lengthening primary school from four to five grades and basic education from eight to nine grades. This had a positive effect on student achievement (Rosa et al., 2019).

In 2006, Cid Gomes was elected governor of Ceará, and in 2007, the state secretariat of education (SEDUC), now led by the Sobral reformers, implemented PAIC in the first three grades of all primary schools in all the state's municipalities. PAIC served (and still serves) as the main vehicle for professional development of primary school teachers, as the focus of primary school success, and as the basis for cooperation between state reform policies and their implementation in municipal primary schools. In 2011, PAIC was expanded to the fourth and fifth grades.

> The PAIC was based on cooperation between the office of the state's Secretary of Education (SEDUC) and the state's municipal governments, the administrative entities most responsible for preschool and early primary education. It was designed to help achieve five interrelated program goals in the early grades of Ceará's municipal schools: 1) reading promotion; 2) supporting municipal literacy strategies; 3) strengthening municipal management; 4) supporting early childhood education; and 5) providing external learning evaluation. In terms of implementation, the program was divided into three broad activities related to three program areas: a) teacher and administrators training; b) municipality network mobilization; and c) provision of books to students. . . . [T]he state's Secretary of Education distributes specific teaching materials and a teaching guide directly to municipalities to be distributed to teachers in schools and provides face-to-face training to early grade teachers. . . . The training is a good example of a well-designed, scripted literacy and numeracy training program initially developed in a single Ceará municipality (Sobral) and successfully scaled up to hundreds of municipalities in Ceará state. (Costa and Carnoy, 2015: 568)

Ceará also introduced an evaluation system (the Permanent System of Evaluation of Basic Education in Ceará [SPAECE] test) beginning in the early 2000s and expanded it to all municipal and state schools in 2004. This was not an easy reform, since municipalities had autonomy and resisted state imposition of a state-mandated evaluation instrument. Nevertheless, the then governor, Lúcio Alcântara, carrying on the educational reform policies of his predecessor, was able to implement the SPAECE in almost all schools by 2004. In that year, more than 180,000 students were tested in mathematics and Portuguese in the fourth (now fifth grade since 2007), eighth (now ninth grade), and twelfth grades. Students, school directors, and about 10,000 teachers also filled out questionnaires (Vieira, 2007). The SPAECE effectively became the state's accounting system and was used as the PAIC assessment instrument.

When PAIC was implemented in Sobral's schools, literacy greatly improved and fifth grade test scores increased substantially (Arruda, 2019). But Sobral's reform-minded governments have continued to implement new improvements in Sobral's schools until today, when new science labs have been introduced in the municipality's middle and high schools, math and science teachers are being trained using advanced training techniques, and there is a continued emphasis in maintaining Sobral as the municipality with the highest fifth grade national test scores in Brazil and with some of the highest scoring middle schools in the country despite Sobral's low income per capita.

Thus, in Ceará, elected officials from different political parties initiated and have since maintained a series of reforms that effectively raised the standards and the quality of teaching in the state's municipal educational systems over the past twenty-five years. They included an early grade literacy program, greatly increased professional development for teachers, a state testing system that focused on monitoring the implementation and outcomes of the reforms at the municipal level, and a long-term effort to organize systematic cooperation between SEDUC and municipal secretariats of education. The latter was key in the constitutional context of Brazil, where municipalities have major control over basic education schools. These reforms were facilitated by increased funding per student, increased funding for school construction and school renovation, and a major emphasis by the state leadership on making education a lead sector in the state's overall development. One municipality, Sobral, under its own reformist leadership, led the way in developing innovative changes that were rather quickly incorporated at the state level and then extended with the election of Sobral's mayor to the governorship. All of this allowed a low-socioeconomic state to greatly outpace the achievement gains of primary and middle school students in other states while greatly increasing enrollment. In both Sobral and Ceará, which see themselves as national leaders in educational improvement, the educational innovation and reform agenda is now in its third decade.

What Do the Cases Teach Us About Leadership?

These three cases are not unique—there are many others that tell a similar story. Educational systems are not easy to improve or to be made more equitable, but they can be, as these cases illustrate. One of the cases—Chile—is a country with a rather centralized educational system, and two cases are states within federal systems, where the states have the power to implement their own reforms—North Carolina in the highly decentralized US system, and Ceará, in constitutionally decentralized Brazil. The Chilean reforms of the 1990s and 2000s were especially complicated because they were preceded by a voucher plan that decentralized much of the control of education (with limited regulations) to individual private schools.

In all three cases, the reforms took time, and measured improvements in results were not immediate in coming. This is important, because in all three cases, the reforms involved significantly large increases in educational spending, which in turn meant that the public's expectations were that this spending would result in visible educational improvements. It is important for a second crucial reason: for the reforms to ultimately result in measured student achievement gains required continuity and persistence in the reform effort, which in turn required continued support from government. In all the cases, curriculum reforms played an important role. In all three, the reforms were also accompanied by student testing systems that, in one form or another, made schools "accountable" for improvement, and, in two of the cases (Chile and Ceará,), accompanied by school monetary incentives to do better on these student tests. Further, in all three cases, the educational reforms put their primary emphasis on improving scores of disadvantaged students, and, at least in Chile, which most increased relative funding for low-income students, the gains for the most disadvantaged students were greater than for more advantaged students.

The impetus and long-term support for these reforms came from progressive leaders who "stayed the course" over two decades or more. In North Carolina, it was a single political leader, his political party, and a progressive business community working together to accomplish major changes in a system coming out of racial segregation, in a state whose traditional industries were being destroyed by international competition. In Chile, it was party coalition that stayed in power continuously for twenty years. In Ceará, it was a group of political-educational leaders from a small rural municipality with a vision for transforming education in the state.

It is positive that the typical leadership in these cases is not a single person, but rather a political party or a coalition of parties that sustains these long-term changes. It is also positive that there are common elements to the reforms in all the cases. These are curriculum change, accountability, support for teachers in the form of higher salaries and professional development, and increased spending on schooling, especially for schools with higher densities of students from low-income families. As important, however, is that during a period of at least two decades, improving education was a major focus of government policy in each of these places. The results in every case were significant increases in student achievement and somewhat greater equity in educational delivery.

My point here is simple: we know the kinds of big reforms that work to improve education, but it takes leadership over the long-term and good economic policies that help sustain growth to finance these reforms. It also takes a focus on improving equity in education and, in Latin America and most other places in the world (including North Carolina), greater equity in the society as a whole.

In this book, I have tried to provide a roadmap for investing not only in schooling but in the other important elements of human and social capital to create a more equitable, truly democratic society prepared for sustained development in the twenty-first century. I believe that every child in Latin America deserves this investment, and every Latin American government should, as its first order of priority, want to do everything possible, for the good of the society it governs, to ensure that all children—no matter their ethnicity or family income—get the very best schooling, health care, drinking water, and living conditions that money can buy. On this our future depends.

References

Alexander, K. L., Entwisle, D. R., and Olson, L. S. (2007). "Lasting Consequences of the Summer Learning Gap." *American Sociological Review* 72: 167–180.

Arruda, C. (2019). "Sobral: Um caminho." Teachers' College Columbia (mimeo).

Attanasio, C. (2015). "Domestic Violence Laws in Latin America: Can Legislation Curb 'Femicide'?" *Latin Times*, June 4. https://www.latintimes.com/domestic-violence-laws-latin-america-can-legislation-curb-femicide-320801.

Ayres, R. L. (1998). *Crime and Violence as Development Issues in Latin America and the Caribbean*. Washington, DC: World Bank, Latin American and Caribbean Studies.

Barnett, W. S. (2008). *Pre-School Education and Its Lasting Effects: Research and Policy Implications*. Boulder: Education Policy Interest Center.

Becker, H. J. (1984). "Computers in Schools Today: Some Basic Considerations." *American Journal of Education* 93(1): 22–39.

Becker, H. J. (1994). "How Exemplary Computer-Using Teachers Differ from Other Teachers: Implications for Realizing the Potential of Computers in Schools." *Journal of Research on Computing in Education* 26(3): 291–321.

Bellei, C. (2009)."Does Lengthening the School Day Increase Students' Academic Achievement? Results from a Natural Experiment in Chile." *Economics of Education Review* 28(5): 629–640. https://econpapers.repec.org/article/eeeecoedu/v_3a28_3ay_3a2009_3ai_3a5_3ap_3a629-640.htm.

Bellei, C., and Vanni, X. (2015). "Chile: The Evolution of Educational Policy, 1980–2014." In Schwartzman, S. (ed.), *Education in South America*. London: Bloomsbury.

Berlinski, S., Galiani, S., and Gertler, P. (2009). "The Effect of Pre-Primary Education on Primary School Performance." *Journal of Public Economics* 93(1–2): 219–234.

Berlinski, S., and Schady, N. (eds.). (2015). *The Early Years: Child Well-Being and the Role of Public Policy*. New York: Inter-American Development Bank–Palgrave Macmillan.

Berman, S. L., Kurtines, W. M., Silverman, W. K., and Serafini, L. T. (1996). "The Impact of Exposure to Crime and Violence on Urban Youth." *American Journal of Orthopsychiatry* 66(3): 329–336. https://doi.org/10.1037/h0080183.

Borofsky, L. A., Kellerman, I., Baucom, B., Oliver, P. H., and Margolin, G. (2013). "Community Violence Exposure and Adolescents' School Engagement and Academic Achievement over Time." *Psychology of Violence* 3(4): 381–395. https://doi.org/10.1037/a0034121.

Bowen, N. K., and Bowen, G. L. (1999). "Effects of Crime and Violence in Neighborhoods and Schools on the School Behavior and Performance of Adolescents." *Journal of Adolescent Research* 14(3): 319–342. https://doi.org/10.1177/0743558499143003.

Bray, M., and Lykins, C. (2012). *Shadow Education: Private Supplementary Tutoring and Its Implications for Policy Makers in Asia* (No. 9). Asian Development Bank.

Brown, R., and Velásquez, A. (2017). "The Effect of Violent Crime on the Human Capital Accumulation of Young Adults." *Journal of Development Economics* 127(July): 1–12. https://doi.org/10.1016/j.jdeveco.2017.02.004.

Bruns, B., and Luque, J. (2014). *Great Teachers: How to Raise Student Learning in Latin America and the Caribbean*. Washington, DC: World Bank.

Buvinic, M., Morrison, A., and Orlando, M.B. (2003). "Violence, Crime and Social Development in Latin America and the Caribbean." In Sojo, C. (ed.), *Social Development in Latin America*. Washington, DC: World Bank.

Carnoy, A. (1962). *Democracia sí! A Way to Win the Cold War*. New York: Vantage Press.

Carnoy, M. (2007). "Improving Quality and Equity in Latin American Education: A Realistic Assessment." *Pensamiento Educativo* 40(1): 103–130.

Carnoy, M. (2011). "As Higher Education Expands, Is It Contributing to Greater Inequality?" *National Institute Economic Review* 215: R1–R14.

Carnoy, M., Brodziak, I., Molina, A., and Socias, M. (2007). "The Limitations of Teacher Pay Incentive Programs Based on Inter-Cohort Comparisons: The Case of Chile's SNED." *Education Finance and Policy* 2(3): 189–227.

Carnoy, M., Cosse, G., Cox., C., and Martínez, E. (eds.). (2004). *Las reformas educativas en la década de 1990: Un estudio comparado de la Argentina, Chile y Uruguay*. Buenos Aires: Ministerio de Educación Ciencia y Tecnología, Banco Interamericano de Desarrollo (BID).

Carnoy, M., and Garcia, E. (2017). *Five Key Trends in U.S. Student Performance*. Washington, DC: Economic Policy Institute.

Carnoy, M., Garcia, E., and Khavenson, T. (2015). *Bringing It Back Home*. Washington, DC: Economic Policy Institute.

Carnoy, M., Gove, A., and Marshall, J. (2007). *Cuba's Academic Advantage*. Stanford, CA: Stanford University Press.

Carnoy, M., Khavenson, T., Fonseca, I., Costa, L., and Marotta, L. (2015). "A educação brasileira está melhorando? Evidências do PISA e SAEB." *Cuadernos de Pesquisa* 45(157): 450–485.

Carnoy, M., Loyalka, P., Dobryakova, M., Dossani, R., Froumin, I., Kuhns, K., Tilak, J. B. G., and Wang, R. (2013). *University Expansion in a Changing Global Economy: Triumph of the BRICs?* Stanford, CA: Stanford University Press.

Carnoy, M., and Marshall, J. (2005). "Cuba's Academic Performance in Comparative Perspective." *Comparative Education Review* 49(2): 230–261.

Carnoy, M., and Samoff, J. (1989). *Education and Social Transformation in the Third World*. Princeton, NJ: Princeton University Press.

Carnoy, M., Santibanez, L., Maldonado, A., and Ordorika, I. (2002). "Barreras de entrade em la educacion superior y a oportunidades profesionales para la población indígena mexicana." *Revista Latinoamericana de Estudios Educativos* (Mexico) 32(3): 9–43.

Carrasco, R. (2014). "Leveling the Playing Field: How Can We Address Educational Inequalities?" PhD diss., Stanford University.

Castells, M. (1996). *The Rise of the Network Society*. Oxford: Blackwell.

Castells, M. (2001). *The Internet Galaxy: Reflections on the Internet, Business and Society*. Oxford: Oxford University Press.

Caudillo, M. L., and Torche, F. (2014). "Exposure to Local Homicides and Early Educational Achievement in Mexico." *Sociology of Education* 87(2): 89–105.

CEPALSTAT. (2021). https://estadisticas.cepal.org/cepalstat/Portada.html?idioma =english. Accessed April 10, 2021.

Chetty, R., Friedman, J. N., Saez, E., Turner, N., and Yagan, D. (2017). "Mobility Report Cards: The Role of Colleges in Intergenerational Mobility." NBER Working Paper 23618. Cambridge, MA: National Bureau of Economic Research.

Chetty, R., Hendren, N., and Katz, L. F. (2016). "The Effects of Exposure to Better Neighborhoods on Children: New Evidence from the Moving to Opportunity Experiment." *American Economic Review* 106(4): 855–902.

Childs, P., and Stromquist, N. P. (2015). "Academic and Diversity Consequences of Affirmative Action in Brazil." *Compare: A Journal of Comparative and International Education* 45(5): 792–813.

Clark, B. R. (1960). "The 'Cooling-Out' Function in Higher Education." *American Journal of Sociology* 65(6): 569–576.

Claro, M., and Jara, I. (2020). "The End of Enlaces: 25 Years of an ICT Education Policy in Chile." *Digital Education Review* 37: 96–108.

Cohn, J. (2014). "Five Things We Can Do to Reduce Domestic Violence." *The New Republic*. September 14.

Coleman, J. S. (1988). "Social Capital in the Creation of Human Capital." *American Journal of Sociology* 94: S95. http://doi.org/10.1086/228943.

Comisión Económica para América Latina (CEPAL). (2012). *Panorama Social de América Latina*. Santiago: CEPAL.

Cordero, G., Contreras, L. A., Ames, P., Dippo, D., Durán, M., Alsop, S., Fynbo, T., Sánchez, M. L., González, T., and García, J. (2005). "Innovación en la educación rural: Reporte de una experiencia de formación de profesores en servicio en el norte de Perú." *REICE. Revista Iberoamericana sobre Calidad, Eficacia y Cambio en Educación* 3(1): 832–845.

Cortina, R. (2014). "Introduction." In Cortina, R. (ed.), *The Education of Indigenous Citizens in Latin America*, 1–18. Bristol, England: Multilingual Matters.

Costa, L. O., and Carnoy, M. (2015). "The Effectiveness of an Early-Grade Literacy Intervention on the Cognitive Achievement of Brazilian Students." *Educational Evaluation and Policy Analysis* 37(4): 567–590.

Cristiá, J. P., Ibarraran, P., Cueto, S., Santiago, A., and Severin, E. (2012). "Technology and Child Development: Evidence from the One Laptop per Child Program." IDB Working Paper Series No. IDB-WP-304. Inter-American Development Bank.

Cuenca, R. (2018). *La cuestión docente en América Latina y el Caribe: Tendencias y desafíos. Informe de apoyo técnico para la Reunión Ministerial E2030 en Sucre, Bolivia*. Santiago: UNESCO-OREALC.

Cunha, F., and Heckman, J. (2007). "The Technology of Skill Formation." NBER Working Paper No. w12840. Cambridge, MA: National Bureau of Economic Research.

Currie, J. (2001). "Early Childhood Education Programs." *Journal of Economic Perspectives* 15(2): 213–238.

Currie, J., and Thomas, D. (1993). "Does Head Start Make a Difference?" Cambridge, MA: National Bureau of Economic Research, No. w4406.

Daude, C. (2011). *Ascendance by Descendants? On Intergenerational Education Mobility in Latin America.* OECD Publishing. http://www.oecd.org/dev/latinamericaandthecaribbean/47237039.pdf.

Dee, T. S., and Penner, E. K. (2017). "The Causal Effects of Cultural Relevance: Evidence from an Ethnic Studies Curriculum." *American Educational Research Journal* 54(1): 127–166.

Del Rosso, J. M. (1999). "School Feeding Programs: Improving Effectiveness and Increasing the Benefit to Education—A Guide for Program Managers." Partnership for Child Development, World Bank. http://documents1.worldbank.org/curated/en/686561468741360505/pdf/multi0page.pdf.

Dercon, S., and Lives, Y. (2011). *Long-Term Implications of Under-Nutrition on Psychosocial Competencies: Evidence from Four Developing Countries.* Young Lives. http://www.dfid.gov.uk/r4d/PDF/Outputs/Younglives/wp72_long-term-implications-of-under-nutrition.pdf.

De Soto, H. (2000). *The Mystery of Capital: Why Capitalism Triumphs in the West and Fails Everywhere Else.* New York: Basic Books.

Dias Lopes, A. (2017). "Affirmative Action in Brazil: How Students' Field of Study Choice Reproduces Social Inequalities." *Studies in Higher Education* 42(12): 2343–2359.

Downie, A., and Lloyd, M. (2010). "At Brazil's Universities, Affirmative Action Faces Crucial Tests." *The Chronicle of Higher Education.*

Drèze, J., and Sen, A. (2002). *Hunger and Public Action.* Oxford, UK: Oxford University Press.

Duarte, J., Gargiulo, C., and Moreno, M. (2011). *School Infrastructure and Learning in Latin American Elementary Education: An Analysis Based on the SERCE.* Washington, DC: Inter-American Development Bank, Technical Note No. IDB-TN-277.

Dudley, S. (2014). "Criminal Evolution and Violence in Latin America and the Caribbean." *InSight Crime.* https://www.insightcrime.org/news/analysis/evolution-crime-violence-latin-america-caribbean/.

Dweck, C. S. (2008). *Mindset: The New Psychology of Success.* New York: Random House.

Economic Commission for Latin America and the Caribbean (ECLAC) and United Nations Children's Fund (UNICEF) Office for Latin America and the Caribbean. (2010). *Child Poverty in Latin America and the Caribbean.* Santiago de Chile: ECLAC. https://www.cepal.org/en/pressreleases/child-poverty-affects-almost-81-million-children-latin-america-and-caribbean.

Elacqua, G., Hincapié, D., Vegas, E., and Alfonso, M. (2018). *Profesión: Profesor en América Latina ¿Por qué se perdió el prestigio docente y cómo recuperarlo?* Washington: Inter-American Development Bank.

Ferreira, F. H., Firpo, S. P., and Messina, J. (2016). "Understanding Recent Dynamics of Earnings Inequality in Brazil." *New Order and Progress: Development and Democracy in Brazil*, 187.

Fonseca, I. (2019). "Structural Inequalities in Education and Their Impact on Student Achievement and Earnings in Brazil." PhD diss., Stanford University Graduate School of Education.

Freire, P. (2018). *Pedagogy of the Oppressed: Fiftieth Anniversary Edition.* New York: Bloomsbury Publishing.

Friedman, M. (1962). *Capitalism and Freedom.* Chicago: University of Chicago Press.

Fuller, B., Bein, E., Bridges, M., Kim, Y., and Rabe-Hesketh, S. (2017). "Do Academic Preschools Yield Stronger Benefits? Cognitive Emphasis, Dosage, and Early Learning." *Journal of Applied Developmental Psychology* 52: 1–11.

Gallego, J. M., and Gutiérrez, L. H. (2015). "ICTs in Latin America and the Caribbean: Stylized Facts, Programs and Policies." Discussion Paper No. IDB-DP-394. Washington, DC: Inter-American Bank.

Garces, E., Thomas, D., and Currie, J. (2002). "Longer-Term Effects of Head Start." *American Economic Review* 92(4): 999–1012.

García de Fanelli, A. (2019). "Exploring Equity in Higher Education Systems: Reflections from Argentina and Chile." *International Higher Education* 97: 27–28.

Gertler, P., Patrinos, H. A., and Rubio-Codina, M. (2006). *Empowering Parents to Improve Education: Evidence from Rural Mexico.* Policy Research Working Paper No. 3935. Washington, DC: World Bank. https://openknowledge.worldbank.org/handle/10986/6686.

Grissmer, D., and Flanagan, A. (1998). *Exploring Rapid Achievement Gains in North Carolina and Texas: Lessons from the States.* Washington, DC: National Education Goals Panel.

GSMA. (2016). "Are Universal Service Funds an Effective Way to Achieve Universal Access?" *GSMA Connected Society Program.* Mobile for Development. https://www.gsma.com/mobilefordevelopment/programme/connected-society/universal-service-funds-effective-way-achieve-universal-access/.

Gutmann, A. (1999). *Democratic Education.* Princeton, NJ: Princeton University Press.

Gutmann, A. (2004). "Unity and Diversity in Democratic Multicultural Education: Creative and Destructive Tensions." In Banks, J. A. (ed.), *Diversity and Citizenship Education: Global Perspectives*, 71–96. San Francisco: Jossey Bass.

Hakuta, K. (1986). *Mirror of Language: The Debate on Bilingualism.* New York: Basic Books.

Hall, G., and Patrinos, H. A. (eds.). (2005). *Indigenous Peoples, Poverty and Human Development in Latin America: 1994–2004.* Washington, DC: World Bank.

Heckman, J. J. (2000). "Policies to Foster Human Capital." *Research in Economics* 54(1): 3–56.

Heckman, J. J. (2006). "Skill Formation and the Economics of Investing in Disadvantaged Children." *Science* 312(5782): 1900–1902.

Heckman, J. J. (2011). "The Value of Early Childhood Education." *American Educator* 35(1): 31–35, 47. http://www.aft.org/pdfs/americaneducator/spring2011/Heckman.pdf.

Heinemann, A., and Verner, D. (2006). "Crime and Violence in Development: A Literature Review of Latin America and the Caribbean." World Bank Policy Research Working Paper 4041. Washington, DC: World Bank.

Hepp, P. K., Hinostroza, E., Laval, E., and Rehbein, F. (2004). "Technology in Schools: Education, ICT and the Knowledge Society." Temuco, Chile: Universidad de la Frontera, Instituto de Informática Educativa (mimeo).

Hernandez, T. K. (2013). "Affirmative Action in the Americas." *Americas Quarterly*, Summer. https://www.americasquarterly.org/affirmative-action-in-the-americas.

Hilbert, M. (2010). "When Is Cheap, Cheap Enough to Bridge the Digital Divide? Modeling Income Related Structural Challenges of Technology Diffusion in Latin America." *World Development* 38(5): 756–770.

Hoffay, M., and Rivas, S. (2016). "The Indigenous in Latin America: 45 Million with Little Voice." The Global Americans. https://theglobalamericans .org/2016/08/indigenous-latin-america-45-million-little-voice/.

Hsieh, C. T., and Urquiola, M. (2006). "The Effects of Generalized School Choice on Achievement and Stratification: Evidence from Chile's Voucher Program." *Journal of Public Economics* 90(8–9): 1477–1503.

Instituto Nacional de Estudos e Pesquisas Educacionais (INEP). (2019). Resultados SAEB, 2019. https://medium.com/@inep/resultados-do-saeb–2017-f471ec 72168d.

ITU (International Telecommunications Union). (2013). "Universal Service Fund and Digital Inclusion for All Study." Geneva: ITU.

Jara, I. (2018). "TIC en la escuelas: Desarrollando habilidades TIC para el Aprendizaje." In Montes, N. (ed.), *Educación y TIC: De las políticas a las aulas*. OEI: Buenos Aires.

Jarillo, B., Magaloni, B., Franco, E., and Robles, G. (2016). "How the Mexican Drug War Affects Kids and Schools: Evidence on Effects and Mechanisms." *International Journal of Educational Development* 51: 135–146. https://doi .org/10.1016/j.ijedudev.2016.05.008.

Justino, P., Leone, M., and Salardi, P. (2013). "Short- and Long-Term Impact of Violence on Education: The Case of Timor Leste." *The World Bank Economic Review* 28(2): 320–353. https://doi.org/10.1093/wber/lht007.

Klein, R. (2011). "Uma re-análise dos resultados do PISA: Problemas de comparabilidade." *Ensaio: Avalação Politica Pública Educação* 19(73): 1–20.

Klette, K., Hammerness, K., and Jenset, I. S. (2017). "Established and Evolving Ways of Linking to Practice in Teacher Education: Findings from an International Study of the Enactment of Practice in Teacher Education." *Acta Didactika Norge* 11(3): 1–22. http://dx.doi.org/10.5617/adno.4730.

Knijnik, G., and Wanderer, F. (2015). "Mathematics Education in Brazilian Rural Areas: An Analysis of the *Escola Ativa* Public Policy and the Landless Movement Pedagogy." *Open Review of Educational Research* 2(1): 143–154. https://doi.org/10.1080/23265507.2015.1052009.

Latinobarómetro. (2018). *Informe 2018*. Santiago de Chile: Corporacion Latinobarómetro.

Levin, H. M., and Meister, G. (1986). "Is CAI Cost-Effective?" *Phi Delta Kappan*, 67(10): 745–749.

López, L. E. (2010). *Reaching the Unreached: Indigenous Intercultural Bilingual Education in Latin America*. Paris: UNESCO, 2010/ED/EFA/MRT/PI/29.

López, L. E. (2014). "Indigenous Intercultural Bilingual Education in Latin America: Widening Gaps Between Policy and Practice." In Cortina, R. (ed.), *The Education of Indigenous Citizens in Latin America*, 19–49. Bristol, England: Multilingual Matters.

Lopez, N. (2007). "Urban and Rural Disparities in Latin America: Their Implications for Education Access." Background paper prepared for the *Education for All Global Monitoring Report 2008. Education for All by 2015: Will We Make It?*

López-Acevedo, G. (2002). "Teachers' Incentives and Professional Development in Schools in Mexico." Washington, DC: World Bank. Latin America and the Caribbean Region/Poverty Reduction and Economic Management Sector Unit.

López-Calva, L. F., and Lustig, N. C. (eds.). (2010). *Declining Inequality in Latin America: A Decade of Progress?* Washington, DC: Brookings Institution Press.

Lora, E. (2008). *Beyond Facts: Understanding Quality of Life.* http://www.iadb .org/en/research-and-data/publication-details,3169.html?pub_id=B-63.

Louzano, P., and Moriconi, G. M. (2015). "Visión de la Docencia y Características de los Sistemas de Formación Docente." *Cadernos Cenpec* 4(2).

Lustig, N., Lopez-Calva, L. F., Ortiz-Juarez, E., and Monga, C. (2016). "Deconstructing the Decline in Inequality in Latin America." In Basu, K. and Stiglitz, J. (eds.), *Inequality and Growth: Patterns and Policy*, 212–247. London: Palgrave Macmillan.

MacGregor, S. (2017). "School Achievement in Drug Violence Contexts: The Case of the Mexican War on Drugs." Master's research paper, Stanford University Graduate School of Education.

Majerowicz, S. N. (2016). *Impacto de educación inicial sobre desempeño académico.* Lima: FORGE.

Martinez Novo, C. (2014). "The Tension Between Western and Indigenous Knowledge in Intercultural Bilingual Education in Ecuador." In Cortina, R. (ed.), *The Education of Indigenous Citizens in Latin America*, 98–123. Bristol, England: Multilingual Matters.

Mato, D. (2008). "Diversidad cultural e interculturalidad en educación superior: Problemas, retos, oportunidades y experiencias en América Latina." In Mato, D. (ed.), *Diversidad cultural e interculturalidad en educación superior: Experiencias en América Latina*, 21–82. Caracas: IESALC-UNESCO.

Mato, D. (2009). "Educación superior, colaboración intercultural y desarrollo sostenible/buen vivir: Experiencias en américa latina, modalidades de colaboración, logros, innovaciones, obstáculos y desafíos." In Mato, D. (ed.), *Educación superior, colaboración intercultural y desarrollo sostenible/buen vivir. Experiencias en América Latina*, 11–64. Caracas: UNESCO-IESALC.

McCowan, T., and Bertolin, J. (2020). *Inequalities in Higher Education Access and Completion in Brazil.* Working Paper 2020-3. Prepared for the UNRISD project on Universities and Social Inequalities in the Global South.

McEwan, P. (1998). "The Effectiveness of Multigrade Schools in Colombia." *International Journal of Educational Development* 18(6): 435–452.

McEwan, P., and Benveniste, L. (2001). "The Politics of Rural School Reform: Escuela Nueva in Colombia." *Journal of Education Policy* 16(6): 547–559.

McEwan, P. J., and Carnoy, M. (2000). "The Effectiveness and Efficiency of Private Schools in Chile's Voucher System." *Educational Evaluation and Policy Analysis* 22(3): 213–239.

McEwan, P. J., and Trowbridge, M. (2007). "The Achievement of Indigenous Students in Guatemalan Primary Schools." *International Journal of Educational Development* 27(1): 61–76.

Medrich, E., and Griffith, J. (1992). *International Mathematics and Science Assessment: What Have We Learned?* NCES 92-011. Washington: DC: National Center for Educational Statistics.

Mentinis, M. (2006). *Zapatistas: The Chiapas Revolt and What It Means for Radical Politics.* London: Pluto Press.

Meza, D., Guzman, J. L., and De Valera, L. (2004). "EDUCO: A Community-Managed Education Program in Rural Areas of El Salvador." Washington, DC: World Bank.

Mizala, A., and Romaguera, P. (2002). "Evaluación del desempeño e incentivos en la educación chilena." *Cuadernos de Economía* 39(118): 353–394.

Mizala, A., and Torche, F. (2012). "Bringing the Schools Back In: The Stratification of Educational Achievement in the Chilean Voucher System." *International Journal of Educational Development* 32(1): 132–144.

Molinas Vega, J. R., Barros, R. P. de, Chanduvi, J. S., Giugale, M., Cord, L. J., Pessino, C., and Hasan, A. (2011). *Do Our Children Have a Chance? A Human Opportunity Report for Latin America and the Caribbean.* Washington, DC: World Bank.

Monteiro, J., and Rocha, R. (2013). "Drug Battles and School Achievement: Evidence from Rio de Janeiro's Favelas." CAF Working Paper.

Mulholland, T. (2005). "Quota System for Blacks at the University of Brasilia. University of Brasilia" (mimeo). Cited in Carnoy, M., Loyalka, P., Dobryakova, M., Dossani, R., Froumin, I., Kuhns, K., Tilak, J. B. G., and Wang, R. (2013). *University Expansion in a Changing Global Economy: Triumph of the BRICs?*, 343–344. Stanford, CA: Stanford University Press.

Murnane, R., Waldman, M. R., Willett, J. B., Bos, M. S., and Vegas, E. (2017). "The Consequences of Educational Voucher Reform in Chile." NBER Working Paper 23550. Cambridge, MA: National Bureau of Economic Research.

Nascimento, P. A. M. (2018). "Higher Education Financing: The Brazilian Case." Stanford University, Lemann Center. https://lemanncenter.stanford .edu/sites/default/files/Paulo%20Nascimento%20presentation%20May %2030th%202017%20.pdf.

National Center of Education Statistics (NCES). (2000). *Digest of Educational Statistics.* Washington, DC: NCES.

National Center of Education Statistics (NCES). (2016). *Digest of Educational Statistics.* Washington, DC: NCES.

Navarro, J. C. (2007). "Education Reform as Reform of the State: Latin America Since 1980. "In Lora, E. (ed.), *The State of State Reform in Latin America.* Washington, DC: Inter-American Development Bank.

Nores, M., and Barnett, W. S. (2010). "Benefits of Early Childhood Interventions Across the World." *Economics of Education Review* 29: 271–282.

Oppenheimer, T. (1997). "The Computer Delusion." *The Atlantic Monthly* 280(1): 45–62.

OECD. (2003). "Reviews of National Policies for Education: Chile." Paris: OECD, CCNM/EDU/EC.

OECD. (2004). "Reviews of National Policies for Education: Chile." Paris: OECD.

Ortiz-Correa, J. S. (2014). Math and Language at War: The Effect of the Colombian Armed Conflict on Math and Language Learning. *International Journal of Developing and Emerging Economies* 2(3): 1–30.

Outes-Leon, L., Porter, C., Sanchez, A., Cueto, S., Dercon, S., and Escobal, J. (2011). "Early Nutrition and Cognition in Peru: A Within-Sibling Investigation." IDB Working Paper Series No. IDB-WP-241.

Pardo, M., and Adlerstein, C. (2016). *Estado del arte y criterios orientadores para la elaboración de políticas de formación y desarrollo profesional de docentes de primera infancia en América Latina y el Caribe.* Santiago de Chile: OREALC-UNESCO.

Patrinos, H. A., and Velez, E. (2009). "Costs and Benefits of Bilingual Education in Guatemala: A Partial Analysis." *International Journal of Educational Development* 29(6): 594–598.

Perez, G. (2020). "Advancing Equity: The Effects of Higher Education Interventions for Improving Underserved Students' Educational Outcomes." PhD diss., Stanford University Graduate School of Education.

Perfetti, M. (2004). *Estudio sobre la educación para la población rural en Colombia.* Santiago: FAO-UNESCO.

Peruvian Ministry of Education [MINEDU]. (2014). "El acompañamiento pedagógico." *Protocolo del Acompañante Pedagógico, del Docente Coordinador/ Acompañante y del formador* [Pedagogical accompaniment. Protocol of the pedagogical companion, the teacher coordinator/companion and the trainer]. Lima, Peru.

Peruvian Ministry of Education [MINEDU]. (n.d.). Soporte pedagógico para la Secundaria Rural. http://www.minedu.gob.pe/soporte-educativo-rural/index .php#top.

Popova, A., Evans, D., Breeding, M., and Arancibia, V. (2018). "Teacher Professional Development Around the World." World Bank, Africa Regional Office, Policy Research Paper No. 8572.

Psacharopoulos, G., and Patrinos, H. A. (eds.). (1994). *Indigenous People and Poverty in Latin America: An Empirical Analysis.* Washington, DC: World Bank.

Psacharopoulos, G., Rojas, C., and Velez, E. (1993). "Achievement Evaluation of Colombia's Escuela Nueva: Is Multigrade the Answer?" *Comparative Education Review* 37(3): 263–276.

Queiroz, V. C., Carvalho, R. C. D., and Heller, L. (2020). "New Approaches to Monitor Inequalities in Access to Water and Sanitation: The SDGs in Latin America and the Caribbean." *Water* 12(4): 931.

Robles, M., Torero, M., and Cuesta, J. (2010). "Understanding the Impact of High Food Prices in Latin America [with Comment]." *Economia* 10(2): 117–164.

Rodríguez, J. S., Leyva, J., and Hopkins, A. (2016). *El efecto del Acompañamiento Pedagógico sobre los rendimientos de los estudiantes de escuelas públicas del Perú* [The effect of Acompañamiento Pedagógico on the achievement of students from Peruvian public rural schools]. Final Report. Lima: FORGE/CIES. www.grade.org.pe/forge/descargas/Informe %20final_AC_PM.pdf.

Rodriguez, J. S., Sanz, P., and Soltau, L. (2013). *Evaluación del diseño y ejecución del presupuesto de la intervención pública "Acompañamiento Pedagógico"* [Evaluation of the design and implementation of the budget to the public intervention "Acompañamiento Pedagógico"]. (No. inf201301). Departamento de Economía-Pontificia Universidad Católica del Perú.

Rosa, L. (2019). "The Organization of Educational Markets and Effects on Individuals' Decisions: An Empirical Analysis Using Brazilian Educational Policies." PhD diss., Stanford University Graduate School of Education.

Rosa, L., Martins, M., and Carnoy, M. (2019). "Achievement Gains from Reconfiguring Early Schooling: The Case of Brazil's Primary Education Reform." *Economics of Education Review* 68: 1–12.

Ruiz-Tagle, J. (1998). "Evidencia sobre la distribución de ingresos en el largo plazo." Departamento de Economía, Universidad de Chile (mimeo). Cited in Hourton, A. (2012). "Income Inequality in Chile: 1990–2006." Kyoto University, Department of Economics, Discussion Paper No. E–12-004.

Salazar-Bondy, A. (1976). *La educación del hombre nuevo: la reforma educativa peruana* (Vol. 201). Buenos Aires: Editorial Paidós.

Scartascini, C., Spiller, P. T., Stein, E., and Tommasi, M. (eds.). (2010). *El juego político en América Latina: ¿Cómo se deciden las políticas públicas?* Washington, DC: Inter-American Development Bank.

Schiefelbein, E. (1991). *In Search of the School of the XXI Century: Is the Colombian Escuela Nueva the Right Pathfinder?* Santiago: UNESCO/ UNICEF.

Schiefelbein, E. (1992). "Redefining Basic Education for Latin America: Lessons to Be Learned from the Colombian Escuela Nueva." UNESCO: International Institute for Educational Planning.

Schmelkes, S. (2006). "La educación intercultural bilingüe en México." Ponencia ante el VII Congreso Latinoamerico de Educación Intercultural Bilingüe. Cochabamba. Octubre 1–4.

Schmelkes, S. (2014). "Indigenous Students as Graduates of Higher Education Institutions in Mexico." In Cortina, R. (ed.), *The Education of Indigenous Citizens in Latin America*, 124–147. Bristol, England: Multilingual Matters.

Schmelkes, S. (2016). "Desempeño docente: Estado de la cuestión." Mexico, D.F.: Instituto Nacional para la Evaluación de la Educación (INEE). https://www.dropbox.com/sh/09hp4k7atx6d4dd/AACijER8jAPuXZTLOIT mRbmna/4.%20Monitoring%20and%20Evaluation/Breakout%204%20 -%20Sylvia%20Schmelkes.pptx?dl=0.

Schmidt, W. H., Tatto, M. T., Bankov, K., Blömeke, S., Cedillo, T., Cogan, L., . . . and Santillan, M. (2007). *The Preparation Gap: Teacher Education for Middle School Mathematics in Six Countries. MT21 Report.* East Lansing: Michigan State University.

Sempé, L. N. (2015). "Balance de la estrategia de Acompañamiento Pedagógico en áreas rurales de Perú en la lógica del presupuesto de resultados." *REICE. Revista Iberoamericana sobre Calidad, Eficacia y Cambio en Educación* 13(4): 35–60.

Sen, A. (1999a). *Development as Freedom.* New York: Alfred Knopf.

Sen, A. (1999b). "Investing in Early Childhood: Its Role in Development." Address to the Annual Meeting of the Inter-American Development Bank, Paris.

Shin, H., Iyengar, R., and Bajaj, M. (2013). "Cross-Country Review of Public Primary Education in Rural Brazil, China, Indonesia, and Mexico: Suggestions for Policy and Practice Reforms in India." Columbia Global Centers, Mumbai Working Paper Series (no. 10). http://globalcenters.columbia.edu /mumbai/files/globalcenters_mumbai/MDEP_WP10_Cross-country %20review.pdf.

Sperling, G. B. (2005). "The Case for Universal Basic Education for the World's Poorest Boys and Girls." *Phi Delta Kappan* 87(3): 213.

Stallings, J. A. (1977). "The Importance of Multiple Data Collection Instruments When Describing the Educational Process." Menlo Park, CA: Stanford Research Institute (mimeo).

Tarlau, R. (2017). "State Theory, Grassroots Agency, and Global Policy Transfer: The Life and Death of Colombia's *Escuela Nueva* in Brazil (1997–2012)." *Comparative Education Review* 61(4): 675–700.

Tarlau, R. (2019). *Occupying Schools, Occupying Land: How the Landless Workers Movement Transformed Brazilian Education.* Oxford: Oxford University Press, Global and Comparative Ethnography.

Tarlau, R., and Moeller, K. (2019). "'Philanthropizing' Consent: How a Private Foundation Pushed Through National Learning Standards in Brazil." *Journal of Education Policy* 35(3):1–30.

Tatto, M. T., Schwille, J., Senk, S., Ingvarson, L., Peck, R., and Rowley, G. (2008). *Teacher Education and Development Study in Mathematics (TEDS-M): Policy, Practice, and Readiness to Teach Primary and Secondary Mathematics—Conceptual Framework*. East Lansing, MI: Teacher Education and Development, International Study Center, College of Education, Michigan State University.

Tedesco, J. C. (2014). *Educación y desigualdad en América Latina y el Caribe: aportes para la agenda post–2015*. Santiago de Chile: OREALC-UNESCO.

Thompson, T., Jr., and Massat, C. R. (2005). "Experiences of Violence, Post-Traumatic Stress, Academic Achievement and Behavior Problems of Urban African-American Children." *Child and Adolescent Social Work Journal* 22(5–6): 367–393.

Toledo, A. (2015). *The Shared Society*. Stanford, CA: Stanford University Press.

Trucco, D. (2013). "The Digital Divide in the Latin American Context. In Ragnedda, M., and Muschert, G. W. (eds.), *The Digital Divide: The Internet and Social Inequality in International Perspective*. New York: Routledge.

UNESCO. (2011). "Regional Report on Education for All in Latin America and the Caribbean." Presented at the UNESCO Santiago 2011, Santiago, Chile: Regional Bureau for Education in Latin America and the Caribbean.

UNESCO. (2012). *ICT in Education in Latin America and the Caribbean*. Paris: UNESCO, Institute for Statistics.

UNESCO. (2013). *Situación Educativa de América Latina y el Caribe: Hacia la educación de calidad para todos al 2015*. Santiago de Chile: UNESCO Regional Bureau for Education in Latin America and the Caribbean.

UNESCO. (2014). "Regional Report About Education for All in Latin America and the Caribbean: Global Education for All Meeting Muscat, Oman, May 12 and 14, 2014." http://www.unesco.org/fileadmin/MULTIMEDIA/HQ/ED/ED_new/pdf/LAC-GEM–2014-ENG.pdf.

UNESCO Statistical Institute. (2021). UNESCO STAT. http://data.uis.unesco.org. Accessed April 12, 2021.

UNICEF and WHO. (2012). "Progress on Drinking Water and Sanitation 2012 Update." UNICEF and World Health Organization, Geneva, Switzerland. https://www.who.int/water_sanitation_health/publications/jmp_report-2012/en/.

United Nations (UN). (2011). *The Global Social Crisis: Report on the World Social Situation 2011*. New York: United Nations.

UNODC (United Nations Office on Drugs and Crime). (2010). "The Globalization of Crime: A Transnational Organized Crime Threat Assessment." Vienna: UNDOC.

UNODC (United Nations Office on Drugs and Crime). (2019). "Global Study on Homicide: Executive Summary." Vienna: UNODC. https://www.unodc.org/documents/data-and-analysis/gsh/Booklet1.pdf.

UNODC (United Nations Office on Drugs and Crime). (2020). "Data Tool." https://dataunodc.un.org/data/homicide/Homicide%20victims%20worldwide.

Valente, C. (2014). "Education and Civil Conflict in Nepal." *World Bank Economic Review* 28(2): 354–383. https://doi.org/10.1093/wber/lht014.

Valenzuela, J. P., Bellei, C., and Ríos, D. D. L. (2014). "Socioeconomic School Segregation in aMarket-Oriented Educational System: The Case of Chile." *Journal of Education Policy* 29(2): 217–241.

van Dijk, J. A. G. M., and van Deursen, A. J. A. M. (2014). *Digital Skills Unlocking the Information Society*. London: Palgrave Macmillan.

Vegas, E. (2018). "Five Lessons from Recent Educational Reforms in Chile." *Brookings Institution Report.* https://www.brookings.edu/research/5-lessons -from-recent-educational-reforms-in-chile/.

Vieira, S. L. (2007). "Management, Evaluation and School Success: Examples from Ceará's Path." *Estudos Avancados* (São Paulo) 21(60).

Vieira, S. L., Plank, D. N., and Vidal, E. M. (2019). "Educational Policy in Ceará: Strategic Processes." *Educação e Realidade* 44(4): 1–24.

Villar, R. (2010). "El programa Escuela Nueva en Colombia: Revista Educación y Pedagogía Nos. 14 y 15." https://aprendeenlinea.udea.edu.co/revistas /index.php/revistaeyp/article/.../501.

Watkins, K. (2000). *The Oxfam Education Report.* Oxford: Oxfam Publications.

Weiler, H. N. (2011). "Knowledge and Power: The New Politics of Higher Education." *Journal of Educational Planning and Administration* 25(3): 205–221.

Wessels, B. (2013). "The Reproduction and Reconfiguration of Inequality: Differentiation and Class, Status and Power in the Dynamic of Digital Divides." In Ragnedda, M., and Muschert, G. W. (eds.), *The Digital Divide.* New York: Routledge, 17–28.

Willis, P. (1977). *Learning to Labour.* London: Saxon House.

Wodon, Q. T. (2000). "Poverty and Policy in Latin America and the Caribbean." Washington, DC: World Bank Technical Paper No. 467.

Wolfe, D. A., Crooks, C. V., Lee, V., McIntyre-Smith, A., and Jaffe, P. G. (2003). "The Effects of Children's Exposure to Domestic Violence: A Meta-Analysis and Critique." *Clinical Child and Family Psychology Review* 6(3): 171–187.

World Bank. (2021). *World Development Indicators.* https://databank.worldbank .org/reports.aspx?source=World-Development-Indicators. Accessed April 10, 2021.

World Bank Group. (2015). *Indigenous Latin America in the Twenty-First Century: The First Decade.* Washington, DC: World Bank.

Zechmeister, E. J., Saunders, E. C., and Brunelle, J. M. (2015). "Internet in the Americas: Who's Connected?" *Americas Quarterly.* May 7. https://www .americasquarterly.org/fulltextarticle/internet-in-the-americas-whos -connected/.

Ziegler, S., Segura, J. A., Boslo, M., and Camacho, K. (2020). *Rural Connectivity in Latin America and the Caribbean—A Bridge to Sustainable Development During a Pandemic.* San Jose, Costa Rica: Inter-American Institute for Cooperation on Agriculture.

Index

About the Book

What will it take to overcome the many challenges that Latin America faces in developing quality, inclusive education for its diverse population? That is the question at the heart of Alejandro Toledo's new book.

Toledo begins from the premise that the uneven caliber of schools and universities in the region is only part of the problem. Drawing on his own childhood experiences living in deep poverty, he addresses the inequalities in health care, the large pockets of economic deprivation, and the discrimination against Indigenous peoples that continue to characterize Latin American societies—conditions of rural education and the pitfalls of privatizing higher education. His examples of successes, and his call for sustained political leadership in reforming education, are both realistic and refreshingly candid.

Alejandro Toledo Manrique served as president of Peru in 2001–2006. During his five-year term, one of his central aims was to fight against poverty through investment in quality education.

During his academic career, Dr. Toledo has been a visiting scholar and research associate at Harvard University; a research associate at Waseda University; a distinguished fellow in residence at Stanford University's Center for Advanced Study in the Behavioral Sciences and a Payne Distinguished Visiting Lecturer at Stanford's Freeman Spogli Institute; a distinguished visiting scholar at the School of Advanced International Studies, Johns Hopkins University; and a nonresident senior fellow in foreign policy and global economy and development at the Brookings Institution. Most recently, he was a visiting scholar at Stanford's Graduate School of Education, where he completed the research for this book.

Dr. Toledo has lectured in more than forty-five countries on issues related to economic growth, poverty and inequality reduction, and democracy, and in 2015 he received the Kalinga Institute's World Humanitarian Award for his work on inequality reduction. His published work includes *Economic Growth for Social Inclusion: Five Years in Which We Planted the Future, 2001–2006* and *The Shared Society: A Vision for the Global Future of Latin America*, which has been translated and published in twelve languages.

Dr. Toledo founded and continues to serve as president of the Global Center for Development and Democracy (www.cgdd.org).